Inside
Commercial Banking

Inside
Commercial Banking

Second Edition

Eric N. Compton

A Wiley-Interscience Publication

JOHN WILEY & SONS, INC.

New York   **Chichester**   **Brisbane**   **Toronto**   **Singapore**

Library of Congress Cataloging in Publication Data:

Compton, Eric N., 1925–
    Inside commercial banking.

    Bibliography: p.
    Includes index.
    1. Banks and banking—United States.   2. Banks and
banking.   3. Bank management.   I. Title.

HG2491.C644   1983   332.1'2'068   83-10278
ISBN 0-471-89561-X

Printed in the United States of America

10 9 8 7 6 5 4 3 2 1

To Maire Cathleen,
who made it possible

Preface

The first edition of this text, published in 1980, focused on the dynamics of change in the commercial banking industry. Banking was then described as in a state of flux, with significant new competitive, regulatory, technological, and market-related developments occurring with great frequency. The point was made that the changes of the preceding twenty years—the introduction of large-denomination negotiable certificates of deposit, the implementing of many applications of electronic funds transfer systems, the growth of bank-card usage, and the organizational restructuring of virtually every major bank under the holding-company concept—were at least as drastic and permanent as those in any two decades in our entire banking history.

In the very brief period that has elapsed since the first edition was published, neither the pace nor the impact of changes in banking has decreased; indeed, both have accelerated. Each business day may bring with it news of developments relevant to the banking industry that create new sets of concerns and anxieties. A partial list of these would include:

The passage of the Monetary Control Act, called the most important piece of banking legislation since 1933;

The tremendous increases in the financial activities of such nonbank competitors as Sears Roebuck, American Express, and Merrill Lynch;

The financial crises affecting many of the nation's leading savings banks and savings and loan associations;

The increases in prime lending rates to previously unheard-of levels;

The introduction of new types of account and quasi-account relationships, including retail repurchase agreements, All-Savers accounts, "sweep" accounts, and expanded IRAs (Individual Retirement Accounts);

The greater competitive pressures caused by the continued phenomenal growth of money market funds;

The increased emphasis on interstate banking activities and acquisitions, including the first interstate mergers of different types of financial institutions;

The rapid expansion of EFTS-related technology, including banking by telephone and banking at home;

The increased public questioning of the soundness of major United States banks because of their heavy involvement in foreign loans.

It is the objective of this second edition to give the reader contemporary information on these and other changes, and to assess their effects. The risk here involves use of the word *contemporary,* for tomorrow's financial press may recount topics and issues that make the term inappropriate. Nevertheless, every effort will be made to provide timeliness.

The institution that chooses to ignore or minimize the number and impact of changes in banking cannot compete effectively, and runs the risk of sharing the fate of the dinosaurs and railroads. The bank personnel who do not keep abreast of the many developments affecting their industry cannot deal with the complexities of today's fiercely competitive financial marketplace.

Commercial bankers today feel, like Hamlet, besieged by a sea of troubles. They have lost their traditional exclusivity in many areas of financial services, and, as a result, their share of the marketplace has steadily declined. From 1949 to 1979, the percentage of assets of all financial institutions held by banks dropped from 52.3 percent to 37.4 percent.[1] The question of actual survival for many banks is posed more frequently today than at any time since the Great Depression. Critics blame the banks for arbitrarily establishing high interest rates on loans. Human rights advocates demand that they disassociate themselves completely from activities in those foreign countries where civil liberties have allegedly been violated. Urban activists complain that banks have not done enough to solve the problems of the cities.

Perhaps most importantly, federal and state banking authorities and agencies continue to enmesh them in entire sets of sometimes overlapping or contradictory, and often anachronistic regulatory constraints, so that

[1]George W. McKinney, Jr., and Robert W. Renner, Sr., "Banking's Dramatic Loss of Market Share," *ABA Banking Journal* (November 1980):66.

unregulated competitors make further gains in the marketplace, while the merits of each case are debated in long, drawn-out hearings.

This last topic of regulation is most often cited as the major problem of commercial banks today. Although bankers may empathize with their peers in other industries on this subject, giving recognition to the fact that some 40 agencies of the federal government alone employ over 100,000 workers to devise and implement regulations—thus creating administrative costs of $5 billion, exclusive of the compliance expenses for the private sector[2]— they never lose sight of the fact that banking remains the most thoroughly and frequently supervised, examined, and restricted of all.

For example, a national bank comes under the jurisdiction of the Comptroller of the Currency, the Federal Reserve, the Federal Deposit Insurance Corporation, and, to some extent, the banking department in its state. If its stock is publicly held, it is subject to the requirements of the Securities and Exchange Commission. All banks are bound by the affirmative action regulations of federal, state, and local governments, and must comply with the Community Reinvestment Act in extending credit in their own geographic areas. Banks cannot make acquisitions, merge, or open branches without the prior approval of all the regulatory agencies that tell banks what they can do, and where and how they can do it. Before any bank can open its doors and accept its first deposits, it must undergo a rigorous chartering process. Throughout its life-cycle, it is subject to examinations that probe its financial condition and determine its compliance with all the laws and regulations that affect it. At all times, it must tie up funds in reserve accounts. Small wonder, then, that a former member of the Federal Reserve Board of Governors expressed this opinion: "Banking, with its three federal and fifty state supervisory authorities and bodies of law to match, is the most overregulated industry in the country."[3]

Yet, in the years that have elapsed since that comment was made, banking has become even more highly regulated, with the formation of new authorities and committees and the adoption of new statutes. Inevitably, erosion of the relative importance of commercial banks has taken place:

> Ten years ago banks provided nearly one-half of all loans made by financial institutions; today, banking's share is only one-third. . . . In 1945, U.S. households held 35% of their financial assets as deposits at banks; today, . . . 20%. Total bank deposits, if adjusted for inflation, actually declined in 1981.[4]

[2]Willard C. Butcher, "Onward the Regulation Revolution," Speech at The Commonwealth Club, San Francisco (September 15, 1978).
[3]Henry C. Wallich, "Banks Need More Freedom to Compete," *Fortune* (March 1970):114.
[4]Lawrence K. Roos, "Deregulation," *American Banker* (June 11, 1982):3.

Granted, much of the current regulatory structure stems from past financial crises that the banks, at least in part, helped to create; yet, as the current cliché states, "the playing field is not level," and bankers continue to raise questions their counterparts in other industries need never ask.

Why can an American bank establish a presence in foreign countries thousands of miles away with relative ease, when it is prohibited from opening a branch one mile away across a state line, and may even be prevented from branching within its own state? Its nonbank competitors face no such restrictions. *Why* were foreign banks, over 350 of which from 51 nations now operate in the United States, allowed to cross state lines and acquire major American Banks?[5] *Why* does one agency of the federal government allow the savings and loan associations to establish automated teller machines across state lines, when all commercial banks are specifically prohibited from doing this?

Along with their concerns over regulation, today's bankers must constantly be aware of the *image* of their profession. An educational effort is sorely needed to convince legislators, members of the press, consumer advocates, and other interested parties that the banks are, in fact, prudently managed, with due responsiveness to customer wants and needs; that their services and products are properly priced; that banks do not make unconscionably high profits when interest rates rise; and that social responsibility is a part of their policies and practices.

The image of banking is closely tied to the dynamics of change. An image of innovative and progressive leadership can be created by a bank that looks at both the present and the future, and thus develops answers to the issues and questions that have resulted from change. What segments of the total market appear to offer the best opportunities for profitability and growth? What type of structuring and what range of services will best meet the needs of those market segments? How can technological change best serve both the bank and its customer? What management techniques are most appropriate?

In this context, bankers must be aware that they deal today with a "new breed" of corporate, retail, institutional, or governmental customer. The mobility of money in our economy has never been greater, because a far more sophisticated clientele has become aware of yield and service options, and does not hesitate to transfer funds—either within the same bank (e.g., from non-interest-bearing demand deposits to those that provide direct income), or from the bank to a competitor.

Some years ago, the thrift institutions coined the term *disintermediation*

[5]"International Banking," *Institutional Investor* (September 1982):273.

to describe the movement of funds away from them and into various attractive investment vehicles. Today, the same term applies to commercial banks as well. Checking account balances, the traditional core of the deposit base, are now kept to a bare minimum by customers who, in increasing numbers, question whether they need a commercial bank at all. The loyalties on which bankers have always depended have declined accordingly. Corporate financial officers proudly report their success in reducing both the number of bank accounts they maintain, and the balances kept in each.[6] The problem caused by the increase in the volatility of money could alone form the basis for a contemporary text.

It has been said that those who ignore the mistakes of history are condemned to repeat them. For this reason, mention must here be made of many aspects of the past performance of banks, especially in times of crisis. Whenever past instances of poor judgment or unsound practices are cited, the intention is not to condemn or to be overly critical of any bank or banker. If, on some occasions, the banks proved to be their own worst enemies, that fact is noted objectively. However, it must also be noted that the banks did not become a key element in the economy, and attract over a trillion dollars in deposits, despite the caliber of their leaders or by accident. Rather, their current soundness and profitability flow from the capability, diligence, and dedication of many past generations of bankers who identified challenges and problems, then devised appropriate responses. No less is called for today. Periods of trial and error may be long and frustrating, but there is reason for hope; banking has successfully coped with many crises in the past, and it can do so again.

Always, the emphasis must be placed on change.

When Stephen Fuller left Harvard's Graduate School of Business Administration to become Vice President in charge of all General Motors personnel, he expressed this thought: "One of the most significant responsibilities of any management is to make sure that the strategies and tactics of the organization are not only perceiving changes, but anticipating them."[7]

His words have as much relevance to the banking industry as to the automotive. Change is intrinsic in today's financial marketplace, and traditionalism will not work. Past generations of bankers did not include such terms as *Eurodollar financing, sweep accounts, point-of-sale terminals, affirmative action,* or *minibranches* in their lexicon, nor did they

---

[6]Suzanne Wittebort, "The Frantic New Pace of Cash Management," *Institutional Investor* (June 1981):179.
[7]"GM Zeroes in on Employees Discontent," *Business Week* (May 12, 1973):28.

have to contend with the dramatic developments that have led to the new supermarkets of finance.

Corporations that historically looked to banks as their major source of credit now bypass them by borrowing from one another, through the commercial paper market, to the tune of $179 billion.[8] Sears Roebuck has announced that the 42,000 customers of its Dean Witter brokerage subsidiary can now cash checks for up to $250 at any of the 851 Sears stores.[9] Beneficial Corporation, no longer merely a small-loan company, now owns First Texas Savings and Loan, with over $2 billion in assets, has received authorization from 26 states to accept deposits at its loan offices, has acquired a 60-branch bank in the United Kingdom, and is implementing an on-line electronic funds transfer system for its 2,000 loan offices.[10] Citytrust, in Bridgeport, Connecticut has introduced an at-home banking system that allows customers to verify account balances, pay bills, transfer funds, and apply for loans; it will also provide current stock market quotes and handle travel reservations.[11] Merrill Lynch has disclosed plans to enter the corporate lending field; it has formed a cadre of former bank officers and plans to add billions of dollars in loans to its assets.[12] The National Credit Union Administration reports that deposits at its 12,125 federally chartered members rose 6.1 percent in 1981, while commercial bank deposits increased only 4.4 percent.[13] National Steel Corporation has acquired the nation's fourth largest savings and loan, which operates in California, New York, and Florida.[14] An editorial in one of the nation's largest newspapers noted that in a single month (September 1982), Chemical Bank announced plans for banking at home by personal computers; the American Can Company bought its third insurance company; the Kroger Company announced that it will sell money market funds in Ohio grocery stores; and Citicorp (the holding company parent of New York's Citibank, N.A.) was allowed to take over a major savings and loan association in California.[15]

[8]*Federal Reserve Bulletin* (August 1982):A25.
[9]Laura Gross, "Sears Outlets Cashing Checks for Dean Witter Customers," *American Banker* (June 17, 1982):1.
[10]M. W. Caspersen, "Whither the Finance Company in a Dynamic Environment?" *American Banker* (May 6, 1982):7.
[11]Megan Gallagher, "Citytrust Turns to Home Banking," *White Plains Reporter–Dispatch* (June 21, 1982):C10.
[12]Lee Smith, "Merrill Lynch's Latest Bombshell for Bankers," *Fortune* (April 19, 1982):67.
[13]Lisa J. McCue, "Credit Union Deposits Up 6.1%," *American Banker* (April 26, 1982):3.
[14]Harry Taylor, "Deregulation, Interstate Powers Vital for Industry Survival," *American Banker* (April 20, 1982):24.
[15]"Saving the Thrifts, and Then Some," *The New York Times* (October 1, 1982):A30.

Each of these developments in itself is evidence of the major changes that characterize today's financial marketplace. It is the objective of this second edition to explore these and the other important topics and issues that face commercial banks today, and to begin the quest for solutions.

As in the past, special acknowledgment is gratefully extended here to Francis A. McMullen, Executive Director of the American Institute of Banking in New York. His encouragement, support, and guidance have been consistent, and his friendship deeply valued.

ERIC N. COMPTON

Hartsdale, New York
August 1983

CONTENTS

Inside
Commercial Banking

1 American Banking: A Historical Overview

Because a commercial bank's customers comprise a cross section of businesses, institutions, entities of government, and individuals, the manner in which the bank interacts with and provides services to them mirrors the environment. A bank's operating philosophy, and the extent to which it is restricted by federal and state laws, can be highly reflective of the outside world. Thus, the mood and spirit of the earliest American colonists can be highlighted and captured if one examines their approach to banking, the institutions they created, and the banking system (or lack of one) existing at the time.

In 1687, when Sir Isaac Newton promulgated the physical law that for every action there is an equal, opposite reaction, he could not have foreseen the applications of that law to many areas outside the purview of the sciences. Yet a moment's thought will demonstrate that this can be done. For example, an era of strict, prudish morality in society gives way to one of license, and vice versa. Fashions go to one extreme, then revert to another. Conservative and liberal political parties often exchange positions of power in governments. Overly sentimental style, soft music, and romantic literary works are replaced by harsh realism, dissonance, and crude language; in turn, the latter fade in popularity, and a new reaction takes place. Such is the case with the historical development of the American banking system.

COLONIAL BANKING

The earliest colonists sought independence and personal liberty in all things. Many came from those countries where a high degree of government control, affecting many aspects of their daily lives, had existed. Typically, the banking scene in those nations consisted of a strong central bank and a handful of commercial banks. To the colonists, this concept was in direct conflict with the broad notion of individual freedom. They reacted by going to the opposite end of the spectrum, extending to banking the same liberty that permitted individuals to establish any type of business they desired.

In direct contrast to the central banking systems in their former countries, for example, England, France, and Sweden, the colonists opted for minimal supervision and government control. Banks were opened through the granting of a charter by the colony (later, the state or commonwealth), but the requirements for charters do not appear to have been onerous. Examinations of a bank's capital adequacy and prudent operations were infrequent and cursory. The notion of a strong central institution as the regulator, "money manager," and examiner of banks was vigorously opposed. As new geographic areas in the expanding nation opened up for settlement, those individuals who wished to start banks were basically as free to do so, as were those who chose other entrepreneurial activities. The same concept of freedom that allowed a person to open a blacksmith's shop, tavern, or general store was applied to the formation and operation of banks.

Many years passed before the colonists accepted the fact that the very nature of banking calls for a *modus operandi* different from that of any other industry. Banks cannot be open and run in a manner that may be valid in another type of business. The early settlers do not seem to have recognized that a system allowing virtually anyone to open and operate a bank, with little or no regulation and supervision, is also a system in which anyone can close a bank. The effects of this system of "free banking" on the nation's economy were disastrous. At a time when a sound banking system, in which the public could place its trust, could have contributed greatly to the nation's progress, it didn't exist.

Success stories of banks that originated in colonial times are unfortunately few and far between. The original Bank of North America (Philadelphia, 1782), along with the Banks of New York and Massachusetts

(1784), are notable exceptions in a general history of bank failures ad widespread lack of public confidence. Many banks went out of business because of outright mismanagement, despite what may have been the best intentions of their organizers. In other cases, the motivation for opening a bank may have been the hope for quick profits, followed by a hasty departure from one town in order to repeat the process elsewhere.

Banks generally hoarded their limited supplies of gold and silver, and disbursed loan proceeds by issuing their own notes to customers. The concept of crediting these proceeds to accounts had not yet taken hold. Each bank's notes presumably were to be used as a medium of exchange, but actually, they were often rejected by merchants who naturally questioned whether the issuing bank was still in existence. In addition, anyone to whom these notes were tendered necessarily wondered if they could be converted into hard currency.

The ease and prevalence of counterfeiting created an added cause for distrust, and thus constituted an additional weakness in colonial banking. By the mid-nineteenth century, over 1,500 individual bank notes were in circulation. Printing and passing bogus notes posed no problem for enterprising counterfeiters.

For many banks, survival and profitability meant taking all possible measures to discourage or prevent redemption of their notes. A system known as "wildcat banking" evolved, in which banks would open redemption offices at remote locations in the wilderness, where only predatory beasts such as wildcats were believed to roam. Noteholders found it difficult, expensive, and time-consuming to travel to such remote sites. This practice enabled the banks to conserve their precious hoards of gold and silver.

Whenever a colonial bank failed, it left behind, in the hands of its customers, a quantity of unredeemable notes. Public distrust of the system increased in direct proportion to the number of bank failures, and was fueled by the questionable value of any given note. A growing economy and an increasing population clearly established the need for an improved banking system.

That need was met on two occasions by establishing a new type of financial institution. In both cases, a beneficial short-term effect was produced. However, in both cases, the new institutions were legislated out of existence. The First and Second Banks of the United States were chartered by Congress for twenty-year periods in 1791 and 1816, respectively. The federal government supplied one-fifth of the initial authorized capital for each, thus making an appearance of financial strength for the public. However, both banks acted as collection agents by accepting from their customers the notes issued by other banks, then presenting these and insisting on settlement in hard currency. This "policeman" function was vehemently resented by the note-issuing banks. In addition, there was strong opposition to the First Bank from the followers of Thomas Jefferson, who questioned its constitutionality, as well as to the Second Bank from the White House itself.[1] In each case, the opposition was so powerful that Congress failed to renew the banks' charters and they were allowed to go out of existence.

The period from 1836 to 1863, following the demise of the Second Bank, has been described as the darkest in American banking history. The problems and weaknesses that had existed in previous years multiplied, and public confidence in the system grew steadily weaker in direct proportion to the number of failures, the prevalence of counterfeiting, and the continued practice of "wildcat banking."

The National Banking Acts

As Secretary of the Treasury under President Lincoln, Salmon P. Chase was given a dual mandate to raise the funds necessary for continuing the Civil War, and simultaneously to devise a solution to the chaotic conditions that existed in the banking system. With ingenuity and diligence, Chase drew up legislation that was passed by Congress in 1863 and expanded and amended in 1864. This legislation is commonly called the National Bank Act, although it technically consists of both the National Banking and National Currency Acts. It is a major landmark in American banking history.

The Act established a new office within the Treasury Department, and created the title of Comptroller of the Currency for the person who was to occupy it. A new form of financial institution, the *national bank,* was created by the Act, and the Comptroller was given responsibility for chartering and supervising all such banks. The organizers of a national bank were required to demonstrate the adequacy of its starting capital.

National banks were empowered to issue a new form of currency, the *national bank note.* All such notes were uniform in appearance throughout

[1]Bray Hammond, *Banks and Politics in America* (Princeton, NJ: Princeton University Press, 1957) pp. 115–117.

the country, except for the name of the issuer. To insure their acceptance by the public, the notes had to be backed by government bonds, which the issuing bank was required to buy in an amount proportionate to its capital. If a national bank failed, the Act made each shareholder personally liable for a sum equal to the value of his holdings.

For the first time in our banking history, a system of bank examination, along with a reporting requirement, came into being. National banks were required to file periodic sworn statements of their financial condition with the Comptroller and were subject to examination by his Office at any time. The Act also mandated a system of reserves, to be maintained by the banks for the protection of their depositors.

Salmon Chase had hoped that existing state-chartered banks would apply for conversion of their charters in order to become "national," and thus gain stature with the public. In actual practice this did not happen. State-chartered banks displayed little inclination to accept the more rigorous terms of national chartering. In an effort to correct this, Congress levied a prohibitive tax on all issues of state bank notes.[2] This accelerated the development of the deposit business, since banks began crediting loan proceeds directly to customers' accounts.

The Dual Banking System

The end result of the National Bank Act was the creation of a dual banking system that has remained essentially unchanged since 1864. Every commercial bank has the option of obtaining its charter from either the federal government or the banking department in its own state. Conversion from either type of charter to the other is possible. Since 1914, while the proportions have varied somewhat from time to time, state-chartered banks have typically accounted for two-thirds of all our commercial banks.[3]

The Period from 1864 to 1913

The National Bank Act did a great deal to eliminate or lessen the weaknesses that had existed prior to its passage. The new system of chartering

[2]Carter H. Golembe, "The Federal Government's Role in Shaping U.S. Banking Structure," *American Banker* (March 6, 1981):22.
[3]David H. Jones, "The National Banking System: Origins and Objectives," *Banking* (October 1975):146.

and supervision promoted public confidence. The fact that national bank notes were known to be backed by government bonds increased this trust. The Act is also noteworthy because it recognized that banking is, *per se*, different from other industries, and cannot be allowed to operate without government supervision and regulation. It is difficult to try to visualize what the effect on the nation's economy might have been if the abuses and weaknesses of colonial banking had been allowed to continue unchecked.

Nevertheless, it can be seen in retrospect that the Act was far less than a panacea for all the financial ills of an expanding nation. In the years following its passage, significant new weaknesses, and problems, either traceable to the Act itself or unforeseen by Chase and his peers, were identified in the banking system. These reached such proportions that the need for new legislation was apparent.

One such weakness lay in the inflexibility of the money supply. National bank notes assumed an increased role as an accepted medium of exchange, and an increase in the supply of these notes would have been desirable and appropriate to meet the needs of a booming, post–Civil War economy. However, by law, the quantity of notes in circulation was limited to ninety percent of the outstanding dollar amount of government bonds. The note supply could not increase unless the government issued additional bonds. A prospering economy produced the opposite result; the Treasury, in order to reduce its debt, called in some of the outstanding bond issues and redeemed them through its increased revenues. The quantity of notes therefore decreased proportionately. A portion of the nationally recognized form of currency was withdrawn from circulation at the very time when it was most needed.

A second weakness resulted from the provision of the Act that required national banks to maintain a specified base of reserves in money center cities, the largest of which was New York. No provision had been made for seasonal fluctuations; the same requirements for reserves applied at all times. In a pyramid effect, reserves from banks throughout the country built up in New York banks and were put to work in the form of investments and loans. When the New York banks were called on to release reserve funds to the banks that occupied lower positions in the pyramid, they were forced to meet their obligation by calling in loans or selling investments. Either action was undesirable from the standpoint of customer good will and highly detrimental from the standpoint of profits.

As subsequently perceived, the third defect in the National Bank Act was its failure to make any sort of provision for the speedy presentation and collection of checks throughout the country. As the population grew and commerce increased, checks became more widely used as a payment medium; however, the Act did not provide a system to expedite their processing. Checks drawn on banks in other cities were usually collected through correspondent banks, but the process—whether by design or because of its inherent weakness—was slow and cumbersome. It was not uncommon for several weeks to elapse before a check drawn on a Boston bank, but deposited with a Philadelphia bank, completed its cycle and was converted into available funds for the depositor.

The depression of 1893 and the financial panic of 1907 hastened recognition of the need for further reform in the banking system and for corrective legislation to address the three fundamental weaknesses. A National Monetary Commission was named to submit ideas for financial reform to Congress, and a series of hearings was held by the House Banking and Currency Committee to examine the state of the nation's financial resources. An American Bankers Association panel, the presidents of forty-seven state banking associations, agrarian leaders, spokesmen for both conservative and progressive factions, and President Woodrow Wilson himself all contributed ideas and exerted influence. After many compromise sessions between the Senate and House, the Federal Reserve Act, reflecting the input of many of the aforementioned groups, was passed and signed into law by Wilson in December 1913.[4]

THE FEDERAL RESERVE ACT

Like the legislation of 1863, which had stemmed directly from the crises and weaknesses of colonial and nineteenth-century banking, the Federal Reserve Act resulted from the government's perceived need for strengthening and reforming the system. It has been identified as the greatest legislative accomplishment of the Wilson era, aside from wartime measures.[5]

The Act represented a blend of elements that were incorporated into

---

[4]The step-by-step progress of the Act is detailed by Roger T. Johnson in *Historical Beginnings: The Federal Reserve* (Boston, MA: Federal Reserve Bank of Boston, 1977).
[5]"The Coming of the Fed," *Banking* (October 1975):148.

it to satisfy the demands of many diverse groups. To those who opposed a strong central bank and resented any form of increased government control, it offered the proviso that the Federal Reserve Banks it created would be privately owned. To those who feared that the President or Congress would be in a position to dictate to the banks, it made the Fed independent of both, and thus conferred on it an autonomy that still exists. To bankers who opposed mandatory membership in the new system, the Act offered a further compromise: all national banks would be required to join, while membership would be optional for state-chartered banks. To those who had voiced concerns over the weaknesses in the banking system that had developed after 1864, it provided specific, viable solutions. The Act made every effort to satisfy not only the Westerners and Southerners who wanted easier credit, but also the Eastern bankers who sought greater stability in the banking industry.[6]

The Federal Reserve Act required member banks to buy stock in the new system in an amount equal to 6 percent of their capital and surplus. It divided the nation geographically into 12 districts, and created a Federal Reserve Bank in each; these were to be the repositories for the reserves that the member banks were required to maintain, and were also to provide facilities for the rapid collection of checks. In this manner, two of the weaknesses of the post–1864 period were addressed. The third weakness, that is, an inflexible money supply, was resolved by giving the Fed authority to issue its notes as legal tender. In addition, the Fed in each district became the distributor of currency and coin for member banks.

The Act specified that the reserves kept with the Fed by its member banks would not earn interest. In return, member banks would gain access to such Fed services as check collection, safekeeping, wire transfers, and the supplying of coin and currency without any direct cost.

To prevent banks from having to call in loans during any period of financial crisis, the Act gave the Fed the power to make direct loans to member banks, and to charge them interest at the *discount rate*. The range of discount rates for all Federal Reserve banks in recent years is shown in Table 1.1. It is this capacity to extend credit that has made the Fed the "lender of last resort" in the United States.[7]

Federal Reserve Banks were also given responsibility for the issuance,

---

[6]William Burke, *"The Fed: The Nation's Central Bank"* (San Francisco, CA: Federal Reserve Bank of San Francisco, 1978), p. 3.
[7]William F. Staats, *Money and Banking* (Washington, D.C.: American Bankers Association, 1982), pp. 74–75.

Table 1.1.   Range of Discount Rates
Selected Dates, 1972–1982[a]

Effective Date	Rate
12/31/72	4½
12/31/73	7½
12/31/74	7¾
5/23/75	6
11/26/76	5¼
10/26/77	6
5/12/78	7
9/22/78	8
10/20/78	8½
11/3/78	9½
8/20/79	10½
10/10/79	12
2/19/80	13
5/8/81	14
4/30/82	12
10/7/82	9½

Source: Federal Reserve Bulletin, various issues.
[a]Intermediate rate adjustments occurred between each of the dates shown.

safekeeping, and redemption of all United States government obligations, and for conducting regular examinations of all member banks. The Fed has authority to issue regulations governing member banks' operations and, most importantly, to control the nation's flow of money and credit. It has three basic tools or techniques at its disposal for this purpose.

By raising or lowering the discount rate, the Fed can make bank credit easier or more difficult to obtain. Similarly, by changing the percentage of required reserves, the Fed can accomplish its objectives. Its Open Market Committee, which meets every week, determines just how much money and credit the economy requires under prevailing business conditions. The Open Market Committee, which regulates the quantity of government obligations in circulation, must also be guided by the necessary level of government borrowing. These three techniques form the foundation of monetary policy in the United States.

The overall operations of the Fed are managed by a seven-member

Board of Governors, appointed by the President of the United States for fourteen-year terms and subject to confirmation by the Senate.

Although the Fed resembles the central banks in other countries in serving as the nation's "money manager" and "the bankers' bank," its private ownership (member banks are the only stockholders in the twelve Federal Reserve district banks) and its freedom from direct control by the President or Congress make it unique among all such institutions. Although member banks control almost three-quarters of the total deposits in the commercial banking system, less than half of the banks are Fed members.[8] In one of the most significant developments in banking in recent years, that percentage of Fed membership has actually been declining.

The ability of the Fed to control the flow of money and credit, and to regulate and examine banks, will obviously be a function of the extent of bank membership in the System. A reduction in membership lessens the Fed's regulatory ability and reduces the amount of bank reserves under its control. The magnitude of this problem surfaced with the drastic increase in money market rates in the late 1970s.

Attrition from the System

As mentioned earlier, the Federal Reserve Act required member banks to keep reserves with their district Bank, earning no interest. As the cost of funds soared in the late 1970s, banks in increasing numbers weighed the value of the Fed services they received against the potential income they could gain if their reserves at the Fed could be freed up and put to profitable use. For example, in 1978 Walter Wriston, Chairman of Citicorp and Citibank, N. A., estimated that his bank could increase its annual pre-tax income by $80 to $90 million if it withdrew from the Fed and used its reserves for loans and investments at 1978 yield rates.[9] During that same year, 99 banks, using similar logic, actually withdrew from Fed membership and thus contributed to a lessening of the Fed's ability to monitor and control monetary policy.[10]

[8]As of June 30, 1982, 37.4% (5,498) of all commercial banks were Federal Reserve members.
[9]"Banking in Transition," *The Bankers Magazine*, (September–October 1978):35.
[10]Peter D. Schellie, *Manager's Guide to the 1980 Monetary Control Act* (Washington, D.C.: American Bankers Association, 1980), p. 23.

The problem of declining Fed membership had actually been identified in 1977 by an informal advisory committee in these words:

> The erosion of membership has become a matter of increasing concern to the Federal Reserve. . . . The present structure and form of System reserve requirements imposed on member banks constitutes a major burden on these banks and is primarily responsible for the increasing withdrawals from membership. . . . These withdrawals . . . have resulted in an erosion . . . of the portion of the money supply under the direct control of the monetary authority.[11]

The Monetary Control Act of 1980, discussed in a later section of this chapter, addressed the problem of attrition from the Fed and attempted to assure that enough deposits would be subject to reserve requirements so that changes in them would influence monetary policy.

The range of activities of the Fed affecting the member banks and the nation's economy is enormous. In addition to all its decisions on the basic tools of monetary policy—Open Market operations, the discount rate, and required reserves—it is involved in all the acquisitions, mergers, and service activities of bank holding companies, the operations of foreign banks in the United States, and the compliance of member banks with all its regulations. A listing of those regulations is contained in Table 1.2.

If the Federal Reserve Act of 1913 had done no more than correct the weaknesses of the post-1863 era by solving the problems of "pyramid" reserves and an inflexible money supply, and establishing a system for the rapid collection of checks, it would still represent a milestone in our banking history. However, the Act went beyond those corrective steps and strengthened the soundness of the banking system through its examining and supervisory functions.

In its role as a lender of last resort, the Fed has provided a vital source of credit when all others have been exhausted. The bankruptcy of the former Penn Central provides a classic example of the Fed's role. By providing unlimited assurance to its members that it would supply funds if needed, the Fed averted a nationwide collapse in the commercial paper market and an accompanying fiscal crisis of major proportions.

Federal Reserve operations also constitute a major source of income

---

[11]"The Problem of Declining Membership: The Elements of a Solution," A Report to the Directors of the Federal Reserve Bank of New York (April 1977):1.

Table 1.2. Federal Reserve Regulations

Regulation	Subject Matter
A	Loans by the Fed to depository institutions
B	Equal credit opportunity
C	Home mortgage disclosure
D	Reserve requirements
E	Electronic funds transfers
F	Registration and filing of securities statements by state-chartered member banks
G	Extensions of credit to finance securities transactions
H	Membership requirements
I	Member stock in federal reserve banks
J	Check collection and funds transfer
K	International banking operations
L	Interlocking bank relationships
M	Consumer leasing
N	Relationships with foreign banks
O	Loans to executive officers of member banks
P	Member bank protection standards
Q	Interest on deposits
R	Interlocking relationships between securities dealers and member banks
S	Reimbursement for providing financial records
T	Margin credit extended by brokers and dealers
U	Margin credit extended by banks
V	Guarantee of loans for national defense work
X[a]	Borrowers who obtain margin credit
Y	Bank holding companies
Z	Truth in Lending
AA	Consumer complaint procedures
BB	Community reinvestment

Source: Board of Governors of the Federal Reserve System, "A Guide to Federal Reserve Regulations" (Washington, D.C., September 1981).

[a] Regulation W pertained to extensions of consumer credit. It was revoked in 1952.

for the United States Treasury. Gross income of the Federal Reserve Banks in 1981 was $15.5 billion, of which $14.2 billion was paid to the Treasury Department after statutory dividends had been paid to the member banks on their stock.[12]

As was true in the case of the National Bank Act, the Federal Reserve Act had become so necessary that one cannot visualize a banking system and a national economy that could have grown and been profitable without it. Nevertheless, because the Federal Reserve operates independently of the White House and Congress, and because there is a lack of agreement among authorities about the wisdom of its actions in monetary policy, it is both a visible and controversial agency of government.

THE GLASS-STEAGALL ACT

The end of World War I and the return of the American economy to peacetime functioning introduced an era of unrestrained optimism and tremendous growth in the private sector. The passage of the Federal Reserve Act had strengthened the banking system by correcting the deficiencies and weaknesses of the pre-1913 era, and during the "Roaring Twenties" banks both reflected and participated in the nation's vitality. Stock market averages soared, businesses reported record profits, and individuals—at least in terms of paper values—became far more affluent. Federal and state authorities liberalized their criteria for chartering and allowed many new banks to open, perhaps on the assumption that the new institutions could not fail to benefit from the nation's economic boom. The banks, in turn, took full advantage of existing laws and became active underwriters of new securities issues, while at the same time building up their own portfolios through heavy investments in common stocks. The commercial and investment banking functions were intermingled. Banks vied with one another in the quest for new funds by offering interest on demand deposits.

Just as the authors of the 1863 National Bank Act could not have foreseen the problems that made its supplementing so necessary in 1913, Wilson and his colleagues also could not have predicted the tragic events

---

[12]*Federal Reserve Bulletin* (February 1982):103.

of the era of the Great Depression, including the near-collapse of the commercial banking industry. The relationship of banks to their economic environment is nowhere more evident than during this period. The Stock Market Crash of 1929 ended the economic boom, and those banks that had tried to capitalize on the climate of unbridled optimism, and in many cases had contributed to it, began to suffer dreadful reverses. The loans they had so optimistically made proved uncollectible as business bankruptcies increased. The paper values of their investment portfolios shrank each day as new stock market declines were posted.

In the ten years preceding 1929, bank failures had averaged about 550 per year. 1930, the year after the stock market collapse, witnessed the closing of over 1,300 banks as their losses mounted and they were unable to meet depositors' demands for payments.[13] The "domino effect" of a single bank failure in a community has often been noted; when over 1,000 banks are forced to close in a single year, a crisis is inevitable as public confidence gives way to outright panic.

A severe blow to that already-shaken confidence was administered by the failure of the Bank of the United States, with over $200 million in deposits, at the end of 1930. This represented the largest failure in our banking history up to that time, and the fiscal crisis was immediately intensified because the bank's name led many individuals to believe that it was the official bank of the federal government. The Fed found its prestige damaged by its inability to keep the bank from failing.

America's financial panic had its counterparts abroad, as Great Britain and twenty-five other countries abandoned the gold standard. During 1932, an additional 2,000 commercial banks, having over $1.7 billion in deposits, failed in the United States.[14] The surviving banks drastically curtailed their credit facilities, and businesses, unable to borrow, were forced to close. Unemployment reached the incredible level of 25%. Because Fed membership was mandatory only for national banks, that agency was powerless in the majority of cases of bank failure; in 1930 there were 17,026 state banks not supervised by any federal agency, and many of these were among the failures. At the end of a five-year period (1929 through 1933), the record showed that a total of over $7 billion in deposits had been lost in over 9,000 bank failures.[15]

[13]Frances E. Wrocklage, "Banking in the Depression," *Banking* (October 1975):40.
[14]Wrocklage, "Banking in the Depression," pp. 41–42.
[15]Carter H. Golembe, "The Organization of Modern Banking," in Herbert V. Prochnow and Herbert V. Prochnow, Jr. (Eds.), *The Changing World of Banking* (New York: Harper & Row, 1974), p. 17.

In one of his first official acts following his inauguration as President in March 1933, Franklin D. Roosevelt ordered a complete shutdown of the banking system for several days. This was intended to provide a cooling-off period, during which the banks could reorganize and the panic could subside. Following this bank holiday, many institutions decided not to reopen. However, in the meantime, Congress had begun a series of hearings that culminated in the 1933 statutes properly known as the Glass-Steagall Act, or the Banking Act of 1933. This legislation, further reforming the banking system, included a prohibition on all interest payments on demand deposits, a prohibition against underwriting of municipal revenue bonds by banks, a prohibition on bank investments in common stock for their own portfolio purposes, and the creation of the Federal Deposit Insurance Corporation (FDIC).

The objective of the FDIC, an official agency of the federal government, is the protection of depositors at insured banks and the promotion of safe and sound bank practices. All Fed member banks (and, therefore, all national banks) were required to join the FDIC; mutual savings banks and state-chartered nonmembers were invited to join. The original insurance coverage of $2,500 per account has repeatedly been raised, and is now $100,000. For the protection of customers at federal savings and loan associations, a parallel agency, the FSLIC (Federal Savings and Loan Insurance Corporation), was also formed.

The operations of the FDIC are supervised by a three-member Board of Governors, two of whom are appointed by the President of the United States. The third member, *ex officio*, is the Comptroller of the Currency. The Corporation's rights and powers include:

1. Setting standards for its member banks
2. Examining them
3. Setting maximum interest rates payable by any FDIC members not otherwise regulated
4. Ruling on merger or branching requests submitted by member banks
5. Taking remedial action to assist an insured bank that is in difficulty
6. Providing insurance coverage for depositors at insured banks
7. Causing the removal of any officer or director who is deemed to have engaged in unsound practices at an insured bank, or to have violated regulations or statutes

The FDIC is authorized to borrow up to $3 billion directly from the

U.S. Treasury at any time, but even when the two largest bank failures in American history occurred in 1974,[16] this borrowing privilege was never exercised. Insured banks pay an annual assessment to the FDIC, equal to 1/12 of 1% of deposits, as a form of insurance premium. If the Corporation's operating results warrant it, a portion of the assessment is subsequently returned to the banks.

The authority of the FDIC and the FSLIC to assume an activist role in dealing with banks and savings and loans that are in financial difficulty was exercised frequently in 1981 and 1982 because of the problems encountered by the thrift institutions. Savings banks and savings and loans have traditionally been the prime sources of home mortgage credit; the loans they extend are long term, and in the past were always made at fixed interest rates that could not be changed during the term of the credit. In 1981 and 1982, they found themselves the victims of an inexorable profit crunch, resulting from the tremendous increases in money market rates. They suffered from a substantial negative spread between their current cost of funds (i.e., interest paid out) and their yield on portfolios of mortgage loans made many years earlier, at far lower rates. In many cases, they sustained losses so severe that survival was impossible. Had they been allowed to fail, the cost to the FDIC and the FSLIC would have been enormous; therefore, both federal agencies acted to prevent their failures by arranging their mergers with stronger insured institutions.

Nine of the ten largest mutual savings banks in New York City posted net operating losses in 1980 totaling $264 million.[17] In a continuation of this trend, thirty-four of New York State's savings banks did so poorly in the first quarter of 1982 that they had to seek State approval before paying any interest to their depositors.[18] As their insurer, the FDIC took action in several of these cases to arrange mergers, six of which caused it direct expenses of $983 million during the first four months of 1982. However, the cost of paying depositors would have been far greater if the banks had been permitted to fail.[19]

The problems of the savings and loan industry were even more severe. As a group, savings and loans (S&Ls) lost over $6 billion in 1981,[20] and

---

[16]Franklin National Bank (New York) and United States National Bank (San Diego).
[17]Karen Slater, "Nine Big NYC Mutuals Lost $264 Million in 1980," *American Banker* (February 10, 1981):1.
[18]Paul J. Browne, "Bank News is Bad News," *Empire State Report* (June 7, 1982):227.
[19]Karen Stater, "FDIC Thrift Aid Nears $1 Billion," *American Banker* (April 6, 1982):1.
[20]William D. Marbach, "The Fidelity Takeover," *Newsweek* (April 26, 1982):68.

the FSLIC spent $81 million in the first quarter of 1982 to assist in the mergers of 10 troubled associations.[21]

As a general rule, these government-assisted mergers took place in the same segment of the total financial marketplace; that is, a thrift institution was merged with another of the same type. Two recent exceptions to this rule established a precedent, and may prove to be the forerunners of further crossings of the boundary lines that have traditionally separated commercial banks from thrift institutions.

In the first merger of its type in our history, Marquette National Bank (Minneapolis) acquired the Farmers and Mechanics Savings Bank in the same city.[22] The FDIC supplied $95 million to help bring about this merger.[23] A continuation of problems in the thrift industry may lead to further takeovers of this type, since the commercial banks may represent the only institutions with sufficient financial strength to become potential partners.

The second exception may prove to be even more significant as a prelude to the eventual relaxing of the rules prohibiting interstate banking. The Federal Reserve approved the acquisition of the $3 billion Fidelity S&L of San Francisco by New York's Citicorp, despite strong opposition from California banks. An estimated $165 million was provided by the FSLIC to assist in the acquisition.[24] The approval marked the first time the Fed had consented to the takeover, across state lines, of an S&L by a bank holding company.

In the banking industry, as in many other areas of everyday life, it is bad news, rather than good, that makes headlines and draws public attention. When the FDIC expends $452 million to bring about the merger of a $2 billion New York City savings bank with one in Buffalo, the problems of the former are emphasized, rather than the fact that the merger created the nation's largest thrift institution, having assets of over $9 billion.[25] When an Oklahoma commercial bank fails and the largest single depositor payoff in FDIC history takes place, tremors shake the entire

[21]Linda W. McCormick, "2 California S&Ls in Assisted Merger," *American Banker* (June 2, 1982):3.

[22]Robert J. Cole, "Bank, Thrift Unit Merge in Minnesota," *The New York Times* (February 23, 1982):D5.

[23]Karen Slater, "First Government-Assisted Merger of Mutual, Commercial Bank Completed in Minneapolis," *American Banker* (February 23, 1982):1.

[24]Linda W. McCormick and Robert E. Norton, "Fed Lets Citicorp Acquire Fidelity Savings & Loan," *American Banker* (September 29, 1982):1.

[25]Robert A. Bennett, "U.S. Sets Big Bank Merger," *The New York Times* (March 27, 1982):30.

financial marketplace and bank stock prices fall. Virtually lost in these news stories is the past record of the FDIC, along with any mention of the financial strength that it still enjoys.[26]

Since 1934, the FDIC has been involved in the failures of 712 banks, with four million depositors. Of these, 99.9% received full recovery within FDIC limits, at a cost to the Corporation of over $6 billion. Yet the FDIC insurance fund, at year-end 1981, still showed $11 billion that could be used for the protection of other depositors if necessary.[27] Similarly, the FSLIC insurance fund, at year-end 1981, amounted to $7 billion.[28] The image of the financial industry in the public mind would be enhanced if these figures were to be noted more frequently and prominently.

THE MONETARY CONTROL ACT

As was noted earlier, the late 1970s were marked by an increasing exodus from the Federal Reserve, along with a corresponding impairment of the Fed's ability to control the flow of money and credit. Chairman Paul Volcker testified in 1980 that 69 banks, with aggregate deposits of $7 billion, had given notice of their intent to withdraw from the Fed, and that deposits at member banks had declined by 3 percent in the preceding three years.[29] The percentage of total bank deposits subject to reserve requirements fell from 86 percent in 1945 to 80 percent in 1970, and to 69 percent in 1979.[30] The Secretary of the Treasury, the Comptroller of the Currency, and banking spokesmen all addressed Congress regarding the need for legislative action.

The Depository Institutions Deregulation and Monetary Control Act of 1980, more commonly known by the latter half of its title, was described by Senator William Proxmire, Chairman of the Senate Committee on

[26]Robert E. Norton, "Bank Stocks, CD Markets Squeezed by Penn Square," *American Banker* (July 8, 1982):1. See also G. Christian Hill, "Penn Square," *The Wall Street Journal* (July 9, 1982):18.
[27]All statistics from Federal Deposit Insurance Corporation, *Annual Report* (1981).
[28]H. Brent Beesley, "Director of S&L Insurer Ponders Agency's Future," *American Banker* (April 19, 1982):4.
[29]Elbert V. Bowden, *Revolution in Banking* (Richmond, VA: Robert F. Dame, Inc., 1980), p. 120.
[30]Schellie, *Manager's Guide to the 1980 Monetary Control Act*, p. 23.

Banking, as "the most significant banking legislation since 1913."[31] The Act had two stated objectives:

> To improve the effectiveness of monetary policy by making the fulcrum on which that policy operates more stable

and

> To provide competitive equity among financial institutions which, given uniform reserve requirements, will be placed on a more equal footing and, given new authorities, will be able to offer more equivalent services to their customers.[32]

As signed into law by President Carter in March 1980, the Act consisted of nine titles:

I   Monetary Control Act
II   Depository Institutions Deregulation Act
III   Consumer Checking Account Equity Act
IV   Powers of Thrift Institutions
V   State Usury Laws
VI   Truth-in-Lending Simplification and Reform
VII   Amendments to the National Banking Laws
VIII   Financial Regulation Simplification
IX   Foreign Control of United States Financial Institutions

The following are some of the major, specific provisions of the Act:[33]

1.   The term *transaction accounts* was coined to include checking and NOW accounts, share draft accounts at credit unions, savings accounts that allow automatic transfers or payments, and accounts that permit more than three telephone or preauthorized payments each month.

---

[31]In *Federal Reserve Bulletin* (June 1980):444.
[32]Board of Governors of the Federal Reserve System, *The Monetary Control Act of 1980* (Washington, D.C., June 1981), p. 1.
[33]A detailed presentation of the Act may be found in *Federal Reserve Bulletin* (June 1980):444–453.

2. *All* depository institutions are required to maintain non-interest-bearing reserves on *both* transaction accounts and nonpersonal time deposits with maturities of less than four years.

3. Institutions with net transaction account balances of $25 million or less must keep reserves of 3% in cash or in a reserve account; those with larger transaction account balances must maintain reserves of 3% on the first $25 million and 12% on the remainder.

4. These new, uniform reserve requirements are to be phased in on a gradual basis through 1987.

5. Membership in the Federal Reserve System remains optional for state-chartered banks and required for national banks. Member institutions must keep their reserves with their district Federal Reserve Bank. Other institutions may use either a Federal Reserve Bank or a member correspondent.

6. A Depository Institutions Deregulation Committee (DIDC), composed of the Secretary of the Treasury and the Chairmen of the Federal Reserve Board of Governors, FDIC, the Federal Home Loan Bank Board, and the National Credit Union Administration, was formed. It must meet at least once each quarter to determine the timing of the gradual phaseout of interest rate ceilings. The controls over interest rates established under Federal Reserve Regulation Q will be eliminated by March 31, 1986.

7. Federal deposit insurance was increased to $100,000.

8. *All* depository institutions were authorized to offer NOW accounts and automatic transfers between accounts and to establish remote service units. All federally insured credit unions were authorized to offer share drafts.[34]

9. All depository institutions offering transaction accounts were given borrowing privileges at the Fed.

10. The Federal Reserve Board was directed to implement a system of explicit pricing for all its services.

11. Expanded lending powers were given to S&Ls, allowing them to invest up to 20% of their assets in consumer loans, corporate debt issues, and commercial paper. Federally chartered savings and loans

---

[34]A *share draft* is a checklike negotiable instrument, used by a credit union member as a payment medium.

were freed from all geographical restrictions on lending, and were authorized to grant mortgage loans in unlimited amounts, offer credit cards, and exercise fiduciary powers.

12. The Federal Reserve Board was directed to issue a revised Regulation Z, streamlining and simplifying the requirements of truth in lending.

Of necessity, many years must elapse before the full impact of the Act on every type of institution can be assessed. Nevertheless, some immediate results have already been identified, and some predictions about the future effects of the Act can be made.

Since all commercial banks will henceforth be subject to reserve requirements, the basic rationale for withdrawing from the Fed will disappear, enhancing the ability of the Fed to conduct its programs of monetary policy.

As a result of explicit pricing, the transaction volume handled by the Fed will decline. Rather than pay specific charges to the Fed, banks will increasingly turn to their correspondents for such services as check collection. At the Federal Reserve Bank of New York, which handles by far the largest volume of checks in the Fed system, the number of items processed fell from an average of nine million per day to eight million per day in 1981.[35] Federal Reserve authorities believe that the income from the new program of explicit pricing will offset the loss of earnings resulting from a decrease in reserves under Fed control. It is also anticipated that new competitive opportunities will exist for correspondent banks, and that there will be new incentives for cost-effective systems at all commercial banks.[36]

As banks find it necessary to pass along to their customers the explicit prices imposed by the Fed, the overall movement toward other forms of payment can be expected to accelerate. Electronic funds transfer applications and systems which allow for payment of bills by telephone will become increasingly popular.[37]

The fact that NOW and share-draft accounts have become available throughout the country will increase the competitive pressures on commercial banks from thrift institutions and credit unions. Evidence is already

[35]Federal Reserve Bank of New York, *Annual Report* (1981):25.
[36]Federal Reserve Board of Governors, *68th Annual Report* (1981):201.
[37]Richard Gilgan, "Deregulation's Impact on Check Processing," *ABA Banking Journal* (June 1982):35.

at hand that testifies to the sophistication of consumers, who appreciate the benefits of a NOW account versus an interest-free checking account. Balances in the former category at commercial banks increased from $8 billion in December 1980 to $46 billion in September 1981, and grew from $1 billion to $6.8 billion at S&Ls during the same period.[38]

Since 1933, Federal Reserve Regulation Q has set ceilings on the interest that member banks may pay on savings and time deposits. Since 1966, a differential, allowing thrift institutions to pay higher rates than commercial banks, has also existed. By 1986, both the ceilings and the differential will have been eliminated. As a result, competition will increase, and long-range strategic planning and effective methods of cost accounting will become even more important in banking.

The increase in federal insurance coverage should allow banks to compete more effectively with uninsured financial intermediaries such as money market funds.[39]

THE BANKING STRUCTURE TODAY

Of all the characteristics of American commercial banking, the most striking is the fragmentation that exists throughout the nation. In other countries, a mere handful of commercial banks dominates the scene; here, over 14,000 abound. This diversification reflects colonial views that the concept of free enterprise applied to all things. These ideals became the basis for the "free banking" laws that were passed in many states in the nineteenth century. Those laws resulted from a deep, widely held concern over the possible concentration of power in a small number of banks, and the ill effects of centralized authority in a federal agency. Thomas Jefferson considered any form of a national or central bank an invasion of states' rights and a violation of the spirit and letter of the Constitution. Conversely, Alexander Hamilton believed that it was the duty of the federal government to intervene whenever necessary to protect a public that would not always act reasonably and justly. Many

[38]Federal Reserve Bank of Richmond, *Annual Report* (1981):8.
[39]Schellie, *Manager's Guide to the 1980 Monetary Control Act*, p. 85.

years later, Hamilton's viewpoint prevailed. The chaotic conditions that "free banking" helped to create formed the justification for the National Bank Act.[40]

Similarly, it was only as a result of the problems and weaknesses such as "pyramid" reserves, the lack of a flexible money supply, and the absence of a program for rapid check collection, which existed after 1864, that the Federal Reserve System was created. Woodrow Wilson made the subject of banking reform part of his 1912 presidential campaign.

Again, it was only in response to the banking crises of the Depression years that the FDIC and the FSLIC came into being. The widespread lack of public confidence caused by thousands of bank failures, with the resulting loss of billions of dollars to depositors, created the need for the Glass-Steagall Act of 1933.

Finally, the Depository Institutions Deregulation and Monetary Control Act of 1980 gave recognition to several problems existing in the financial marketplace: that is, the diminished ability of the Fed to conduct monetary policy when dealing with a reduced number of member banks, the need for thrift institutions to be given additional competitive powers, the inadequacy of the existing limits on federal insurance for deposits, and the problems resulting from interest rate ceilings and differentials between commercial banks and thrift institutions.

This brief overview of the historical evolution of our present banking system, then, admittedly pays more attention to past failures than to successes. It stresses crises, unstable financial conditions, and industry weaknesses as the causative factors leading to the major legislative actions that have shaped the system.

The rationale for this emphasis on the negative aspects of American commercial banking lies in the learning process that examines the past and tries to apply its lessons to the present. Our current system of chartering, supervising, restricting, and examining commercial banks has been severely criticized as anachronistic, duplicative, excessive, and unresponsive to the changing needs of a competitive environment. At the same time, it has been justified on the grounds that much of it is designed to prevent banks from repeating past mistakes. If there is actual overregulation, bankers must temper their resentment of it by realizing that if they desire a large degree of public trust, and want their actions to maintain a

[40]Diane G. McConnell, "Central Banking in the New Nation," *Banking* (October 1975):34–35.

strong impact on the economy, they cannot be given the same amount of freedom as other businesses.[41]

Banks have this in common with other industries: their effectiveness can be measured by their ability to recognize deficiencies and problems and to react in a timely and effective manner. Much of the framework of legislation affecting them results from their own past failures to initiate corrective action. Today's bankers must be developed, trained, and motivated to serve their industry in a more professional way. They may never enjoy the same degree of freedom that their predecessors had, but bemoaning that fact is fruitless. Rather, they must be problem-oriented and prepared to contribute to the nation's well-being, even within a framework of externally imposed constraints. All the factors needed for effective management must work together if that contribution is to be made.

One quality that will make bankers more effective is an ability to consider banking's need to meet a set of obligations to various constituencies. For some of these obligations, no precedent can be found; they did not exist in the past. In other cases, the obligation may have existed, but went unrecognized and therefore unsatisfied. In today's banking, this concept of a set of obligations that directly affect management's approach, the range of services offered, and the daily operations of an institution may be considered essential to the growth and profitability of the industry and its components.

[41]Howard D. Crosse and George H. Hempel, *Management Policies for Commercial Banks,* 2nd Ed. (Englewood Cliffs, NJ: Prentice-Hall, 1973), p. 18.

(June 1981):179.
[7]"GM Zeroes in on Employees Discontent," *Business Week* (May 12, 1973):28.

2 The Constituencies of Commercial Banks

The individuals who supply the capital needed to form a new company, fund a research project, or help produce a new Broadway play find that the process is relatively simple. By executing the necessary legal documents and issuing checks as their contributions to the new venture, they meet the basic requirements and need do little more. However, when a group applies for a charter for a new bank, additional and very different procedures are required. The organizers must prove to federal and/or state authorities that there is a real need for a new bank in the community, and that it is being started with sufficient capital to meet both its legal and practical needs. Their personal and business backgrounds must show that they are of unimpeachable character, and that they have a track record of success, with expertise that will contribute to the new bank's future growth and profitability.

In short, the previously expressed theme repeats itself: banking *is* different from all other industries, and its inherent obligations to various groups can be identified from the outset.

Martin Mayer[1] has noted that the free enterprise system gives any individual the unquestioned right to open the business of his or her choice, *except* when the formation of a bank is at issue. It is the same topic, that is, the obligations of banks, that makes the observation valid. Our commercial banks are part of the private sector, owned by many investors.

[1]*The Bankers* (New York: David McKay Co., 1974), p. 67.

They owe their existence to their *stockholders,* who make up the first group to which certain definite obligations exist.

There are three reasons why *units of government* impose their own set of obligations on banks. First, through their credit function, banks have the ability to create money; that is, by approving loans and crediting the proceeds to customers' accounts, they give those customers money that, in effect, did not exist before. Second, banking as an industry is tremendously important to the national economy. Businesses, consumers, and agencies of federal, state, and local governments rely upon banks for their deposit, payment, and credit functions. Third, by far the largest portion of our total money supply takes the form of demand deposits, which for the most part are held by commercial banks. The soundness of the banking system and the policies and practices of banks are a source of concern to agencies of the federal, state, and local governments.

Depositors, and the public in general, form a third constituency for commercial banks. They demand the protection of deposited funds at all times, as well as certain levels of performance and certain services which must be provided on a prompt, efficient, and cost-effective basis.

Most banks today have embarked on entirely new approaches to the area of personnel management. This reflects recognition of their obligations to the *staff,* both official and clerical.

Finally, banks, like most corporations today, find themselves ever more deeply involved in questions pertaining to the entire broad area of social responsibility. They are in the spotlight in terms of meeting their obligations to the *community.*

The effective bank is the one that recognizes all these obligations and makes every effort to meet each one. The bank that ignores them is destined for a short and unprofitable existence.

STOCKHOLDERS

Individuals who buy bank stocks generally accept the essential conservatism of the industry, and do not expect the growth records of their holdings to match those of the more glamorous and exotic issues in the marketplace. This generalization has traditionally been offset by a second, which holds that bank stocks are usually not subject to the same wide fluctuations as those seen in the equity issues in other industries.

A third generalization may be made, based on stock market analyses. There appears to be a lack of confidence among investors regarding the banks' ability to meet all their contemporary challenges and generate adequate profits. Thus, although a price/earnings ratio of approximately 10 is viewed as a norm in the marketplace, it does not apply to bank stocks. Shares in the major bank holding companies can generally be purchased today at prices that are only five or six times annual earnings. As noted earlier, the problems reported by one or two major banks tend to have a "ripple effect" in the market, spilling over into investors' perceptions of the entire industry, and thus depressing the prices of bank stocks in general.

In an age of consumerism, "sunshine laws," and full disclosure, bank stockholders display a greater tendency than ever before to be inquisitive and vocal regarding all phases of the institution's performance and activities. The bank can no longer satisfy its obligations to the stockholders by reporting increased profits and management successes, along with occasional increases in the dividend rate. Rather, management must be ready to answer stockholder questions about lending policies in areas of the world where civil rights violations have allegedly taken place, about expense accounts and incentive plans for senior officers, about political contributions, about loans to less-developed countries, and about new security measures that appear necessary in reaction to the publicized problems of other banks. Like the annual stockholders' meetings, bank annual reports have become far lengthier. Additional charts and graphics, five- and 10-year comparative summaries, and detailed statements of policy and practices appear.

GOVERNMENTS

A bank's obligations to federal and state governments are both statutory and ethical. These agencies will take all possible steps to assure that every bank under their jurisdiction is operating in a prudent manner and is conforming to all appropriate laws and regulations. Ethically, the bank incurs an obligation to the government by the mere act of obtaining its charter and conducting a banking business. It is accepting a public trust, and its actions must reflect that trust.

Whenever a bank is examined by a government agency, a report of the examiners' findings is sent to the bank's directors, with suggestions for any remedial action that may be necessary. The Comptroller of the Currency, the Federal Reserve, the FDIC, and the state banking departments may issue cease-and-desist orders whenever they find a bank engaging in unsound practices, and they can cause the removal from office of any bank officer or director who has been deemed guilty of contributing to such practices. Repeated violations or management shortcomings can result in the closing of a bank by government fiat and the assuming of its liabilities and assets by another bank (e.g., in an assisted merger), or by an entity of the government itself (e.g., the FDIC). For example, in April 1982, federal regulators seized the Fidelity Savings and Loan Association, fired the president and senior officers, dissolved the institution, and established a new association in its place. This marked the first instance in our history of the actual seizure and reorganization of a savings and loan.[2]

In the abstract, a bank is obligated to understand and implement all the statutes affecting it because only in this way can the interests of all parties be properly served. In concrete terms, a bank is obligated to do so because it will not be allowed to continue in operation if it does not.

DEPOSITORS

Depositors expect transactions to be handled promptly, courteously, and accurately. They must be made to feel that their funds are protected with the utmost care. They look to their banks as a prime source of credit, and consider that their relationship gives them the right to call on the banks in time of need. They expect banks to make it convenient and easy for them to conduct their financial transactions. They are far more sophisticated than their predecessors, and far more aware of their new, expanded freedom of choice in the competitive financial marketplace. The loyalty on which banks depended in the past is difficult to find today. The

[2]As noted earlier, in September 1982, the Federal Reserve approved the takeover of this savings and loan by New York's Citicorp.

"new breed" of depositor recognizes the value of the funds under his or her control and will quickly move them, if necessary, to another institution that offers more or better services at more attractive prices.

Nondepositors, that is, the public in general, also expect certain performance from the banks. They assume that any institution with the word "bank" in its title will automatically be willing to provide them with a whole host of financial services. Bankers are often expected to serve as consultants on all types of financial matters. Their predictions of economic trends, legal opinions, aid in drawing up wills, and investment advice are often sought, and it is often difficult for them to explain why these requests cannot be met.

STAFF

The attitudes of stockholders, the requirements of government authorities, and the expectations of customers have all undergone changes in recent years, but the dynamics of change are nowhere more apparent than in the area of human resources management. The term itself is indicative of this change. *Human resources management* is now used instead of *personnel operations* to reflect the bank's awareness that the staff is as much a resource of the organization as are its deposits, technology, and assets. Banks today generally accept an entirely new set of obligations to their staff members. Their programs for recruiting and training, salary and benefit administration, performance reviews, job enrichment, and supervisory and sensitivity training exemplify this.

In any bank or corporation, the board of directors is the active, governing body, at the apex of the entire organization. It is therefore logical to expect that a bank can best know and appreciate its obligations to all its constituencies by giving them some voice on the board. This is exactly what has happened during the past 10 years. Board membership at many of our largest and most prestigious banks is now held by members of minority groups, among others, who would never have been admitted in prior years. The objective is to have these individuals bring new insights to board meetings—insights that might never have been supplied by the very limited hierarchy from which bank directors traditionally came.

Another aspect of change in the staffing picture has resulted from a discarding of the provincialism and parochialism displayed by bankers in the past. Those attitudes led them to believe that they were uniquely qualified to solve the problems of banking without any help from other professions or industries. Today it has become commonplace for bank management to conduct extensive outside recruiting, not merely at colleges and universities, but also from nonbank companies and disciplines. The mid-career hire has become an integral part of today's banking. Specialists in such fields as marketing, cost accounting, systems analysis, data processing, financial controls, and training have been added to the staffs of major banks to bring them an expertise that was not available internally.

Bankers have also displayed a drastic change in their thinking about the entry-level skills and qualifications, life styles, and attitudes of staff members. Questions are posed today as to the validity of past requirements and management techniques. Must each new employee display the level of educational attainment that banks formerly demanded? Is a criminal record an absolute barrier to any type of employment in a bank, as it formerly was?[3] Can officers, managers, and supervisors interact with their subordinates on a purely authoritarian basis, as they did in the past?

Candidates for bank employment today place far less emphasis on the security and prestige of the job, and are well aware of opportunities outside banking. They look for immediate benefits, rather than the long-range attractiveness of pension and profit-sharing plans.

Similar attitudinal changes prevail among those who are candidates for management positions. They look for jobs that will offer them early promotion, a voice in the management of the organization, and opportunities for decision-making as quickly as possible; if these expectations are not met, they have no hesitation in leaving.[4] The rate of turnover among these individuals creates a significant problem for banks that have invested large sums of money in recruiting and training them, only to have them resign in a relatively short time. The expense factor is exacerbated by the fact that each resignation deprives the bank of a person who had been identified as a future manager.

An even more costly problem in banking is caused by the turnover rate among tellers—the first line of interface with customers, and the cadre whose actions can do so much to create a favorable or unfavorable image

---

[3]In 1973, Chemical New York Corporation, in its Annual Report, cited its special program for hiring and training ex-convicts.

[4]Interviews cited by John Haynes and Nathan Glassman in *New Generation*, (1970), 4:52.

of the bank. In other businesses, a 20 percent rate of turnover could easily be disastrous; in banking, the rate of teller turnover is commonly 40 percent and, at some institutions, 60 percent.[5] From 1965 to 1981, the consumer price index rose over 170 percent, yet average teller salaries increased only 60 percent and suffer by comparison with entry-level pay in the typical major corporation, even though the latter may impose far less responsibility on the new employee.[6]

The maintenance of computers and other inanimate resources is a major expense factor on a bank's annual income statement. No less important should be the "maintenance" of the staff, which is the most important component of the organization. Emphasis on efficiency and productivity must always exist, but should be tempered by a realizatiion that no type of automation or mechanization will eliminate the human element that makes such efficiency possible.[7] The training given to supervisors in banking today frequently recognizes the validity and importance of the work of Abraham Maslow, Frederick Herzberg, and Douglas McGregor.[8] Their analyses of the interface between managers and their subordinates have made a real contribution to the field of management psychology by suggesting approaches that can create better interpersonal relationships and result in a higher degree of achievement of common goals. No bank can hope to build a productive and reliable work force around dissatisfied employees. First-line managers have the best view of employees in the work environment; they should be expected to identify potential problems before they occur, and should attempt to prevent those problems through the use of human resource strategies.

Detailed performance reviews and comprehensive exit interviews play an important part in banking's modern programs of human resources management. They are increasingly used as a means of identifying the causes of dissatisfaction among employees. The concept of a specialized unit, designed to listen to individual grievances on a confidential basis, has also gained wide acceptance.[9] Finally, most banks today emphasize suggestion contests and similar incentive plans that reward employees for their constructive ideas.

[5]Robert O. Metzger, "Teller Turnover," *Bank Administration* (October 1981):39.
[6]Metzger, "Teller Turnover," p. 39.
[7]William M. Berliner, *Managerial and Supervisory Practice: Cases and Principles,* 7th Ed. (Homewood, Ill.: Irwin, 1979), p. 488.
[8]The bibliography lists specific works by these three individuals.
[9]Robert Kirkpatrick, "Employee Retention in Changing Times," *American Banker* (October 5, 1981):13.

Terms such as *motivation* and *job enrichment, career pathing* and *participatory management* have now become part of the vocabulary of banking as new and different obligations to the staff are identified. Many banks have implemented programs that combine various job functions, allow staff members to innovate, and emphasize decision-making at lower levels.[10] In other cases, banks have adopted programs for the specific benefit of members of minority groups in order to address their cultures, value systems, and short- and long-term aspirations.[11]

Affirmative Action

High on the list of contemporary topics in the area of human resource management is the need for specific programs aimed at eliminating all forms of discrimination. Historically, the American banking industry was dominated by native-born, white Protestant males.[12] The barriers to opportunity and career advancement for all others began to break down during World War II, as women assumed many bank positions previously reserved for men. Later, the Civil Rights Act of 1964 provided the impetus, supplemented by legislation in 1967 prohibiting discrimination based on age, and further supplemented by Presidential Executive Orders 11141 and 11246. As is evidenced by a Conference Board report published in 1979, commercial banks gradually assumed a leading position among all industries in complying with the goals of Equal Employment Opportunity.[13] In that same year, federal government statistics disclosed that women and members of minority groups had at least doubled their representation among bank officers and managers since 1970.[14]

As part of this overall effort, the human resources departments in major banks typically have prepared and implemented detailed affirmative action plans, providing information on all their antidiscriminatory practices. In

---

[10]"Bankers Trust Broadens Jobs to Improve Efficiency and Morale," *American Banker* (March 19, 1973):3.

[11]Berliner, *Managerial and Supervisory Practice: Cases and Principles,* p. 368.

[12]Robert M. Fulmer, *Practical Human Relations* (Homewood, Ill.: Irwin, 1977), p. 365.

[13]Daniel Cowles, "Banks Top Industry in EEOC Compliance," *American Banker* (May 4, 1979):2.

[14]J. Veronica Biggins, "Banks Show Significant Progress for Women and Minorities," *ABA Banking Journal* (September 1979):22.

many cases, a bank's performance in this area is directly audited by agencies of federal, state, and local government, and detailed reports are required. The regulations of the OFCC (Office of Federal Contract Compliance) state that these affirmative action plans must itemize the actual steps taken or planned in attaining the goal of complete equality in all respects for all employees.[15]

COMMUNITIES

America's business history is replete with tales of corporations that routinely polluted the environment, acted unethically in forcing competitors out of business, and paid no attention to health or safety standards for their employees. The task of management consisted exclusively of achieving greater profits,[16] and the tycoon who is reported to have said, "The public be damned!" had a great many counterparts among industrialists to whom the concepts of social and civic responsibility meant little or nothing.

Conversely, the twentieth century, and especially the latter part of the 1970s, has become known as an age of consumerism and a period when the pressure for socially responsible actions steadily increased. A corporation's policies and practices today are subject to critical analysis by its stockholders (who are more numerous and vocal than ever before), consumer advocates (who have become far more visible in society), entities of government (who claim to act in the public interest), the media, and a host of activist groups. It no longer suffices for a bank or business to simply point to its bottom-line earnings and corporate successes; it is expected to use its skills and resources to improve the quality of life for all citizens,[17] and there is widespread demand for both banks and businesses to make social concerns a matter of paramount importance.[18]

Commercial banks frequently find themselves called on to display even

[15]The OFCC oversees all employment practices of nonconstruction companies with 50 or more employees and with federal contracts for $50,000 or more.
[16]Robert M. Fulmer, *The New Management*, 2nd Ed. (New York: Macmillan, 1978), p. 259.
[17]Ibid., p. 441.
[18]Peter F. Drucker, *Preparing Tomorrow's Business Leaders Today* (Englewood Cliffs, NJ: Prentice-Hall, 1969), p. 77.

more social responsibility than their corporate peers. This results from the premise that they use money taken from a community, and therefore should be required to return and reinvest it in a wide variety of tangible benefits. Supporting the local Little League or Chamber of Commerce, or having bank officers serve on local hospital or school boards, is simply not enough. The former Chairman of the Bank of America has noted that banks and businesses no longer enjoy their former privilege of merely providing those programs that are implemented "with one eye on . . . self-interest. Those in corporate life are going to be expected to do things for the good of society just to earn their franchise, their corporate right to exist."[19]

Yet an element of self-interest always exists in any program of social responsibility that a bank may introduce, simply because the profitability and growth of the institution are so closely tied to those of the community in which it operates. If a town or city displays symptoms of urban decay and blight, other businesses may move away; banks generally lack this option and must rise or fall with their communities. A major bank has stated this as a matter of policy:

> The well-being of the environment in which a bank functions economically and socially is critical to its profitability, and therefore to the discharge of stockholder responsibility. Both are very dependent on each other.[20]

Social responsibility, then, has become one of the recognized obligations of banks; yet it cannot be viewed in isolation and without regard for all the other obligations inherent in the banking business. The actions taken to meet it may not be immediately compatible with the institution's profit objectives. In addressing this question, David Rockefeller has pointed out that living up to its social responsibility may be even more important for a bank than maximizing its earnings.[21] Indeed, fears have been noted in some quarters that the latter goal may be neglected if the banks and businesses overreact to community and social pressures. Milton Friedman, for example, has been quoted as saying that "the social responsibility of

[19]In *Future Without Shock,* Louis B. Lundborg, p. 84. Copyright 1974 by W. W. Norton & Co., Inc., New York. Reprinted by permission.
[20]Chemical New York Corporation, *Annual Report* (1977).
[21]*Creative Management in Banking* (New York: McGraw-Hill, 1964), p. 83.

business *is* to increase profits,"[22] and he foresees dire consequences for the economy of a free society if the profit motive becomes secondary to the notion of social responsibility.[23]

The programs undertaken by banks for the benefit of the community may entail significant expenditures. One major bank allocates 2 percent of its after-tax earnings to social responsibility, and makes over 200 annual contributions to educational institutions, cultural organizations, neighborhood projects, housing and redevelopment associations, and environmental protection groups at an annual cost of $7 million.[24]

Thus, although social consciousness may be seen as an absolute necessity and a direct obligation for banks, it requires a delicate balance to keep it within the context of overall profitability. An outstanding record as a corporate citizen will not necessarily guarantee liquidity and profits but, conversely, a bak that is unwilling to take socially responsible actions because of their effect on profits can be the target not only of public criticism, but also of some form of reprisals.

Motivation

Whenever a highly visible bank or business adopts a plan of social action, questions may logically be raised about its reasons for doing so. Did it act in a socially responsible way because it believed this was the morally correct course to follow, because it realized its options were limited, or because one of its branches was burned by militants who opposed its power and viewed it as a hostile component of the "establishment"?[25] Do major corporations discontinue polluting because they are good citizens, because they gain tax benefits by installing new equipment, or because they fear sales will drop as a result of bad publicity? Expediency and altruism often go hand in hand; cynical questions are easily posed, and motives are not always readily discernible.[26]

---

[22]In Lundborg, *Future Without Shock*, p. 81 (emphasis added).
[23]In Fulmer, *The New Management*, p. 444.
[24]Willard C. Butcher, "Chase's Philanthropic Activities," Speech delivered at the University of North Carolina (October 16, 1981).
[25]Lundborg, *Future Without Shock*, pp. 20–21.
[26]Richard J. C. Roeber, *The Organization in a Changing Environment* (Reading, MA: Addison-Wesley, 1973), p. 115.

In many cases, the answers come from a combination of factors, including the following:

1. Government regulations
2. Direct pressure from various groups
3. Voluntary commitments

Government Regulations.   In addition to federal, state, and local laws requiring equality of opportunity in every aspect of personnel practices, prohibiting all forms of discrimination in lending, and regulating the forms used in loan processing and the techniques used to collect delinquent loans, all financial institutions are now subject to the terms of the Community Reinvestment Act (CRA). This Act was a response by Congress, in 1978, to the many charges of "redlining" that had been brought against thrift institutions and other lenders, primarily in the home mortgage field. *Redlining* is the pejorative term coined to describe the banks' alleged policy of drawing boundaries in red ink around a neighborhood to outline those areas where loans would not be considered.[27] Prior to the Act, fifteen lawsuits had been brought against federal regulatory agencies by civic groups, charging them with failure to comply with the enforcement provisions of the 1964 Civil Rights Act. The CRA may prevent further litigation of this type.[28]

The Act requires that all federal agencies, in considering a request from a commercial bank or thrift institution for a new branch, acquisition, or holding company activity, must give effect to all that the institution has done or failed to do in meeting the needs of its community. The basic premise is that an institution that is deemed not to have done enough should be enjoined from further growth. Comments *pro* or *con* a bank's lending policies and practices are invited from the public, and all such comments become part of the institution's official dossier, on file with each regulatory agency.

For example, irate civic groups in one area of New York City led a movement resulting in withdrawals of over $600,000 from a bank that had been accused of systematic redlining. Under the terms of the CRA, the FDIC Board of Governors subsequently rejected an application by that

[27]Donald T. Savage, "CRA and Community Credit Needs," *The Bankers Magazine* (January 1979):51.
[28]Steven Pastore, "Redlining—or Red Herring," *The Bankers Magazine* (January 1979):43.

bank for an additional branch, on the grounds that it had taken deposits from the area but had not put those funds to work for the benefit of the same community.[29]

Direct Pressure. As in the preceding example, civic groups may withdraw funds from banks and register complaints with units of government. Community leaders may demand meetings with a bank's management to insist on better treatment. Lawsuits are filed in increasing numbers by bank employees who allege that some form of discrimination has been practiced. Picket lines, led by activists who object to a bank's action or inaction, may appear. Each of these can detract from the institution's image, and ultimately affect the balance sheet.

A further dilemma confronts the banks in the area of social responsibility, since civic leaders and labor unions may demand direct financial help for a troubled community; that is, they claim that a bank *must* invest in the municipality's debt issues. This raises serious questions about the degree of risk a bank can reasonably be expected to take. It is a common misconception that banks have large pools of money, consisting chiefly of their own funds, to lend and invest as they see fit. Nothing could be further from the truth. In actuality, $90 out of each $100 that banks lend or invest comes from depositors, rather than from capital and surplus. Prudence in lending and investing these funds is directly tied to the concept of responsibility to the depositors. Since 1975, reports of the financial difficulties of many major cities have appeared with alarming frequency. Social responsibility might call for banks to support those cities by buying their bonds and notes; yet considerations of risk cannot be ignored for the sake of fulfilling that responsibility.

The basic policy decision that must be made addresses the question of applying normal credit criteria in lending and investing when municipal debt issues, mortgage loans in deteriorating neighborhoods, or loans to small, minority-owned businesses are at issue. To relax those criteria may be tantamount to assuming otherwise unacceptable risks, placing the funds of depositors in jeopardy, and incurring criticism from federal or state bank examiners.

Voluntary Commitments. A nationwide survey conducted in 1972 disclosed that 42 percent of the respondents were ''not sure'' what contri-

[29]Ibid.

butions commercial banks were making to the well-being of their communities. In the same study, 64 percent of the respondents indicated a desire for greater bank involvement in community programs.[30]

There is strong evidence that a positive message from the banks to the public is now being conveyed. Whether a bank provides bullet-proof vests for police officers or sponsors cultural projects, whether it conducts information seminars for widows, retirees, and investors or creates training programs for disadvantaged adults, a bank can contribute to the quality of life and the well-being of its community. The American Bankers Association has published a detailed list of purely voluntary measures, similar to those mentioned above, taken by banks throughout the country to meet the needs of their communities.[31]

The Social Audit

Because socially responsible actions have become such an important part of the overall operations of banks and businesses, attempts have been made to quantify the extent to which these organizations have actually discharged their obligations. These efforts at performance measurement have been described as "social audits." They are designed to show the sensitivity with which an organization has adapted to social change:

> The evolving means by which the corporation and others have striven to appraise the impact of its actions on society, and the manner in which it has discharged its social responsibility, have generally been described as a *social audit*.[32]

The social audit may be a listing of the expectations of social groups as identified by the bank or business, and a statement of the organization's priorities in addressing these, a description of the activities that will be undertaken, or an updated report of accomplishments versus goals. Five

[30]Louis Harris, *The Second Study: The American Public's and Public Opinion Leaders' Views of Banks and Bankers* (Philadelphia, Penn.: The Foundation for Full Service Banks, 1972), P. 74.
[31]American Bankers Association, *Bankers and Community Involvement,* (Washington, D.C., 1978).
[32]John J. Corson and George A. Steiner, *Measuring Business's Social Performance: The Corporate Social Audit* (New York: Committee for Economic Development, 1974), p. 23.

such audits have been reported by nationally known firms, two of which were among the nation's leading banks.[33] Many major corporations have established special committees to supply input into and review the social audit. To ensure objectivity and enhance credibility, members of the corporate board of directors are usually appointed to these committees from outside the organization. In effect, they have made the civic and social contributions of the organization part of its overall balance sheet, and their work reflects the view that a business enterprise today must take into account all its responsibilities as a corporate citizen, even when these affect its profits.[34]

COMMUNICATIONS

The final obligation of each commercial bank crosses all the boundaries that separate constituencies, and it directly affects every group with which the bank is involved. It is the obligation to generate effective communication, in every sense of the word.

Oral and written communications of every type fill a business day and have a direct bearing on the way an organization functions. They connect human beings to one another and form a foundation and bridge upon which the institution is built.[35]

Every day, members of the bank's management team must direct the staff, deal with representatives of the community, answer questions posed by the media, interact with depositors, and develop advertising messages. Every exchange of correspondence with or call on a customer, every internal memorandum on procedural changes or matters affecting the staff, every conversation between manager and subordinate, and every staff meeting can be an example of the effective or ineffective transmitting of desired information. The need for clarity in communication, whether oral or written, internal or external, has never been greater.

[33]Ibid.
[34]Rockefeller, *Creative Management,* pp. 22–23. The concept is also addressed by Neil H. Jacoby in *Corporate Power and Social Responsibility* (New York: Macmillan, 1973), p. xvii.
[35]Raymond V. Lesikar, *Business Communications: Theory and Application,* rev. ed., (Homewood, Ill.: Irwin, 1972), pp. 3–4.

The autocratic manager of the past felt little need to develop communication skills. His message was usually terse, authoritarian, and nonnegotiable. Similarly, the bank's communications with its shareholders, depositors, and community were usually brief and impersonal. Advertising was kept to a bare minimum, information about the bank's basic policies was not widely disseminated, and the role of a bank in its community was taken for granted by both parties. Today, enlightened self-interest demands that all possible steps be taken to encourage and enhance communication in every direction.

Whenever stockholders have been led to understand why certain policies were adopted, whenever depositors have been told why specific actions affecting them are being taken, whenever staff members have been made to feel that they are a most important part of the organization and that their ideas and reactions are welcomed, and whenever civic groups have been informed of the direct contributions of the bank to the well-being of the community, there is a positive and direct effect on both the efficiency of the institution and its image, and the obligations that it has to each group are being recognized. Conversely, if any of the constituent groups is kept in the dark, and if management conveys the impression that it has no real interest in listening, the organization is bound to suffer. Table 2.1 provides some concrete examples of positive and negative communication that may occur in routine bank operations.

Table 2.1. Examples of Communication

Effective Communication	Ineffective Communication	Noncommunication
Supervisor and subordinate jointly agree on the terms of a business plan and budget.	A staff memorandum is unclear and filled with jargon; readers throw it away without understanding it.	Subordinates cannot discuss their job-related problems with superiors.
A file memorandum documents all details of a discussion with a customer regarding a proposed loan.	A clerk fails to realize the importance of each step in a job procedure.	An important telephone message is not delivered to the right party.
Employee publications clearly spell out all the details of each benefit plan.	A depositor is confused about the method used to calculate interest on a loan or account.	A clerk is never told about the bank's policies regarding absenteeism.
An annual performance review gives a full, quantitative picture of an individual's progress versus goals.	A supervisor is unsure about the limits of his or her authority in the position.	Employees are not told in advance about changes that affect them.
The Annual Report states and explains policies regarding the bank's involvement in and loans to certain nations.	Publications and press releases are vague or slanted so that only one view is presented.	No effort is made to publicize the bank's socially responsible actions.

3 Effective Management

If bank managers today occasionally look back over their shoulders and wistfully speak of "the good old days," one can understand their nostalgic feelings by recalling the years when their industry was rather static and relatively trouble-free. Resistance to change characterized banking in general. Banks offered a very limited range of services to a very limited market, and faced very little competition. Management's main task was to put to profitable use the demand deposits that flowed in steadily. The *status quo* produced annual profits that were satisfactory, so that innovations in approaches or techniques did not seem necessary. Attempts to visualize the future and to prepare ways of coping with the changes it might bring were not considered worth the effort and expense. Whatever limited planning had occurred focused on the purely financial objectives of the organization, with little or no attention to marketing strategies and specific action plans.[1]

The contemporary student or observer may have difficulty in imagining a banking industry that made such minimal efforts to develop new services, market existing ones, and recognize the potential value of the consumer as a bank customer. Yet those words summarize the prevailing philosophy. Commercial banking was the prototype of the stable, consistently profitable industry. Its profits could not compare with those of many others, such as the high-technology industries, but it was also free from the severe fluctuations in earnings that they experienced. It was only in the years

[1]James E. Bryan, Jr., "Changing the Internal Organization," *The Bankers Magazine* (May–June 1982):67.

following World War II that basic, drastic, and permanent revisions took place in banking.

In marked contrast to the past, banking today is an affirmation of Parmenides' axiom that "Everything is change." The exclusivity on services that banks formerly enjoyed has disappeared. New technology is simultaneously making new services possible and cost effective, and is changing the internal operating procedures of the past; those new services are being offered by banks to newly perceived markets in many areas of the world, but, at the same time, are being offered in the United States by a host of competitors who, years ago, posed no threat to the banks. Today, new problems in human resources management crop up as the work itself changes, the pressures for increased productivity grow, and new skills are required not merely for the profitability of the institution, but in many cases for its actual survival. Coping with the new financial environment may prove too difficult for many banks and bankers. If they cannot make the necessary adjustment to an era of intense competition and high-cost deposits, they may be forced to look for partners who will help them preserve at least part of their stockholders' stake in the institution, and those who cannot do so are likely to disappear completely from the scene. If banking was ever an industry unto itself, it no longer is. Rather, it is part of a total financial industry that includes many other actual or quasi-"financial institutions."

New regulations from federal and state authorities affect commercial banks, sometimes allowing them to innovate in serving customers, but on many other occasions inhibiting their ability to compete. The president of a Maryland bank has stated that

> The myriad changes that are inevitably dictated by Federal regulatory agencies interpreting new legislation are critical problems facing the banking industry today. We have a lack of confidence in Congress's ability to understand the nature of our business and to make intelligent decisions that will have a lasting effect on our industry.[2]

In terms of numbers, aggressiveness, and a full range of financial services, the competition facing commercial banks was never greater. Both the banks and their new competitors must deal with a new breed of customers who are infinitely more knowledgeable and mobile than any of

[2]Jerome P. Baroch, Jr., in "The Important Problems Facing Banks Today," *The Bankers Magazine* (May–June 1980):47.

their predecessors. The former Chairman of the Federal Deposit Insurance Corporation has identified the decade of the 1970s as productive of as much change in banking as were the previous fourteen decades.[3] There is no reason to expect that the size and scope of the changes will diminish in the future. The specifics and timing are unknown, but further changes in competition, technology, regulation, and money market conditions can most assuredly be predicted to occur.[4]

The luxury of traditionalism is one that today's bankers cannot afford, unless they are prepared to face a still greater decrease in their relative position versus that of their competitors. Effective management today mandates that banks assume a position far different from that which so many of them adopted in the past, when they simply permitted the future to happen and made no attempt to anticipate it or react to the events that might be foreseen.[5] In addition, bankers must discard the former parochialism that seemed to preclude their accepting into the industry those individuals with skills or backgrounds in nonbanking disciplines or areas, and to prevent their applying the management techniques that had succeeded in other industries.

One of the ironies that characterized past management attitudes in commercial banking lies in the fact that bankers expected far more from customers than they were prepared to implement in their own institutions. A corporate borrower was required to present forecasts of revenues, cash flows, and profit margins, and display an ability to plan for and adjust to change. Yet the bank imposing those criteria probably did nothing comparable itself.

If bankers today are in fact willing to learn from others, they can give proper weight and credence to a survey of 280 chief executives, two-thirds of whom said *planning* was their most important single activity, and that they devoted 44% of their time to it.[6] The need for planning is recognized throughout the corporate world,[7] and the direct costs of failure to plan

[3]K. A. Randall, in Herbert V. Prochnow and Herbert V. Prochnow, Jr., Eds., *The Changing World of Banking* (New York: Harper & Row, 1974), p. 322.

[4]Thomas W. Thompson, Leonard L. Berry, and Philip H. Davidson, *Banking Tomorrow: Managing Markets Through Planning* (New York: Van Nostrand Reinhold, 1978), p. 18.

[5]John M. Mason, *Financial Management of Commercial Banks* (Boston: Warren, Gorham & Lamont, 1979), p. 110.

[6]John W. Humble, *How to Manage by Objectives* (New York: AMACOM, A Division of American Management Associations, 1972), p. 45.

[7]Thomas R. Williams, "Competitive Business Strategy," *American Banker* (August 14, 1980):20.

may include neglect of markets, loss of market share, wide swings in earnings, and an inability to take advantage of external developments. Planning is the management technique that looks at an organization as it now stands, attempts to predict the external and internal factors that may affect it in the future, and leads to committing resources to certain courses of action after coordinated and comprehensive decision-making has taken place. It should occur before any other managerial function, since it will decide the scope and nature of those functions.[8]

Unfortunately, there are many indications that bankers in general give lip service to this concept but do little to put it into practice. The president of a Connecticut bank speaks for many of his peers:

> In order to meet both the demands of the savers and . . . the needs of the borrowers, we must intelligently plan and package our services. . . . Banks with good management and an intelligent plan for survival will be able to stand the test of time. However, many smaller banks will be merged into others or put out of business entirely.[9]

Yet one bank consultant notes that two of the largest institutions on the West Coast did not have a formal strategic planning process until 1980, and that others among the fifty largest commercial banks fall into the same category.[10] In another survey of 302 banks having assets of $10 million or more, two-thirds of the respondents said they made no effort to plan beyond a two-year time frame, and 40 percent of the largest banks (i.e., those with over $500 million in assets) made the same admission.[11] Another study, also conducted by a bank consultant, disclosed that only three of the 107 respondents had developed clear, specific objectives for the ensuing three years, and that only 13 percent of them had a definite statement of purpose or mission.[12]

These results are disheartening at best. Bankers cannot claim ignorance of the benefits of the planning process; they know that it provides direction, forms a basis for action and reaction instead of mere passive acceptance,

[8]Robert M. Fulmer, *The New Management,* 2nd Ed. (New York: Macmillan, 1978), p. 94.
[9]Edward G. Farrell, in "The Important Problems Facing Banks Today," *The Bankers Magazine* (May–June 1980):48.
[10]Robert O. Metzger, "Barriers to Bank Productivity Improvement," *The Bankers Magazine* (January–February 1982):58.
[11]Richard W. Sapp, "Banks Look Ahead: A Survey of Bank Planning," *The Magazine of BANK ADMINISTRATION,* (July 1980):12.
[12]Phillip L. Zweig, "Smaller Banks Called in Need of Strategic Planning," *American Banker* (June 24, 1982):2.

and assigns tasks in order to provide grounds for performance reviews. It is also closely allied to the concept of social responsibility; by preparing to meet the anticipated future needs of customers, the planning function can contribute to community well-being and progress.[13] Yet the same bankers who would admit these facts may also be among those who have developed a wide variety of excuses to explain their failure to give the necessary emphasis to planning.[14]

One institution may claim that the fluctuations in the money market, which are entirely beyond its control, make forward planning futile. A second may cite the plethora of government regulations affecting it, and point out that so much time and effort are required to keep up with, implement, and report on these regulations that proper attention simply cannot be paid to planning. A third institution may offer the excuse that it lacks expertise in planning and does not have the trained personnel who can perform the necessary planning tasks.[15] In effect, each of these banks is contributing to the negative image of the industry mentioned earlier: "Bankers are highly resistant to innovation . . . [and] nothing will change until they are brave enough to enter these new worlds of management science."[16] Each is also helping to perpetuate a system of crisis management, in which no action is taken unless or until actual disaster looms on the horizon. There is a clear need today for banks to learn from the corporate example and to try to anticipate and manage change. That need arises from the equally clear fact that their competitors, particularly today's non-banks, will not stand idly by in the meantime.[17]

THE PLANNING PROCESS DEFINED

In its most simplistic form, the planning process is one that could be followed by any individual who is in the process of considering a future

---

[13]John W. Ennest and Gerald E. Patera, "Planning and Control Systems for Commercial Banks," in Prochnow and Prochnow, Jr., *The Changing World of Banking*, p. 259.
[14]Ibid., p. 266.
[15]Eric N. Compton, "Bank Planning: A Status Report," *The Bankers Magazine* (May–June 1981):75.
[16]Metzger, "Barriers to Bank Productivity Improvement," p. 61.
[17]George G. C. Parker, "Now Management Will Make or Break the Bank," *Harvard Business Review* (November–December 1981):140.

course of action, or any organization that is concerned about its present and its potential. Basically, planning consists of posing three questions:

Where are we now?
Where do we want to be?
How will we get there?

Each of these in turn leads to subsets of further questions that go into considerable detail. For example, "Where are we now?" forces the bank or corporation to evaluate the true nature of its business, appraise its existing degree of success, determine the wants and needs of its market and the components of that market, assess the manner in which it is perceived by outsiders, and understand the many regulatory and legal constraints that may inhibit its effort to satisfy customer needs and wants. This process has been identified as one reason for the success of corporations, while a failure to undertake such planning has been cited as one of the causes of bankruptcies.[18]

Similarly, the question, "Where do we want to be?" provokes many secondary and corollary sets of inquiries. These may include:

What are the specific objectives of the organization?
What rate of growth does it wish to attain?
Will it endeavor to be all things to all people?

The last-named question is especially relevant for banks today. Decisions as to which segments of the total marketplace are to be served with which products and services in which geographic areas are critical to achievement of the bank's objectives.[19]

The questioning process is not one that should be followed only by the largest banks; indeed, there may well be a greater need for it in the community institutions of limited size than in the money-center giants. If one predicts attrition from the banking system, with a substantial reduction in the existing number of institutions, it is clearly the largest that can most effectively meet the competition, adjust to changes, and survive. The

---

[18]Peter F. Drucker, *The Practice of Management* (New York: Harper & Row, 1954), p. 50.
[19]Williams, "Competitive Business Strategy," p. 20.

smaller banks have an even greater obligation to plan ahead and develop ways of differentiating themselves from competitors.[20]

To ask "How will we get there?" is tantamount to questioning the appropriateness of any strategies that flow from the answers to the first two questions. Once management has determined the targets it should aim for, the methodology must be developed. Planning cannot be divorced from managing. The most effective managers in banking are those who have given thought to the possible shape of the future, who create scenarios based on that thought, who identify the actions to be taken in conformity with these scenarios, and who truly believe that their own decisions and approaches will help improve their institutions' future.[21] Bank managers today are expected to make short-term decisions that contribute to organizational long-term programs.[22]

Organizing is a managerial decision. It calls for managers to clarify their challenges and business strategies, and then to outline the critical tasks and working relationships that are needed to meet the challenges and implement the strategies.

Without a planning process, management may never give sufficient thought to the strengths and weaknesses of the organization as it now exists. Without a planning process, management does not make a real determination of what the bank should be, as opposed to what it is now. Without a planning process, the strategies and tactics for growth and profitability are not identified.

However, when planning takes place, a bank places itself in a position to gain a competitive advantage in one or more areas, and its management knows what must be done in order to make this happen. If it believes that future legislation will make interstate banking or intrastate branching possible or more extensive, it will act in advance by identifying the key locations for expansion and taking preliminary steps toward establishing a presence in them. If the bank believes that federal laws may be revised so that underwriting revenue bonds is again allowed for commercial banks, it will have the necessary personnel and systems in place ahead of time. If its market research unit identifies significant demographic changes in

[20]Phillip L. Zweig, "Strategic Planning for Smaller Banks," *American Banker* (June 24, 1982):2.

[21]Thomas R. Williams, "Competitive Business Strategy: The Art of the CEO," *American Banker* (August 14, 1980):20.

[22]Mason, *Financial Management of Commercial Banks,* p. 110.

the customer base, the bank can then reshape its policies and become a leader in providing services aimed at specific market segments.

Planning, then, directly influences the image of the bank as it is perceived in the marketplace, and affects the bottom line by indicating the steps that are required to maximize profits. It is also a management vehicle for communication, since it conveys the fact that the institution has a definite sense of direction and that the performance of staff members should always focus on it. It leads to a correlation of growth with discipline and selectivity with quality.

THE PLANNING PROCESS IMPLEMENTED

In order to put the process into operation, a specific commitment to it must take place at the highest level of management. The bank's Chief Executive Officer establishes the pattern and provides the leadership. He or she must make it absolutely clear to the staff that the process is necessary, that it will lead to specific benefits, that it has the complete support of the senior officers, that it is not merely a paper or "make work" exercise giving lip service to the concept, that the results of the process will be closely monitored, and that one effect of the process will be the measuring of individuals' contributions to the fulfillment of the organization's stated objectives.

Given this top-level commitment, the group or committee responsible for implementing the process can then review those factors, external and internal, known and probable, that affect the bank now and will affect it in the future. The following list makes no attempt to be all-inclusive, but suggests some of the most likely topics:

1. *Social and economic conditions.*   The projected rate of inflation, predicted government reactions to it, projections of consumer income and personal savings, interest rate assumptions, social responsibility concerns, and consumer and activist movements.

2. *Government policies and legislation.*   The impact of the Monetary Control Act (elimination of ceilings on interest rates with the phaseout of Regulation Q, explicit pricing for Fed services, new requirements for reserves), new regulations on electronic funds transfer systems

(EFTS), increased authorization for NOW accounts, Federal Reserve restraints on holding company operations, expansion of foreign bank activities and those of non-bank competitors, and Congressional action to permit interstate banking or revenue bond underwriting.

3. *Financial considerations.* Capital constraints, liquidity problems, tax status, existing and proposed components of income, ability to allocate funds to specific areas and "match fund" assets and liabilities, and the existing and anticipated size and "mix" of deposits.

4. *Human resource factors.* Existing and required staff, provision for management succession, and development and training needs.

5. *Technological considerations.* Existing versus desired capabilities, anticipated consumer reactions to EFTS applications, systems revisions, and the estimated benefits and costs of technological change.

6. *Marketing.* Identification of international, retail, corporate, commercial, institutional, and government market segments on which to focus, determination of services to be emphasized for each, appraisal of extent and effectiveness of competition, and determination of type and scope of advertising campaigns and promotions.[23]

Some banks have found it helpful for in-depth analytical discussions of this type to take place in a conference center or other location away from the premises. In this way, the brainstorming sessions can be held without distractions or interruptions.

The next step in the implementing of the total planning process entails formulating *objectives*. These are broad, long-term, nonquantitative statements that answer the basic question, "Where do we want to be?" Examples of objectives might include:

1. Enhancing of the bank's reputation as innovative and responsive to the needs and wants of its markets

2. Improvement in the quality of the loan portfolio

3. Leadership among peer and local banks in annual growth in earnings per share

---

[23]A more comprehensive description of the analytical process may be found in Thompson et al., *Banking Tomorrow: Managing Markets Through Planning*, pp. 51–60 and in Prochnow and Prochnow, Jr., Eds., *The Changing World of Banking*, pp. 263–264.

Objectives, in turn, lead to *goals,* which are more specific and quantitative, and are usually to be attained within a shorter time. Objectives generally apply to the entire organization, whereas goals may pinpoint areas in which certain measurable progress is sought. Examples of goals might include:

1. Stated percentages of improvement in return on equity, return on assets, and earnings per share over the next five years
2. Increases in penetration of identified segments of markets, as determined by specific percentages of market share
3. Reductions in critical expense areas

Goals should be ambitious but attainable, and should contribute directly to stated objectives. They must take into account the strengths and weaknesses of the bank, as identified through the analytical process. If goals require a commitment of money and equipment, management must be prepared to supply both.

Participatory management has a high priority in this process. Individuals must be made to feel free to speak openly about existing problems of any type. The bank's senior officers must create the proper climate for this. If the planning process is designed merely to have key personnel tell members of senior management only what they want to hear, and if staff members are afraid to pinpoint weaknesses in the organization known to them or perceived in the marketplace, there is actually no process at all. At some of the larger banks, this problem has been addressed through the formation of task forces, composed of groups of officers who have been given the specific responsibility of preparing the institution for the future, and whose recommendations go directly to the most senior level of management.

Policies

The next step in the planning process requires the formulation of *policies.* These are official statements, supportive of goals and objectives, drawn up to provide guidelines for performance and to spell out the "rules of the road" for staff members to follow. They may be of a nature that reflects the overall philosophy and ethics of the organization such as the following:

1. Material inside information shall never be used by the bank or any staff member in recommending to others the selling or buying of certain securities.

2. Members of the bank's staff shall neither solicit nor accept fees, gifts, lavish entertainment, or other benefits intended to influence their business transactions with customers.

3. The bank shall not attempt to obtain any form of agreement from a customer that its purchases of the customer's products or services will be tied to the amount of business the customer gives to the bank in the form of deposits.

In other instances, policies may be prepared and made known to the staff in direct consequence of agreed-upon goals. These are concrete, rather than philosophical or ethical. Examples might include:

1. To improve our competitive position in the retail market, we will expand our installment loan and mortgage loan activities.

2. To achieve our goals of social responsibility, we will provide equal opportunities for employment and advancement for all, without discrimination of any kind. The same nondiscriminatory standards will be applied to all requests for credit.

3. To improve management controls over key areas of the bank, we will implement a system of individual profit centers, identifying all income and expense factors.[24]

One advantage of the "brainstorming" type of session is that it gives participants many chances to discuss contingency plans and alternate courses of action. In many cases, policies must be designed with provisions for rapid change. Fully participative discussions can assist in creating "what if" and "worst case" scenarios, so that possible adverse consequences and external factors are fully considered and responses fully developed.

Many bank policies are predicated on highly volatile conditions, for example, changes in money markets, the world situation, or the economy, and therefore may have to be changed on short notice. An international

[24]The concept and implementing of profit center planning are discussed in Oliver G. Wood, Jr., *Commercial Banking: Practice and Policy* (New York: D. Van Nostrand, 1978), p. 51–59.

crisis creates the need for a new policy in response. The 1979 developments in Iran exemplify this. When the new Iranian government repudiated all existing debts and announced that all Iranian deposits outside the country would be withdrawn and repatriated, American banks quickly exercised their right of offset of deposits against loans—a policy developed in prompt response to crisis. Similarly, news of a major problem at one bank brings about a reassessment of the policies at others. For example, the failure of the Penn Square Bank, N.A., in 1982 led other banks to reexamine their lending policies regarding certain categories of customers.[25]

Strategies

As extensions of agreed-upon policies, the bank should then prepare specific *strategies*, consistent with goals and contributing to objectives. Thus, for example, lending officers will apply certain criteria to each situation as a means of improving loan portfolio quality. Branches will develop marketing strategies to develop new business. The installment loan and bank card divisions will take appropriate action to improve their market share.

Practices

The bank's policies and strategies are reflected in the daily *practices* of all levels of management. A staff member acts in a certain way in order to carry out those policies and strategies. For example, a bank may establish an objective of improving its market share in the insurance industry. A quantified, specific goal is then formulated: during the coming year, new demand deposits of $_____ will result from the opening of accounts by _____ insurers and existing balances from insurance companies will increase by _____ percent. The strategies to be employed in attaining these goals will then be embodied in a marketing plan that details officers' call programs and identifies the services to be offered to each customer or prospect, in response to what is known about each company's situation and needs. The operations units whose production will

---

[25]Robert E. Norton, "Seafirst Hikes Penn Square Loss Estimate," *American Banker* (July 14, 1982):1, and Douglas Martin, "Penn Square: The Residue," *The New York Times,* (July 23, 1982):D-1.

be affected by the new activity will be altered so that any needed equipment and staff can be acquired. The entire process culminates in the practice, which is the work performed by calling officers in soliciting new accounts and enhancing existing ones.

Planning amounts to little more than an expensive and time-consuming paper exercise, unless the ongoing performance of each unit is monitored against the plan. A bank establishes certain objectives and incorporates them into annual operating plans. Every level of its management is then expected to make measurable, direct contributions to the fulfillment of the plan. Annual or semiannual performance reviews of each officer can be designed to include the specific controllable results he or she achieved compared to goals.

None of the foregoing should be construed to mean that planning is merely a mechanism by which higher levels of management impose arbitrary strategies and goals on subordinates without the benefit of input from the latter. Communication, again, is an essential part of the process. Line managers must be free to supply their ideas, and must be given some degree of latitude in interpreting corporate goals for their own particular circumstances and environments. Whenever it becomes necessary to revise plans, line managers should be able to document the reasons and justify the changes.

A branch manager, for example, may have agreed to certain deposit and profit goals for a particular year. However, owing to changes in the neighborhood through population shifts or the departure of a major company, or as a result of an aggressive promotional campaign mounted by a nearby competitor, the branch's deposits may decrease. By midyear, it is apparent that original targets cannot be met. It would be grossly unjust to penalize the manager for a combination of external factors that are beyond his or her control; therefore, the goals must be reviewed in the light of contributory circumstances and factors.

STRUCTURING

As a result of the planning process, management may decide that the existing organizational structure of the bank is not one that is most likely to achieve the objectives that were set. It may be appropriate to redesign the structure so that the components are better positioned to focus on specific market areas.

For example, major banks in most money market cities were traditionally structured along geographic lines. A National (or United States) Division was responsible for all accounts outside the bank's own area, while a Metropolitan Division handled all local accounts. Where legally possible, the latter division used a network of branches as the vehicles for servicing every type of business—major corporations, smaller enterprises, and consumers.

This division of responsibilities has undergone a complete change at several of these banks in recent years. Instead of following purely geographical boundaries, the banks are now organized according to customer type. Thus a Corporate Banking Department would be created along "wholesale banking" lines, which would handle every phase of the bank's relationships with its major corporate customers, regardless of their location. This entity might be subdivided further along specific industry lines, so that teams of officers specialize in the transportation, food, petroleum, tobacco, or other sectors, according to the volume of business handled. Under this type of organization, geography is irrelevant; a single team may handle the accounts of corporations whose offices are many miles apart.

The banks that follow this course of action also create new entities to handle the needs of smaller businesses and consumers, who represent the market that the branch network addresses.

The creation of organizational structures with so many levels, however, would logically occur only among the largest banks. In small institutions a much simpler structure would suffice. It is a fundamental responsibility of management to determine what major divisions of the organization should be formed, aside from such basic ones as Human Resources, Auditing, and Trust.

The structure of the organization and the forming of profit centers within it may be viewed as a logical adjunct to the concept of management by objectives. Officers who are placed in charge of each unit must understand the roles their areas play in the overall bank, and must recognize that their performance will be reviewed according to their contributions to the total bottom line. There should be no doubt in any employee's mind that performance leading to goal fulfillment will also lead to rewards. While job satisfactions result from this, they are not the purpose. Rather, management's objective is to bring the individual's goals into harmony with those of the organization, and to motivate the level of performance that makes it possible for both to be realized.[26]

Profit centers create the need for separate and distinct accounting systems in a bank, in order to have all income and expenses properly allocated. If a branch or other functional unit has sources of funds (e.g., deposits), exceeding its uses of funds (e.g., loans and investments), it can be considered as supplying the excess to a bank "pool," and it should therefore be credited with interest income. If the converse is true, the profit center is charged at the established internal rate for its use of funds over and above its sources. In essence, profit center accounting considers entities within the bank as if they were individual banks, generating and using funds.[27]

ACCOUNTABILITY

New approaches to effective management in banking often include the preparation of job descriptions for various staff levels. These clearly outline the areas of responsibility that the job embraces, the number of individuals supervised, the importance of the job in the overall picture, and the position objectives. Job descriptions may be classified according to a system of points, synthesizing the above factors on a weighted basis. Levels of compensation then become functions of the number of points assigned to each position.

An important aspect of the job description lies in the assigning and accepting of accountability. An officer is expected to delegate tasks; those who fail to do so are automatically poor managers because they have not allowed juniors to assume more responsibility and thus have not provided for proper management lines of succession. Every manager's performance review should indicate what he or she has done or failed to do in training and preparing a replacement.

Delegation, however, does not absolve managers at every level from

[26]Wayne B. Lewin, "Banking Productivity Versus Personal Goals," *The Magazine of BANK ADMINISTRATION* (October 1979):10.
[27]Ennest and Patera, "Planning and Control Systems for Commercial Banks," p. 251.

accountability. The end results produced are the yardstick by which performance is evaluated. An individual cannot point to the errors or shortcomings of subordinates as an excuse for the performance of a unit. This concept of accountability may have first been clearly identified in professional sports; a coach or manager is fired or rewarded as the team succeeds or fails and cannot use the ineptness of the players or the poor performance of assistants as an explanation for failure when it occurs. This same principle is being applied to corporate and bank management at every level, including those of a Chairman or President. Outright terminations, and resignations "by mutual consent," of officers at the most senior levels of nationally known corporations and banks have become commonplace whenever their organizations failed to perform. An individual who is promoted must accept the fact that he or she will now be judged according to eventual bottom-line results. If weaknesses or problems exist and inhibit goal attainment, the manager must take prompt and decisive corrective action.

SYSTEMS AND CONTROLS

Each refinement of computer capability brings an increase in the number and scope of reports that are available to bank management, covering every aspect of the institution's operations. Monthly reports can be generated showing all income and expenses for a branch, department, or other unit and relating these to goals or budgeted figures. These reports can be subdivided to give details of official and clerical salaries, interest expense and income, and the charge or credit for funds used and supplied. On a daily basis, data on account balances, overdrafts, loans, and accruals can be provided. *Pro forma* figures can be projected to show trends and the end results of decisions. Loan portfolio reports can be subdivided to show types of outstandings, concentrations of collateral, or by industry, amounts and ageing of delinquencies, or other meaningful data. Simulation techniques can be used to assist in decision-making.

However, these technological advances serve no real purpose unless management uses them to initiate appropriate actions and implement necessary controls. If computer reports show that a certain service has become unprofitable, that a branch is steadily losing money, or that a particular policy has worked to the detriment of the organization, management must respond. This is not to say that computers run the bank; rather, they should be considered as the tools that provide timely and relevant data, facilitating and justifying the managers' decisions.

A relationship manager, to whom a group of accounts is assigned, uses the monthly reports generated by the computer to ascertain whether each account is carrying compensating balances sufficient to support the level of activity. If a shortfall exists, the manager is then expected to use the information to negotiate with the customers and correct the problem. If the management information system clearly shows that one unit of the bank regularly fails to meet its goals, there must be an explanation and a move to correct the situation. If computerized analysis of the loan portfolio indicates that an undue concentration of loans has taken place in certain countries or industries, management can act at once.

RESPONSIBLE UNITS

In varying degrees and to varying extents, three units are involved in the planning process. They play roles of greater or lesser magnitude in determining the strategies that flow from objectives and goals, in putting policies into effect, in monitoring results, and in making the decisions that result from monitoring. The three units consist of the bank's *stockholders, directors,* and *officers.*

In smaller banks, the number of *stockholders* may be limited to members of a single family; in the largest banks, there may be 50,000 or more. This distinction makes the degree of stockholder participation in the management process quite different in each case. At the major money center banks, the shareholder base is so large and diversified that, with the exception of a vocal minority that raises questions, criticizes, and introduces resolutions for change, shareholder involvement is minimal. At the opposite end of the spectrum are those banks where the senior officers, major stockholders, and dominant figures on the board are one and the same, and these few individuals, in effect, are the bank.

However, the extent of stockholder involvement is immaterial. The important fact is that the bank's basic and ongoing obligation to them, as outlined earlier, makes them a *de facto* element in all considerations of bank management. Shareholders elect the directors, and look to them to draw up proper policies for the bank's profitability and growth. They want and expect their stake in the bank's future to appreciate and be fully protected over the course of time.

Directors, as was noted earlier, are at the apex of the organization chart and are legally responsible for supervising the bank's affairs. They are expected to know the bank's mission, define its objectives, set its policies, ensure the legality and prudence of its decisions and actions, be accountable for the results, select the managers who will implement policies and monitor their performance, and, under certain circumstances, accept personal liability for losses the bank may sustain.

Beyond their responsibilities to assure that the bank is in sound financial condition and to possess the necessary management skills, directors must also make certain that the bank is competitive and that it meets the needs of its market(s). For the guidance of individuals serving as directors of national banks, a bulletin is available, enumerating and detailing their responsibilities and liabilities;[28] other texts are available on the same subject.[29]

The concept of accountability is an important one for board members to understand. They cannot escape their obligation by pleading ignorance of what has been done in the bank, or by using their own absences from meetings as an excuse. Liability can stem from action *or* inaction; if directors fail to look into any area where prudence dictates they investigate, they may face substantial penalties.[30]

Bank boards typically include committees, either as required by law or as designated in the by-laws. Members of these committees supervise the credit, investment, auditing, and trust functions.[31] When a bank is examined by representatives of a government agency, the directors must review a copy of the report of their findings, then take any necessary action to correct deficiencies and make improvements.[32] The directors are the representatives of all the various constituencies to which the bank is

[28]The Comptroller of the Currency, *Duties and Liabilities of Directors of National Banks* (Washington, D.C.: American Bankers Association, 1972).

[29]*Focus on the Bank Director: The Job* (Washington, D.C.: American Bankers Association, 1977).

[30]Ibid., p. 74.

[31]Howard D. Crosse and George H. Hempel, *Management Policies for Commercial Banks*, 2nd Ed. (Englewood Cliffs, N.J.: Prentice-Hall, 1973), p. 52.

[32]Wood, *Commercial Banking: Practice and Policy*, p. 33.

obligated, and as such they must set policies, oversee practices, and assess results.[33]

National banks must have at least five, but not more than twenty-five, directors; state laws vary. Both federal and state statutes require them to own stock in the bank and prevent their serving as board members for any competing commercial bank within the same geographic area.[34]

Although both the stockholder and director units play important roles, it is the third component, the *bank's officers,* to which major attention must be directed in any consideration of effective management. It is the basic role of the official staff not only to carry out the policies set by the board and senior management, but to propose new ones that may be more appropriate. Officers must keep the directors informed, take advantage of their expertise, and utilize them as a court of last resort in those instances in which decisions cannot be made at any lower levels. The officers have a daily involvement in all the functions of the bank and an exposure to the attitudes and needs of the marketplace that no other group can have. Their input to higher levels of management, and through the latter to the board, is invaluable.

The daily actions of bank officers as they explain, interpret, and implement policies must be consistent with the goals of the bank, and contribute in a positive way to the success and profitability of their own units. They must review and coordinate, train and develop, establish accountability for their subordinates, and assure quality performance.

The last-named task is especially critical in the banking industry because the huge daily volume of transactions and documents creates inherent statistical probabilities of error. The costs of quality control and the methods used to achieve it can be considered as integral parts of the planning process. Senior management must constantly look not only at those errors that leave the bank (e.g., the misposted check, the incorrect advice, or the statement sent to the wrong customer), but also at those errors caught before a task is completed. The former category causes expensive, time-consuming inquiries and adjustments, can be detrimental to the bank's image, and may result in the actual loss of accounts. The latter category requires that time and money be allocated to a system of superimposed layers to inspect and verify work. The errors themselves create forms

[33]Edward W. Reed, R ichard V. Cotter, Edward K. Gill, and Richard K. Smith, *Commercial Banking* (Englewood Cliffs, N.J.: Prentice-Hall, 1976), p. 59.
[34]Crosse and Hempel, *Management Policies for Commercial Banks,* p. 52.

expense and necessitate repetition of work. The goals that were established during the planning process can be frustrated if enough attention is not paid to the matter of quality control, and the lack of quality control can eventually be far more expensive than the costs of implementing it.[35]

CONTROLS AND AUDITING

No discussion of the tasks and problems of bank management today would be complete without some reference to the measures that must be taken to minimize risks and thus to safeguard the bank's own funds and those entrusted to it by customers. The measures themselves are referred to as *controls;* the process by which their completeness is measured, their effectiveness assessed, and the financial condition of the bank determined, is known as *auditing*. The objectives include protection of all assets, accuracy and reliability of all accounting data, operational efficiency, and total adherence to all prescribed managerial policies. For example, a policy of dual control may have been established in certain work situations; this requires that two employees be involved so that each may verify the other's work and is a form of control. Auditing will determine, among other things, whether the required procedures are being followed in order to protect the bank.

Federal Bureau of Investigation reports show that the number of bank robberies is consistently increasing. In New York City, 141 such robberies took place in a single month (August 1980), and statistics compiled by the American Bankers Association show an average of 177 defalcations of $10,000 or more at banks over a 10-year period.[36]

Newspaper stories repeatedly publicize cases of missing or stolen securities at banks, wire transfers of funds that were fraudulently entered through bank computers, improper loans made by or for bank officers, and speculative trading in foreign exchange. Each of these incidents serves both to demonstrate the scope of the problem and the need for improved systems to try to prevent further losses. As the active, governing body of the corporation, the board must accept responsibility for implementing

[35]William J. Latzko, "A Quality Control System for Banks," *The Magazine of BANK ADMINISTRATION,* (November 1972):17.
[36]Crosse and Hempel, *Management Policies for Commercial Banks,* p. 239.

all needed policies and systems relevant to bank security. It usually designates one officer to supervise the program of internal controls and to conduct all internal examinations; this person is commonly called the auditor. He or she, appointed by the board, also reports directly to the board on all matters involving the safety and efficiency of operations and the accuracy and completeness of all records.

Auditors must be completely independent and have absolute control over their own performance. They cannot take the position that frequent examinations of the bank by federal or state authorities suffice; those agencies are primarily concerned with the bank's compliance with all laws and regulations, and are not specifically trying to locate frauds or embezzlements. The auditors must be the internal watchdogs and policemen.

Any bank employee who has been involved in both an internal and an external examination usually states that the former is the far more rigorous and detailed of the two. This is exactly as it should be. No bank can afford the luxury of waiting for a federal or state examining team to identify problems and suggest ways to improve security.

In addition to conducting unannounced examinations within the bank, the auditor may also address specific questions affecting the overall safety and efficiency of the organization. For example, he or she may check to see if fingerprints and references of job applicants are being verified. The auditor may institute controls over numbered forms or documents, and examine the records of overdrafts. His or her approach to the question of bank risk tries to determine how great that risk is, why it is being incurred, and what is being done to minimize it. In summary, audit programs are designed to insure that whatever *can* be done for protection *is* being done.

Unfortunately, no foolproof system has ever been devised to protect every aspect of a bank's operations in every branch and department. Disgruntled employees will often find some loophole in a system and use it to their own advantage. A bank robber or other criminal will always manage to frustrate the security systems that have been implemented. Regulatory officials agree that efforts to defraud and embezzle will continue, and that new techniques and schemes will be developed to meet the new technological and new protective methods.[37] That fact, however, should not deter bank management from an equal, unceasing, and thorough effort

---

[37]Curt Miller, "The $1.5 Million Embezzlement Case," *Bank Systems and Equipment* (May 1973):35.

of its own, in which all possible controls are installed for the protection of the institution's assets and those of its customers.

MANAGEMENT IN ACTION

The "management by crisis" thinking that seems to have prevailed among many banks in the past is simply unacceptable in today's dynamic, competitive environment. The former passive attitude, resistant to change and characterized by such expressions as "Wait and see" or "We never did it that way before" must give way to a far more enlightened philosophy.

In essence, commercial banking seeks to generate profits by rendering services. To accomplish this twofold objective, a commitment to change is required. That commitment is a necessary part of the total process of

Table 3.1.   Program Summary and Work Plan

SEGMENT: (1) _RETAIL BANKING_ _____ ATTACK PLAN: (1) _EXPLORE PROFITABILITY + MARKET NEEDS_

PROGRAM: (1) _FEASIBILITY OF BRANCH EXPANSION_ _____ MANAGER: _W.R. SMITH_

SPECIFIC PROGRAM OBJECTIVE:
DETERMINE IF ADDITIONAL BRANCHES ARE   1) NECESSARY FOR MARKET
                                       2) POTENTIALLY PROFITABLE

CRITICAL ASSUMPTIONS TO MONITOR:
1. NEIGHBORHOODS WILL REMAIN ESSENTIALLY UNCHANGED
2. CUSTOMERS WILL PREFER ACTUAL BRANCHES TO AUTOMATED FACILITIES.

IS THE TIMELY EXECUTION OF THIS PROGRAM ESSENTIAL FOR MEETING THE   YES NO
FINANCIAL OBJECTIVES OF THE SEGMENT STRATEGY   ☒ ☐

#	PHASE ONE MILESTONE	DATE
1.	CONDUCT MARKET RESEARCH RE EXISTING COMPETITION IN AREA; SHOW EACH ON MAP	6/30
2.	IDENTIFY ANY POTENTIAL CHANGES IN AREA (NEW HOUSING, OFFICES, ETC.)	6/30
3.	COMPLETE DEMOGRAPHIC STUDY OF AREA (POPULATION, INCOME, ETC.)	8/1
4.	CONDUCT MARKET RESEARCH RE NEEDED/WANTED BANKING SERVICES IN AREA	9/15
5.	IDENTIFY BRANCH PROFIT POTENTIAL FOR FIRST THROUGH FIFTH YEARS	10/1
6.	SELECT OPTIMUM LOCATIONS ON BASIS OF ALL ABOVE FACTORS, OR JUSTIFY "NO GO"	11/1
7.	IF "GO" QUANTIFY HUMAN RESOURCES NEEDS AND	11/15
8.	INITIATE REAL ESTATE NEGOTIATIONS	

planning—which, in turn, is an essential component of contemporary management in action.[38]

The process entails a series of bench marks and principles. Management must develop and disseminate clearly defined objectives and goals. There must be a clear understanding of the nature of the organization and a statement indicating what its mission is and how it intends to serve its markets. Those elements in the future that will have an impact on the bank's tasks must be identified, and basic policies and strategies must be drawn up to meet them. Management must consider the bank as an entity that must change with its customers, its environment, and the economy, of which it is an important part. Thus, planning can create a work climate in which managers and subordinates know where the bank wants to be, and understand the steps that they must take to lead it in that direction.

Effective planning makes possible a system by which staff members not only know what is expected of them, but also the time frame within which they should accomplish certain goals, along with the specific contributions that are expected of them so that the desired bottom-line results can be attained. Table 3.1 illustrates a specimen work plan in which an objective is stated and each milestone leading toward its completion is identified.

Through receptivity to new ideas and flexibility in thinking, as well as willingness to admit mistakes (and correct them when they occur), a bank's directors, stockholders, and officers are all involved in planning, each in different ways and to varying extents. Their joint efforts can shape the course of the bank's future, instead of merely perpetuating the present.[39]

[38]Mason, *Financial Management of Commercial Banks*, pp. 120–121.
[39]Douglas V. Austin and Gene S. Booker, *Modern Techniques in Bank Management* (Boston: Warren, Gorham & Lamont, 1969), p. 14.

4 Sources of Bank Funds

An apocryphal story claims that four officers, each representing a different commercial bank, met to discuss the planning processes initiated by their respective banks and the management focus that had been placed on future activities. "Our biggest concern," said the first banker," is *liquidity*. We're prepared to pay far less attention to other considerations because we know many of our customers are really worried over recent bank failures and problems. They want absolute assurance that they can withdraw their funds from us at any time. We see our main job as emphasizing that availability for them. No matter what else we neglect, we're going to guarantee liquidity at all times."

"That's all well and good," said the second, "but we're much more conscious of the need for *safety*. Our customers have heard one scare story after another about all the bad loans, domestic and foreign, that banks have made in the past few years, and how much they have had to charge off. Liquidity can take second place in our thinking. We're focusing on risk, and we're determined to let the world know how prudent and conservative we've become. We simply refuse to take the risks we took last year and the year before. Besides, how in the world can your bank possibly build up liquidity to that extent? What exactly do you plan on doing? Will you fill up every inch of space in your vault with currency so that you gain maximum liquidity?"

"You're both on the wrong track," said the third bank officer. "We're in business purely and simply to make money. Everything else must be secondary. *Income* is the key ingredient in our game plan. The stock-holders, newspapers, money brokers, investment analysts, and everyone else all look at our bottom line. They all know we've had some substandard earnings, and it makes no sense for us to worry about anything else until we improve our image by showing an increase in net income. You'll see the difference this year. It's no secret: our focus is on a very ambitious profit plan, because *that's* the real name of the game today. Forget everything else; just tell me about earnings per share."

Like the three blind men in the fable who tried to describe an elephant, each of the three bankers was partially correct, yet each was unable to see the complete picture. It was only the fourth officer who was able to put the entire problem into the proper perspective.

"All three of you have lost sight of the basics of today's bank management," he said. "Of course, you're right when you say that no bank can neglect considerations of liquidity and safety, and of course, you're correct when you say that income is extremely important. But whenever you overemphasize any one of those three elements at the expense of the other two, you're doing nothing but creating problems for yourselves. If you can't manage your bank's funds by balancing all three objectives, you've lost the war."

His comments summarize one of the most vital issues facing the bank management team today. The banker is no longer an *asset* manager, whose chief job is to selectively put to profitable use the funds that steadily flow into his bank on an interest-free basis. He is now a *liability* manager, dealing in purchased money. Generally speaking, banks today find that they must *buy*—and pay a competitive price for—whatever funds they need. Only then can they use the funds in a way that combines the three principles of *safety, liquidity,* and *income.*

The banker, then, has come to resemble a manufacturer who had somehow been able to obtain the necessary raw materials for his business at no cost, but suddenly found that he had to begin paying a high price for them. Demand deposits formed the traditional raw material of commercial banking, and the unpleasant but inescapable fact is that those deposits no longer flow into, build up in, and remain with the banks as they once did. Banks must recognize that they cannot count on demand deposits to fund their daily operations and provide the basis for their loans and investments.

Since the early 1960s, the most dramatic shift in our entire banking history has taken place in the "mix" of deposits. In 1950, demand deposits accounted for 71% of total commercial bank deposits; by 1974, they made

Table 4.1. Time Deposits at Commercial Banks

Year	Total Time Deposits	Ratio to Total Bank Deposits
1950	$36.7 billion	29%
1955	50.0	32
1960	72.9	39
1962	97.8	46
1964	126.6	50
1966	158.6	55
1967	183.8	57
1975	459.0	59
1978	616.0	61

Sources: Figures through 1967 from *Savings and Time Deposit Banking* (Washington, D.C.: American Bankers Association, 1968), p. 4–17. Subsequent figures from *Federal Deposit Insurance Corporation, Annual Reports.*

up only 43%,[1] and the change in ratio continues. Table 4.1 displays the trend away from demand deposits in selected years from 1950 through 1967; and Table 4.2 analyzes the 1980 annual reports of the ten largest American commercial banks to show the emphasis on savings and time deposits. As of August 1982, only 24.8% of total bank deposits were in the form of interest-free checking accounts.[2] Demand deposits are no longer the bank's basic stock-in-trade; savings and time deposits dominate, and bring with them problems in the management of funds that prior generations of bankers never had to face.

This evolutionary—or perhaps revolutionary—trend causes the banks to pose new and challenging questions about their business. They must identify the sources of funds on which they now depend, and know the costs of those funds in a highly competitive marketplace. They must offset those costs through their loan and investment policies, practices, and pricing. Their profit planning must reflect the new structure of their deposit base.

[1]Edward W. Reed, Richard V. Cotter, Edward K. Gill, and Richard K. Smith, *Commercial Banking* (Englewood Cliffs, N.J.: Prentice-Hall, 1976), p. 84.
[2]*Federal Reserve Bulletin* (September 1982):A17.

Table 4.2.   Time to Demand Deposit Ratios Ten Major Banks, 1980

Bank[a]	Time/Demand Ratio
Citibank (New York)	86 / 14
BankAmerica (San Francisco)	79 / 21
Chase Manhattan (New York)	74 / 26
Manufacturers Hanover (New York)	67 / 33
Morgan Guaranty (New York)	70 / 30
Continental Illinois (Chicago)	81 / 19
Chemical Bank (New York)	68 / 32
Bankers Trust (New York)	68 / 32
Western Bancorporation (Los Angeles)	65 / 35
First National (Chicago)	83 / 17

Source: "Annual Scoreboard of 200 Banks," *Business Week* (April 13, 1981), 94. Data supplied by Standard & Poor's Compustat Services, Inc.
[a]Listed according to total asset size.

As mentioned earlier, *disintermediation* is the generic term used to describe the flow of money from lower-yielding or interest-free deposits to various vehicles that provide better rates of return. The Monetary Control Act of 1980, by authorizing all financial institutions to offer NOW accounts, will further accelerate the movement of funds away from demand deposits into these interest-bearing relationships.

HISTORICAL DEVELOPMENT

Prior to the Great Depression, commercial banks in America were allowed to pay interest on demand deposits, and many of the major institutions in money market centers aggressively vied with one another for new business by offering attractive interest rates to their corporate, institutional, and governmental customers and prospects. In periods of economic prosperity and increasing competition, the rates offered as a means of gaining new accounts rose accordingly. However, to meet the expense created by rising interest costs, banks in many cases had to sacrifice loan portfolio quality to some extent. Safety became less important than income. By booking higher-risk loans, the banks could charge higher interest rates and thus offset their increased costs.

Loans of substandard quality were a causative factor in the collapse of many banks during the early 1930s.[3] Those failures, numbering in the thousands and causing losses of billions of dollars, were taken into account by Congress when the Glass-Steagall Act, calling for major reforms in the banking system, was being considered in 1933. That legislation, as enacted in its final form, contained several restrictive features, one of which prohibited all payment of interest on demand deposits.

The Banking Act of 1935 expanded on this by giving the Federal Reserve the power to establish maximum interest rates on various forms of savings and time deposits at member banks. Under this Act, Federal Reserve Regulation Q came into being. It remains operative today as a critical and, more recently, highly controversial element in the network of controls over the banking system.

As noted in Chapter 1, the Depository Institutions Deregulation Committee (DIDC) was authorized, under the terms of the Monetary Control Act of 1980, to establish the timetable for gradual elimination of all interest-rate ceilings. The Garn-St. Germain Bill of 1982 further directed the DIDC to establish a new account with *no* rate ceiling.[4] This will be discussed in detail in Chapter 6, as part of the overview of Retail Banking. The effects of the legislation, as regards free and open competition for deposits, will have to be assessed over the course of time.

As long as the banking system was able to maintain an ample reservoir of interest–free demand deposits and selectively put them to work, the banker was an asset manager in a funds-using industry. Whenever loan demand from preferred customers increased, the banks simply sold portions of their government bond holdings and used the proceeds to fund the loans. There was always an adequate supply of available money to meet the banks' needs.

However, in the years following World War II, the commercial banks as a group began losing ground relative to other financial intermediaries. Their major customers—affluent individuals and a "new breed" of sophisticated financial officers in corporations, agencies of government, and

---

[3]Paul S. Nadler, *Commercial Banking in the Economy* (New York: Random House, 1968), p. 61.
[4]"A Rundown of the New Banking Law," *ABA Banking Journal* (November 1982):38.

institutions—started to recognize the many opportunities that had opened up for them. Increasingly, they found that there were many ways of putting their funds to work at a profit, instead of leaving those funds in an interest-free checking account. From 1946 to 1956, total deposits at all insured commercial banks increased 38 percent; during the same period, deposits at mutual savings banks and savings and loan associations grew by 172 percent.[5]

Perhaps the most significant characteristic of the commercial banks' approach to this situation was shown by how slowly they recognized their relative decline in the marketplace and attempted to respond. For many years, while their competitors were steadily attracting deposits at their expense, the banks stubbornly insisted on maintaining their traditional posture, disdaining the consumer as a customer and neglecting any major, systematic marketing effort. Most commercial bank officers seem to have felt that customers and prospects knew them, knew their bank, and would come to them whenever necessary. No attempt was made to encroach on the savings account or mortgage loan field, since these were viewed as the exclusive province of the thrift institutions, which capitalized on the needs of a postwar civilian population and aggressively sought the deposits with which to fund their loans.[6] The commercial banks saw themselves as corporate-oriented holders of demand deposits and, despite the statistical evidence, seem to have assumed that they would always remain in a preferential, funds-using position.

Commercial banks, as a group, were also by far the largest holders of United States government obligations. At the end of World War II, they held almost 60% of their total assets in this medium, and their total holdings represented over one-third of the national debt.[7] By law, the Fed was required to buy back, at par value, any such obligations from the banks, at any time. Hence any investments in government bonds could be converted into usable funds, at fixed prices, with no difficulty. The inflationary cycle that the nation experienced in the early stages of the Korean War (1950 and 1951) resulted in the abolition of the laws on this subject.

[5]Carl T. Arlt, "The Changing Character of Bank Deposits," in Herbert V. Prochnow and Herbert V. Prochnow, Jr. (Eds.), *The Changing World of Banking* (New York: Harper & Row, 1974), p. 59.

[6]George W. McKinney, Jr., William J. Brown, and Paul M. Horvitz, *Management of Commercial Bank Funds,* 2nd Ed. (Washington, D.C.: American Bankers Association, 1980), p. 4.

[7]Martin Mayer, *The Bankers* (New York: David McKay Co., 1974), p. 187.

The Accord of March 4, 1951, between the Treasury Department and the Federal Reserve, gave the Fed total freedom in its open-market purchases and sales of government obligations, and eliminated the concept of fixed-price support.[8] Government bonds, therefore, were trading freely. As the government found it necessary to pay higher interest rates to attract investors, futher disintermediation from the banks took place at the same time that credit demands were rapidly increasing. The two factors combined to create steadily rising ratios of loans to deposits at commercial banks.[9]

The savings and loan associations, as a group, displayed the greatest increases in growth, relative to that of the commercial banks. Total bank deposits in 1946 were $144 billion, while the savings and loans held $8 billion. During the ensuing twenty-five years, the former had grown to $543 billion, increasing 3.76 times, while the latter grew to $175 billion, increasing 21.8 times.[10]

The competition for funds increased in type as well as in asset size. For example, the total assets of life insurance companies tripled, and those of trusteed pension funds increased fifteen times.[11] Corporate treasurers were legally prohibited from opening savings accounts with corporate funds at member banks,[12] but could easily select from many other investment media that provided them with interest income on what formerly had been sterile funds in checking accounts. Even more opportunities existed for individuals. They could readily transfer funds from commercial banks to thrifts, or invest in federal or municipal obligations at attractive yields. Those with larger amounts of available cash could generate income through bankers' acceptances or prime commercial paper. The decade of the 1950s showed an 80 percent growth in America's gross national product (GNP), but only a 21 percent increase in demand deposits at commercial banks.[13]

Eventually, the Federal Reserve responded to the twin pressures on commercial banks (i.e., slow growth of demand deposits while demands for credit were increasing) by revising Regulation Q so that members could pay higher interest rates on savings and time deposits in order to attract

---

[8]McKinney, Jr., Brown, and Horvitz, *Management of Commercial Bank Funds*, p. 14.
[9]Nadler, *Commercial Banking in the Economy*, p. 153.
[10]Carter H. Golembe, "The Organization of Modern Banking," in Prochnow and Prochnow, Jr., *The Changing World of Banking*, p. 14.
[11]Mayer, *The Bankers*, p. 190.
[12]Federal Reserve regulations were revised in 1975 so that this restriction was eliminated and corporate savings accounts up to $150,000 were permitted.
[13]Nadler, *Commercial Banking in the Economy*, p. 158.

funds. The Fed also restructured its reserve requirements for members, thus encouraging them to compete for such deposits with thrift institutions. Today, required reserves on savings and time deposits are approximately one-fourth those on demand deposits, and the Monetary Control Act of 1980 provides for a continuation of this differential.

Further complicating the problem of attracting and retaining funds in the postwar period was the rise to prominence of the credit unions. These organizations were originally confined to use by employees of the same company or unit of government. Today, it is legally possible for any group of individuals having some common bond or purpose to obtain a charter and form a credit union. Once established, this type of financial institution can offer a wide range of services in competition with commercial banks and thrifts. In addition to their traditional functions of attracting members' deposits and making loans to them at preferential rates, credit unions now offer check-like instruments, known as "share drafts," for bill paying,[14] and have entered the home mortgage and credit card fields.

The competitive advantages enjoyed by credit unions in the competition for depositors' funds stem from their low operating costs and from the fact that they are exempt from taxation on their income.[15] Credit unions often receive free office space from the corporate or government employer with whom their members are affiliated, and may be able to take advantage of volunteer help, payroll deduction plans offered by the employer, free accounting services, and other ancillary aids.[16]

In 1950, total deposits at credit unions were $1 billion; in the ensuing decade, the unions doubled in number and their deposits reached $5 billion. In the 1960s, membership doubled again and assets tripled.[17] By mid-1982, total assets of the 22,000 credit unions were over $84 billion, and their outstanding consumer loans were over $45 billion.[18] They have become the third largest source of consumer credit, exceeded only by commercial banks and finance companies.[19] Bankers necessarily ask how much of this deposit and loan activity might have been placed with them, had it not

[14]The Monetary Control Act authorizes these drafts.
[15]Robert W. Davis (ed.), *Comparative Digest of Credit Union Acts* (Washington, D.C.: Credit Union National Association, 1981), p. 5.
[16]Mark J. Flannery, *An Economic Evaluation of Credit Unions in the United States* (Boston: Federal Reserve Bank of Boston, 1974), p. 7.
[17]Reed et al., *Commercial Banking,* p. 86.
[18]*Federal Reserve Bulletin,* September 1982, p. A29.
[19]Eric N. Compton, *Savings and Time Deposit Banking* (Washington, D.C.: American Bankers Association, 1982), p. 57.

been for the credit unions' aggressive competition. At the same time, there is resentment over the inherent advantages the credit unions enjoy. In 1978, President Carter proposed that credit unions be subjected to federal taxation, but his proposal was never enacted into law.[20]

THE CERTIFICATE OF DEPOSIT

In 1961, the then-First National City Bank of New York (now Citibank, N.A.) introduced a revolutionary new type of money market instrument, the *negotiable certificate of deposit,* in direct response to the need to attract new funds. The CD, as it has become commonly known, must be granted a permanent position of prominence among the major developments in the American banking system. Its growth has been truly remarkable. From a zero base in 1960, negotiable CDs, in large denominations (i.e., over $100,000, and therefore exempt from all interest rate ceilings), attained a nationwide figure of over $12 billion in 1964, and over $72 billion in 1974.[21] By July 1982, these same instruments accounted for $336 billion, or 18 percent of the total deposit liabilities of all commercial banks.[22]

In addition to their attractiveness in terms of interest rates, the fact that FDIC coverage applied within standard insurance limits, and their status as direct and guaranteed obligations of the issuing banks, these certificates gave investors an important benefit that previous types of CDs had lacked: they were issued in negotiable form, so that the holder could readily sell the CD in the secondary market at any time.

The large-denomination, negotiable CD has given the banks an option: instead of selling assets in order to raise cash, they can simply issue CDs.[23] It has enabled them to attract funds that would otherwise have been placed with competitive intermediaries, and the statement has been made—perhaps in the form of an oversimplification—that were it not for CDs, the

[20]Mario A. Milletti, "Credit Unions Attract More Assets," *The New York Times* (April 3, 1978), p. D1.
[21]"The Changing Deposit Structure," *Bank Stock Quarterly* (May 1974):2.
[22]*Federal Reserve Bulletin* (September 1982):A13.
[23]McKinney, Jr., et al., *Management of Commercial Bank Funds,* p. 69.

commercial banking system might display no deposit growth at all.[24] However, it must be regarded as somewhat of a mixed blessing.

More than any other factor, the CD has been the cause of a remarkable change in the typical bank's expense statement. Interest paid to depositors has become the largest, fastest-growing, and least controllable item of bank expense. Table 4.3 shows the growth of interest expense over a recent five-year period.

In 1981, total operating expenses for all insured commercial banks were $227.7 billion. Of that amount, $138.9 billion (61 percent) consisted of interest paid; a further breakdown discloses that $39 billion was paid to holders of large-denomination CDs.[25] In 1950, salaries and wages accounted for 50 percent of all bank operating expenses; by 1960 that percentage had shrunk to 40, and in 1981, salaries and wages constituted only one-seventh of total operating expenses.[26]

As a liability manager today, the commercial banker is a buyer of funds in a highly competitive financial marketplace. The "new breed" of customer is a shopper who recognizes the value of his or her funds to the bank, and therefore goes from one financial intermediary to another, seeking the highest interest rate. Any bank wishing to curtail its growth in annual interest expense can do so only by lowering its posture in the CD area; any bank wishing to increase its base of deposits can do so only through interest-bearing relationships. In a complete departure from tradition, commercial banking today is oriented toward time, rather than demand, deposits.

MONEY MARKET CERTIFICATES

The trend toward various forms of time deposits received further impetus when the various federal regulatory authorities—the Federal Reserve, the FDIC, and the Federal Home Loan Bank Board—issued regulations in 1978 that authorized the institutions under their respective jurisdictions to begin offering a new form of instrument known as the money market certificate (MMC).

[24]Nadler, *Commercial Banking in the Economy*, p. 164.
[25]"Profitability of Insured Commercial Banks," *Federal Reserve Bulletin*, August 1982, p. 463.
[26]David I. Fisher, *Cash Management* (New York: The Conference Board, 1973), p. 21.

Table 4.3.   Interest Expense at Commercial Banks

Year	Interest Expense as a Percent of Total Operating Expenses
1975	45.5
1976	49.5
1977	49.3
1978	51.1
1979	54.3

Source: "Profitability of All Insured Commercial Banks, 1979," *Federal Reserve Bulletin* (September 1980):691.

The regulations specified that MMCs could be issued for periods of exactly 26 weeks, and that the minimum denomination would be $10,000. The ceiling rate of interest payable by commercial banks was the discount rate for the most recently issued six–month Treasury bills; compounding of interest was permitted, and all thrift institutions were allowed to pay interest at a rate ¼ percent higher than the commercial bank rate. On March 15, 1979, the three authorities revoked the permission to compound interest on MMCs, and eliminated the rate differential whenever the T-bill rate was 9 percent or more.

The growth of MMCs during a very short period parallels that of the negotiable CD. One year after they were first issued, MMCs outstanding were $62 billion; by year-end 1980, the nationwide figure was $410.2 billion, of which insured commercial banks held $177.6 billion—an increase of $74 billion in one year.[27] The largest savings and loans in America reported similar growth in MMCs, and at year-end 1981, 260 of those institutions reported MMCs totaling $84.7 billion, or 35.8% of their total deposits.[28]

OTHER INTEREST-BEARING RELATIONSHIPS

During 1981 and 1982, Congress and regulatory authorities took further steps to enhance the ability of depository institutions to attract funds. The

[27]"The 300 Largest Commercial Banks," *American Banker* (March 6, 1981) p. 1.
[28]Harvey Glassman, "Deposit Growth Grinds to Virtual Halt at Biggest S&Ls," *American Banker* (February 23, 1982) p. 1.

one–year "All-Savers Certificate" was authorized by Congress for issuance during the 15-month period from October 1, 1981 to December 31, 1982; it carried a yield (always exempt from federal income tax, and possibly exempt from local taxes) set at 70 percent of the investment yield on new one–year United States Treasury bills. In 1981, the Depository Institutions Deregulation Committee (DIDC) removed interest rate ceilings on 30-month "small saver" certificates, and on Keogh and Individual Retirement Accounts (IRAs) with deposits maturing in 18 months or more.[29]

Additional types of new account and quasi-account relationships (e.g., retail repos, "sweep" accounts, and accounts specifically designed to compete with money market funds) will be described in Chapter 6, under the heading of Retail Banking.

PROFIT PLANNING

The increased importance of the time and savings deposit function, with its accompanying increase in interest expense, has forced commercial banks to make major changes in their profit planning. They now recognize that the term "profit margin" can be applied to banking as well as to any other industry. The "spread" at any time between the cost of funds to a bank, and the yield it derives from loaning or investing them, has become one of the most significant factors affecting the bottom line of bank performance.

The fact that today's banker is described as a liability manager who deals in purchased rather than interest-free money does not diminish the need for effective asset management. Indeed, the two concepts should be united so that asset *and* liability management take place in tandem. Many banks have attempted to implement a program known as "matched funding" wherever possible. Under this program, interest-rate-sensitive assets (e.g., loans) are matched against liabilities (e.g., deposits) that are also interest-rate-sensitive. Time frames are likewise matched in an attempt to avoid the classic problem of borrowing on a short-term basis in order to fund long-term debt.

[29]"Profitability of Insured Commercial Banks," *Federal Reserve Bulletin* (August 1982) p. 456.

Unfortunately, the sheer size of many banks makes it impossible for them to perform matched funding on a dollar-for-dollar basis. Therefore, they adopt various strategies designed to restructure their asset "mix" and increase the rate sensitivity of those assets. Interest rates in recent years have been the highest in our history, and also have been far more variable.[30] The deposit base has steadily swung toward those types of time deposits that are sensitive to rate changes. To offset what is occurring on the liability side of its balance sheet (with a consequent effect on its income statement), a bank may try to increase the rate sensitivity of its assets and restructure their "mix." For example, it might use the financial futures markets for hedging, or reduce its portfolio of fixed-rate, long-term loans. It might shorten the maturities in its investment portfolio.[31] It might offer new types of floating- and variable-rate loans, including home mortgages. It might take various steps to increase the yield on its consumer credit outstandings.[32]

Decisions involving huge sums of money must be made each day about whether the quoted rate for CDs and other forms of time deposits should be raised or lowered. The current interest rate a bank quotes on time deposits is often the *quid pro quo* that determines which bank a customer selects. At the same time, pricing decisions must be made on loans and interest rates, which are adjusted as market conditions change. The prime rate charged by banks to their largest, most creditworthy customers changed seventeen times during 1981, with a high of 20.5 percent and a low of 16 percent.[33] CD rates were changed even more frequently, according to conditions in the money markets.

OBJECTIVES OF FUNDS MANAGEMENT

The fundamental change in deposit structure that has taken place in the commercial banking system heightens the pressure to achieve that critical

[30]McKinney, Jr. et al., *Management of Commercial Bank Funds,* p. 7.
[31]Abraham Serfaty, "Financial Futures in Liability Management," *American Banker* (April 21, 1981):6.
[32]F. Lee Jacquette, "Bank Balance Sheet Planning for the 1980s," *The Bankers Magazine,* (September–October 1980):38.
[33]*Federal Reserve Bulletin* (January 1982):A26.

balance among the three objectives of funds management—liquidity, safety, and income—that is necessary if the bank is to meet all its obligations to all its constituents. The fourth banker in the story told at the beginning of this chapter recognized that any overemphasis on one objective at the expense of the other two would be highly detrimental to the entire bank. It is appropriate to explore this in greater detail here.

Liquidity

Liquidity for a bank describes its ability to meet customer demands for the withdrawal or payment of funds. It is absolutely essential if the bank is to remain in operation. Any refusal by a bank to honor a customer's demand at any time can start a run on that bank and trigger a financial crisis.

Yet no bank considers it realistic to expect that all its customers will issue checks at the same time for the sum total of their demand deposit balances. Similarly, not all passbook customers will withdraw their entire savings account balances on the same day, nor will all holders of time deposit instruments seek payment at the same time. Absolute liquidity would require that the bank be prepared for just such an eventuality, but practical considerations dictate otherwise. If a bank were to try to meet this ultimate goal, it would be forced to keep its vaults overflowing with currency, its balances with correspondent banks at absurdly high levels, and its non-interest-bearing reserves at the Fed in amounts far beyond the required figure. These three items constitute the bank's *primary* reserves. They represent cash or its immediate equivalent, and are the principal source of liquidity for the bank; however, they produce no income.

Secondary reserves are less liquid, but have the advantage of contributing to liquidity while generating income. There is a slightly higher degree of risk involved in them. The most common examples of these reserves include short-term federal government issues (e.g., Treasury bills), bankers' acceptances, and other highest-quality, noncash assets that can be sold at once, if necessary.

In addition to providing for withdrawals of funds, liquidity in a bank must also consider the demand for loans. The credit function is an integral part of banking; long-standing customers with good credit expect the banks to make funds available to them when needed, and there will always be unused commitments and unused portions of credit lines that may be exercised at the customer's option. Provision must be made for these. Therefore, when a bank calculates its liquidity needs, it tries to project both a "floor" for deposits and a "ceiling" for loans. Using all available data, the bank tries to estimate—usually for a twelve-month period—the level to which existing deposits can be expected to drop, and the level to which existing outstanding loans will probably increase.[34] Because the bank must be prepared both to pay out money to depositors and accommodate those customers who have a legitimate claim on it when borrowing needs arise, the combination of the dollar figure needed for withdrawals, along with the amount needed for an increase in loans, represents the total liquidity requirement.

The process of calculating liquidity needs can never be reduced to an exact science; there are too many imponderables that can affect it. However, a bank can employ a wealth of known material in order to make the best possible "educated guess" about its future requirements. For example, to meet the projected demands for payments of funds, it can chart the seasonal patterns of deposit inflow and outflow over past business cycles, and it can determine from its own records the dollar amounts of maturing time instruments over a period of time. Similarly, there are cyclical and seasonal patterns of borrowing, and these provide some clue about probable future needs. The basic nature of a bank's business is perhaps the most important factor in considering probable loan demand. A bank in an agricultural area must consider the farmers' needs for credit prior to the local harvest time. Conversely, a bank located in a resort community expects loan demand to be minimal during the off season.

Safety

No less than liquidity, safety in every phase of a bank's operations is an essential part of its effort to achieve proper management of funds. Each investment and loan basically represents a commitment of customers' funds, and those funds must be protected; yet loans and investments carry inherent degrees of risk. If a bank were to overemphasize the concept of safety and therefore assumed only minimum risks, it would necessarily

---

[34]McKinney, Jr., et al., *Management of Commercial Bank Funds*, pp. 220–230.

curtail its credit operations. Its only loans would be those that were completely secured by collateral of unquestioned value and marketability, and its only investments would be those that could be sold at a moment's notice. This conservativism would reduce income to unacceptable levels, harm the bank's image, and adversely affect many borrowers. By failing to meet the credit needs of its community, the bank would find itself in violation of the basic requirements of the Community Reinvestment Act.

Safety, then, is a *sine qua non,* but it must take into account the prudent assumption of certain risks. It can never be considered at the expense of, or to the exclusion of, the other two objectives of management of funds.

Income

Neither can income be overlooked in this effort. Survival and growth depend on profits. Interest payouts each year, labor costs, and the basic expenses of operating the bank continue to escalate, and there must be a profit margin that enables the institution to offset these and display satisfactory earnings.

However, the fundamental truth that interest on loans is the most important single income factor again comes to the fore. If funds management policies opted to maximize income at the expense of the other two objectives, the bank would be forced to relax its normal credit standards and increase its income by accommodating every category of applicant under every conceivable set of borrowing conditions. Safety would suffer and liquidity would decrease. Although the bank's short-term profits might appear excellent, its eventual charge-offs of imprudent loans would, on a long-term basis, create a drain on the entire structure. Further, the bank in question would come under severe criticism from federal and state examiners for its liberal credit policies, along with its failure to enforce normal credit standards.

BASIC SOURCES

How do commercial banks obtain the funds necessary to conduct their daily operations? There are only three fundamental sources of funds: *capital, deposits,* and *borrowings.*

An institution's *capital funds* include the amounts that its incorporators originally invested through their purchases of stock. Retained earnings (often subdivided into undivided profits and surplus) and subsequent issues of common and preferred stock are also part of the capital base. Many banks have also issued interest-bearing notes and debentures in order to build up their capital funds. Instruments of this type have a fixed claim on assets and earnings, and have priority over common and preferred stock in the event of a bank's liquidation, but are subordinate to depositors' claims.[35] In many cases, bank debentures carry the privilege of conversion into stock under predetermined time and rate conditions.

The amount of a bank's capital is usually thought of as the basis for assessing its financial strength. Capital is the ultimate safeguard against insolvency, protecting the safety of deposits.[36] Minimum capital requirements for establishing a new bank are set forth in federal and state laws; the amount varies according to the size of the community to be served. Examinations of any bank by a government agency always include a determination of its capital adequacy. To bolster stockholders' confidence, most banks stress the amount of their capital funds in their reports and statements, and show the additions to those funds that took place during the year.

Under federal and state regulations, the amount of a bank's capital is also a determining factor in its credit function. Generally, 10 percent of capital and surplus is the maximum a bank may lend to any one obligor on an unsecured basis.[37]

Deposits constitute the basic raw material of a bank, put to work each day to generate profits and render services. Banks today are funds-gathering organizations that must compete in an increasingly wide and aggressive marketplace for the deposits they wish to attract. Commercial banks remain the prime suppliers of credit to every segment of the economy—businesses, governments, and consumers—and their customers look to them to provide funds in time of need. To meet these customer demands for credit, banks must depend largely on deposits; but in today's environment they cannot adopt a passive role and wait for new deposits to appear.

Corporate, institutional, individual, and governmental customers are quick today to take full advantage of the many opportunities available to

---

[35]Crosse and Hempel, *Management Policies for Commercial Banks,* p. 301.
[36]McKinney, Jr. et al., *Management of Commercial Bank Funds,* p. 17.
[37]State laws usually permit state-chartered banks to include undivided profits in calculating their legal lending limit.

them. They tend to leave deposits *only* where there is an attractive rate of interest or range of needed services, or both. The movement of money in our economy from one form of financial intermediary to another has never been more rapid. Disintermediation occurs quickly whenever customers identify some type of more profitable situation. The introduction of MMCs again illustrates this point. When commercial banks were at a competitive disadvantage because of the interest rate differential, funds flowed from them to the thrift institutions that offered a better yield. When the differential was eliminated, the flow was reversed.

The competitive problem extends across the traditional lines that separate financial institutions. During a single month (April 1979), New York's mutual savings banks experienced the largest single outflow of funds in their history, suffering decreases in deposits of $779 million because their depositors found that money market funds, commercial paper, or federal or municipal obligations were offering higher yields than the banks were legally permitted to extend.[38]

In seeking additional funds, banks may find it difficult to attract new capital at times when the investment community has strong reservations about their financial strength and, therefore, about their stocks. Efforts to increase deposits may also appear unpalatable if the end result will be a direct growth in interest expense, as is usually the case today. For both these reasons, many banks now turn to various forms of *borrowing* as a means of obtaining the funds they need.

Bank borrowings include any direct loans made by one institution to another, loans made by the Fed, and federal funds transactions.

Regulation A of the Federal Reserve System pertains to the privilege, originally held only by member banks, of seeking short-term loans directly from the Fed to meet unusual situations or seasonal needs. The Regulation states that the use of this borrowing privilege over lengthy periods, or on a frequently recurring basis, is not considered appropriate, and in such cases the Fed may simply decline the request. The Monetary Control Act of 1980 extended the borrowing privilege to all financial institutions that offer transaction accounts, so that thrift institutions and credit unions now have access to the Fed for loans. Whenever the Fed grants credit to an applicant, the loans must be secured either by federal government obligations or other eligible paper. As noted earlier, the discount rate applies to all such credit extended by the Fed.

---

[38] *Daily Bond Buyer* (May 15, 1979):3.

Because the reserve accounts maintained at the Fed do not earn interest, each member attempts to keep its reserve balances at the required minimum level, and to put any excess reserves to profitable use. A bank that needs federal funds ("fed funds") to meet its reserve requirement borrows them from another bank that happens to have surplus reserves at the time, and pays the prevailing daily rate of interest.

In 1963, the then Comptroller of the Currency, James Saxon, issued a ruling that drastically revised the federal funds market by allowing all national banks to consider transactions of this type as purchases by the borrowing bank and sales by the lending bank. National banks, therefore, were no longer required to show federal funds borrowings as loans on their balance sheets.

With the Saxon announcement, an entirely new market opened up. Banks that needed funds for their own profit purposes began actively seeking out others that had excess reserves, and the latter found that they could readily sell their surplus reserves to the highest bidder.

MEASURES OF BANK PROFITABILITY

Because America's commercial banks are neither nationalized nor subsidized like their counterparts in other countries, and because they are organized directly for profit, the measures of their profitability are important to all their constituents—stockholders, depositors, units of government, and the public in general—as well as to their own managers and those who analyze their performance for stock market purposes. A set of ratios has been developed to determine the success or effectiveness of banks in managing the resources under their control, and these ratios are frequently used to determine how well a given bank is functioning. The most common ratios are:

1. Return on assets (ROA)
2. Return on equity (ROE)
3. Capital adequacy
4. Earnings per share (EPS)

Return on assets (ROA) is derived by dividing a bank's earnings before securities transactions by its average total assets during a period. Table 4.4 displays the ROA figures for two major commercial banks in selected years from 1968 through 1976. A detailed analysis of these ratios shows that Bank "A" has experienced excellent growth in sheer size of its assets, but that those assets were not being put to proportionately profitable use. On the other hand, Bank "B" not only showed asset growth, but utilized its assets far more effectively and therefore showed steady improvement in its rate of return.

Return on equity (ROE), the second measure of profitability, divides the bank's earnings before securities transactions by the dollar amount of its stockholders' investment in it; therefore, it shows the rate of return on the capital base. Table 4.5 uses the same two commercial banks used in the earlier example, and shows the ROE figures for them over the same period of time.

Both of these ratios illustrate that mere bottom-line profits alone do not provide an adequate basis for judging the performance of a bank. Rather, ratios must be used to show the bank's effectiveness in putting resources to work.

Table 4.6 shows the ROE and ROA data for the nation's largest bank holding companies in comparable 1982 and 1981 periods.

Table 4.4.   Return on Assets

Year	Earnings Before Securities Transactions[a]	Average Total Assets[a]	Return on Assets
Bank "A"			
1968	$35.0	$3,580	0.98%
1970	41.6	4,411	0.94
1972	42.1	5,341	0.79
1974	55.5	8,577	0.65
1976	42.9	8,332	0.51
Bank "B"			
1968	$10.7	$1,566	0.68%
1970	12.7	1,668	0.76
1972	16.7	2,018	0.83
1974	23.3	2,573	0.91
1976	29.5	2,978	0.99

[a]Dollar figures are in millions.

Table 4.5. Return on Equity

Year	Earnings Before Securities Transactions[a]	Average Shareholders' Equity[a]	Return on Equity
Bank "A"			
1968	$35.0	$316	11.1%
1970	41.6	347	12.0
1972	42.1	398	10.6
1974	55.5	467	11.9
1976	42.9	513	8.4
Bank "B"			
1968	$10.7	$100	9.4%
1970	12.7	111	11.4
1972	16.7	128	13.1
1974	23.3	153	15.2
1976	29.5	187	15.8

[a]Dollar figures are in millions.

Table 4.6. Comparative ROA/ROE Data
The 15 Largest Bank Holding Companies

	ROE 2nd Qtr., 1982	1981	ROA 2nd Qtr., 1982	1981
BankAmerica Corp.	11.7	13.1	0.41	0.47
Citicorp	13.1	10.6	0.50	0.37
Chase Manhattan Corp.	(4.0)	15.8	(0.08)	0.54
Manufacturers Hanover Corp.	12.6	12.5	0.44	0.41
J. P. Morgan & Co., Inc.	15.4	17.2	0.71	0.75
Chemical New York Corp.	14.0	15.0	0.53	0.50
Continental Illinois Corp.	(13.9)	14.7	(0.51)	0.54
First Interstate Bancorp.	14.1	17.0	0.63	0.75
Bankers Trust New York Corp.	14.1	14.0	0.55	0.51
Security Pacific Corp.	14.4	16.7	0.57	0.68
First Chicago Corp.	9.8	9.4	0.37	0.38
Wells Fargo & Co.	10.7	10.0	0.45	0.39
Crocker National Corp.	5.0	11.1	0.26	0.45
Marine Midland Banks	8.3	10.8	0.37	0.46
Mellon National Corp.	12.8	12.2	0.69	0.69

Source: American Banker, July 27, 1982, p. 3.

Capital adequacy is the third ratio of profitability, traditionally known as the capital ratio. It is obtained by dividing total stockholders' equity by total assets. Every examination of a bank by federal or state authorities assesses its capital adequacy. The stronger a bank's capital position (and, therefore, its capital ratio) the greater its projected appearance of financial strength. Capital ratios for all insured commercial banks averaged 5.8 percent for 1981. During that year, the banks showed total increases of $11.2 billion in their capital, 80 percent of which came from retained earnings.[39]

However, in 1982, the Federal Reserve revised the basis for calculating a bank's capital ratio, and used a new term, primary capital, to describe the total amount an institution has available for the protection of its depositors. The new term includes all common and perpetual preferred stock, surplus, undivided profits, contingency and other capital reserves, and allowances for loan losses. As a result, Salomon Brothers calculated the leverage—that is, primary capital as a percent of average total assets—for the same 15 major banks used in Table 4.6. The average for the 15 banks was a leverage figure of 21.3.[40]

Earnings per share. (EPS) is the final ratio, arrived at by dividing the bank's bottom–line income by the average number of stock shares outstanding. Growth in EPS is commonly thought of as a key indicator in analyses of bank performance. EPS figures also provide a means of determining how highly a bank's stock is regarded in the marketplace. If its EPS for a given year is $5 and the stock is selling at $25, the price-earnings ratio is five and this can be compared with P/E ratios for other institutions.

A complete analysis of a bank's profitability requires review of all its performance ratios over a lengthy period of time, rather than a focus on any one ratio for any one year. A bank may have incurred a highly unusual, non-recurring loss during one year, or its strategies in that one year may have made a heavy commitment of resources for expansion purposes. The results of policy decisions directly affect its profitability ratios for the year in question, but must also be analyzed over time. Short-term strategies cannot be viewed alone; they should be considered in the light of long-term results.

[39]*Federal Reserve Bulletin* (August 1982):461.
[40]Robert A. Bennett, "New York Bank Profits Surge," *The New York Times* (October 25, 1982):1.

5 Uses of Funds: Wholesale Banking

During 1979, the American Bankers Association embarked on a major new advertising campaign, using television commercials and magazine advertisements to stress the point that the financial needs of every type of customer can be completely satisfied *only* through our 14,000 commercial banks. This advertising was in direct response to the intensive campaigns conducted by thrift institutions, brokerage firms, money market funds, and other competitors as a means of attracting funds away from the "Full Service" banks.

In using the term *Full Service* to describe the basic nature of their business, the commercial banks are displaying an approach to the market that differs substantially from their traditional limited posture. For most of its history, American banking has been essentially *wholesale* in nature. Networks of bank branches, providing a wide range of services to every category of customer, were largely nonexistent until the post-World War II period. The average working person was not thought of as a potential customer, and the entire thrust of banking lay in gaining and keeping deposits from corporations, agencies of government, and correspondent banks, and in lending and investing those funds to generate annual profits. To today's observer, who may be surrounded by banks operating hundreds of branches and doing everything possible to market a full spectrum of services to every type of customer, it may come as a surprise to learn that such widespread *retail* banking is a relatively new development in the industry.

By arbitrary definition, the wholesale bank makes no attempt to be all things to all people. It focuses on the three categories of customer mentioned in the preceding paragraph. If branching is permitted in the wholesale bank's state, it will take advantage of that law only to a very limited extent, although its retail competitors may be constantly expanding their branch systems. The wholesale bank's range of services to individuals will not include the small installment loan, the Christmas Club, or the low-balance checking account, but will address the investment, trust, and related needs of the more affluent. Only 15 to 20 percent of the wholesale bank's customer base will generate 75 to 80 percent of its deposits.

With the end of World War II, the wholesale banking that had historically characterized the system came under serious questioning. Management teams at many institutions began to ask whether that type of banking actually represented the optimum approach to growth and profitability. The consumer came to be perceived as a neglected segment of the total market, and commercial bankers in increasing numbers gradually accepted the notion that installment lending need not be left to finance companies, that savings accounts for individuals need not remain the exclusive province of the thrift institutions, and that personal checking accounts, even with nominal balances, could reasonably be offered to society at large. The relative growth of such competitors as savings and loan associations and credit unions could no longer be ignored, and a movement that may justifiably be called revolutionary took place in the postwar years and has accelerated ever since.

Where state laws restricted or prohibited branch banking, pressures for legislative change increased as the banks sought permission to function wherever their customers might be. Many banks that had been entirely wholesale in philosophy recognized the profit potential of the retail market and thus merged with other institutions that had already adopted a retail posture, and in so doing, succeeded in capturing a share of the consumer business.

This movement was most noticeable in New York City in the late 1950s, as one after another of the nation's largest banks announced the completion of merger negotiations. The former Chase National Bank, the former Chemical Bank and Trust Company, the former Hanover Bank, and the former Bankers Trust Company merged with the Bank of the Manhattan Company, the Corn Exchange Bank and Trust Company, the Manufacturers Trust Company, and the Public National Bank, respectively. In each case, the merger represented a departure from a wholesale identity for the first-named bank and enabled it to position itself on the retail side of banking. Simultaneously, the merged bank was able to continue its service to and cultivation of corporate, government, institutional, and correspondent bank accounts. It may be said that the concept of Full Service banking truly began at this time.

WHOLESALE BANKING: BASIC CONSIDERATIONS

From the management standpoint, wholesale banking offers certain inherent advantages. It allows a bank to operate with a relatively small staff, since large numbers of tellers and clerks are not required. It avoids the problem of escalating rent and occupancy costs at large networks of branches. Since wholesale banking does not generate the transaction volume that retail banking requires, it allows the bank to operate with less equipment, requiring less floor space. Perhaps most importantly, the wholesale bank creates an image of highly professional specialization and personalized attention to customer needs.

These putative advantages must be carefully weighed against other considerations. By definition, a wholesale bank must address the needs of large corporate, institutional, and government customers; therefore its staff must be prepared to deal with the increased sophistication and expertise displayed by those customers in today's financial environment. The wholesale bank depends heavily for its profits on a portfolio of loans made to these major customers, but financial officers today are increasingly prone to bypass commercial banks wherever possible and borrow from one another through the commercial paper market. During 1982, for example, the economic downturn, with its accompanying shrinkage in corporate liquidity and profits, forced businesses to borrow in steadily increasing amounts, and the total of commercial paper outstanding increased during every one of the first seven months, reaching a July figure of $181 billion.[1] The issuer of commercial paper can combine his activity in that area with a modern cash management program to minimize the demand deposit balances that the wholesale bank would otherwise gain.

[1]*Federal Reserve Bulletin* (September 1982):A25.

An additional risk in wholesale banking lies in the relatively small number of accounts that are involved. The loss of any one of these carries very significant risk, since it often represents a meaningful portion of the bank's total deposit base. The same reasoning may apply to the credit function in such a bank. The largest customers are inevitably the largest borrowers. Default on any single loan will have a far greater impact on earnings than a charge-off at the retail bank, whose credits are far more numerous and diversified.

The increasingly multinational aspect of the wholesale bank's corporate customers compels the bank to become a global lender, possessing a firm grasp of the current economic conditions in all the areas of the world where its clients operate. It must be prepared to provide its credit facilities and expertise through such services as international loan syndications, and to face the challenges and risks entailed in extensive foreign exchange transactions.

The concept of risk diversification also extends to the concentration of funds from particular industries. A wholesale bank may find that it has become largely dependent of aerospace, automobile, steel, or petroleum firms for its deposits, loans, and income, and a recession or other problem in these segments of the economy will then significantly affect the entire bank.

A final consideration for management on the subject of wholesale and retail banking is the degree of deposit structure volatility in each case. Savings deposits fluctuate less widely than demand deposits; business accounts display far larger day-to-day balance changes; and major corporate, correspondent bank, and government accounts are subject to the highest rate of turnover of all. At New York City banks during the 1970s, the turnover rate for demand deposits was seven times higher than the rate in 1945. Liability management and liquidity needs are prime concerns in wholesale banking because of this increase in money mobility.[2]

This presentation of the positive and negative factors in wholesale banking may prompt the question of whether a purely wholesale bank can actually succeed in today's financial marketplace at a time when so many competitors are aggressively seeking to increase their retail activity. Two well-publicized contemporary situations may provide an answer.

[2]Howard D. Crosse and George H. Hempel, *Management Policies for Commercial Banks,* 2nd ed. (Englewood Cliffs, N.J.: Prentice-Hall, 1973), p. 128.

VIABILITY

Morgan Guaranty Trust Company in New York has long been regarded as the prototype of the wholesale bank. A list of its clientele would include the largest of the "Fortune 500" corporations, as would its loan portfolio. A bank spokesman has said that it lends to those "Fortune" firms "to whom we *choose to lend*."[3] His statement reflects the bank's philosophy, which calls for providing the highest quality of in-depth service throughout the world *only* to those market segments with which Morgan Guaranty wishes to deal. It operates a relatively small number of New York City and foreign branches, each of which is in an area where its major customers are domiciled or operating. It makes no effort to reach the consumer market with installment loans or low-balance checking accounts. During the credit shortages of 1969–70, 1974, and 1980, Morgan Guaranty refused to cut its lines of credit to major corporate customers, although others were retrenching.[4]

What have been the bottom-line results of this operating philosophy? From 1971 through 1980, Morgan Guaranty outperformed 16 of the nation's largest banks in per-share earnings growth, averaging 13.4 percent per year.[5] If return on assets (ROA) is used as the yardstick of performance, Morgan Guaranty, with $0.81 per $100, ranked first among the fifteen largest U.S. banks in the third quarter of 1982.[6] It is also far more heavily capitalized than the other fourteen banks on that list, with total equity 5.22 percent of average total assets; and if net income alone is to be used as the measure of success, the bank showed a 45 percent gain from third-quarter 1981 to third-quarter 1982.[7] Its accomplishments as the epitome of wholesale banking are self-evident.

The second situation is noteworthy in that it evidences a reversal of the general trend away from purely wholesale banking and a significant move in the opposite direction. Bankers Trust Company, through its own growth and its merger with the then-Public National Bank, transformed

---

[3]Martin Mayer, *The Bankers* (New York: David McKay Co., 1974), p. 259 (emphasis added).
[4]John Carson-Parker, "Why the Blue Chips Bank on Morgan," *Fortune* (July 13, 1981):38.
[5]Ibid., p. 37.
[6]Robert A. Bennett, "New York Bank Profits Surge," *The New York Times* (October 25, 1982):D1.
[7]Ibid.

itself over the course of some 25 years from a "carriage trade" wholesale bank into an institution serving the needs of every type of customer through a network of 106 branches in the New York City area. However, its Annual Report for 1978 announced management's decision that providing all financial services to all markets was no longer considered the optimum course to follow for future profitable growth. Therefore, the Annual Report and subsequent disclosures stated that Bankers Trust would sell as many as 89 of its branches, and would implement a policy of focusing on and providing services to corporations, governments, financial institutions, and high-income individuals through the remaining branch offices and through the bank's overseas presence in twenty nations.[8] By year-end 1980, 80 branches, with $900 million in deposits, had been sold, and the bank had completed a cycle from wholesale to both wholesale and retail and back to its original wholesale character.[9]

One year later, the bank had completed the sale of its bank card business to The First National Bank of Chicago. Exclusive of any gains resulting from its disposition of that activity and the sale of its branches, it reported an increase in ROA from $0.42 in 1979 to $.57 in 1981, and an increase in ROE from $12.78 in 1979 to $15.52 in 1981. Accompanying the publishing of those figures was this statement:

> Our corporate strategy is to concentrate resources selectively on what we can do well and profitably. We have chosen commercial banking, money and securities markets, corporate finance, and fiduciary as our four core businesses and have identified corporations, governments, financial institutions, and certain individuals as our primary markets.[10]

Bankers Trust's decision resulted from a planning process similar to that described in the previous chapter. The bank conducted a self-examination to identify its strengths, and then selected the market segments to which those strengths were best suited.

None of the foregoing should be construed as an effort to polarize the wholesale/retail concept and thus to claim that banks must make an either/or decision in this regard. Indeed, commercial banks today usually want to be known as "Full Service" institutions that do not focus on wholesale business to the exclusion of other types of customers. The typical bank

[8]Robert A. Bennett, "Bankers Trust: Corporate Focus," *The New York Times* (April 16, 1979):D1.

[9]"Wholesale Banking's New Hard Sell," *Business Week* (April 13, 1981):82.

[10]Bankers Trust New York Corporation, *Annual Report* (1981):3.

attempts to combine the best elements of both wholesale and retail banking. At the same time, the trend is toward some degree of market segmentation; that is, the bank identifies those types of customers with whom it feels it can most effectively deal, and then selects the services that can best be rendered to them on a profitable basis.

A somewhat different approach can be seen in those large banks that have restructured internally to create Corporate Banking units. An officer in one of those departments works in a manner parallel to that of his or her counterparts at a purely wholesale bank, but this officer's unit is only one part of a larger organization whose other components address the needs of smaller or "middle market" businesses, lower-income individuals, and other customers in the area served. If a bank is described as retail, it need not be thought of as one that neglects corporate, government, institutional, or correspondent bank relationships. Rather, it should simply be considered more diversified than the purely wholesale bank.

USES OF FUNDS: CREDIT

Archaeologists have uncovered evidence of a loan made by representatives of a temple in ancient Babylon some 5,000 years ago to a local farmer, who promised to repay with interest after the harvest. The same lending situation occurs today in American banks in agricultural areas. In *The Merchant of Venice,* Shakespeare created Shylock as the archetype of the moneylender who accommodated merchants. Goldsmiths in England often acted as private bankers, extending loans to their customers. Truly, the credit concept is as old as history itself, and never disappears from the business scene.

Innovative methods of borrowing were necessary in order to finance the American Revolution,[11] and ever since that time our country has, to an increasing extent, been one that largely operates on various types of credit. The commercial banks, which came to replace the temples, goldsmiths, and other lenders, are the major suppliers of that credit. Measured against our gross national product of over $3 trillion is the fact that total

[11]M. L. Bradbury, "Financing the Revolution," *Banking* (October 1975):115–117.

loans at American commercial banks in July 1982 were $1 trillion.[12] Whether a bank is described as wholesale or retail, large or small, and regardless of the size and nature of the geographic area in which it operates, it must always recognize an obligation to satisfy the legitimate credit needs of its community and customers. In doing so, it not only provides a needed service, but also generates the profits necessary for its own survival and growth.

Which bank customers create these demands for a continually increasing supply of credit? The question can be conveniently answered by considering three segments of our society: governments, businesses, and consumers.

Governments—federal, state, and local—must resort to various forms of borrowing in order to meet their increased expenditures. The federal government, of course, is the bellwether in this respect, since its revenues have exceeded its expenditures in only three of the years that have elapsed since 1951. In 1981, the national debt passed the trillion-dollar mark, and Congress has found it necessary to raise the statutory debt limit six times since 1976 to make additional federal borrowing possible. The Open Market Committee of the Federal Reserve is responsible for issuing all Treasury bills, notes, and bonds, and the commercial banks, as a group, are the largest holders. In mid-1982, they held $116 billion of these obligations.[13]

State and local governments face the same chronic problem. They cannot increase taxes or develop new sources of income to keep pace with expenditures. During 1979, they issued $43.4 billion in new obligations; in 1980, $48.4 billion; and in 1981, $47.7 billion.[14] Again, commercial banks are the major suppliers of the funds these governments need. At year-end 1981, they held over $48.3 billion in these debt issues, for which the generic term is *municipals*.[15] Tax-anticipation and revenue–anticipation short-term notes and long-term bonds are the most common offerings.

Like their corporate counterparts, officials of various agencies and authorities of governments have turned to the commercial paper market to raise funds. Their issues, which carry an exemption of interest from federal taxes, include those offered by the Illinois Education Facilities Authority, the Government Development Bank for Puerto Rico, and the South Dakota

[12]*Federal Reserve Bulletin* (September 1982):A15.
[13]Ibid.
[14]Ibid., p. A36.
[15]Alan Longley, "Largest Banks Increase Bond Holdings 4.5%," *American Banker* (May 14, 1982):55.

Housing Development Authority,[16] and carry shorter maturities (usually 15 to 45 days) than notes. Repayment to the holder is made directly from operating revenues.[17]

Businesses of every size and type continually resort to borrowings from commercial banks to meet their seasonal, working capital, capital expansion, or other needs. Despite the efforts of many corporate financial officers to use the commercial paper market or other sources of funds, the commercial banks remain in a preeminent position as the supplier of business credit. Total commercial and industrial loans at all commercial banks were $386 billion in July 1982.[18]

Individuals make up the third category of bank borrowers and use various forms of credit far more readily and extensively today than ever before. The total installment debt of consumers amounted to $332 billion in July 1982, of which $147 billion was owed to commercial banks.[19] This figure does not include $1.1 trillion in mortgage debt on one-to-four family homes, of which commercial banks held $178 billion.[20]

The financing of these three major categories of borrowers, therefore, has largely been provided by the commercial banks despite the extent and accessibility of their competition. Thrift institutions, retailers, credit card issuers, commercial and personal finance companies, credit unions, brokerage firms, and insurance companies are all active in the lending field in a variety of ways; yet commercial banks continue to dominate, chiefly because they alone have the capability to offer every size and type of loan to every segment of the borrowing marketplace, under every conceivable set of conditions. As our inflation-fueled economy has grown steadily in the years since World War II, so has the overall credit function at commercial banks, and the emphasis that was once placed on investments as a source of bank income and as a use of depositors' funds has declined proportionately. A bank's first obligation in the use of funds is to its creditworthy customers, especially those who have maintained relationships with the bank for years, and who naturally look to it for credit. All other uses of bank funds have lower priority.

[16]"Municipal Commercial Paper," *Perspective* Standard & Poor's Corporation (September 17, 1980):3.
[17]Byron Klapper, "Municipal Commercial Paper," *Governmental Finance* (September 1980):23.
[18]*Federal Reserve Bulletin* (September 1982):A15.
[19]Ibid., p. A42.
[20]Ibid., p. A41.

Although loans and investments may both be considered by a bank as extensions of credit, they must be ranked in that order. When banks allocate funds, loans have first priority; investments rank below them because, in many cases, the bank is not dealing directly with the customer/depositor.

In 1950, the total of loans at all insured commercial banks was 31% of total assets. By 1960, that percentage had risen to 47; when nationwide demand for credit escalated dramatically in 1974, total loans were 60% of total assets. August 1982 figures show assets of $1.7 trillion for banks, with $1.0 trillion (59%) in loans and leases.[21]

Although the credit function is an integral part of the daily operations of all "Full Service" banks, and although these institutions regularly make many sizes and types of loans to the three basic categories of customers, it is invariably the corporate segment that generates the largest domestic and global volume. For this reason, the credit function is considered here as most relevant to wholesale banking. International lending and consumer credit warrant separate treatment, and will be dealt with in subsequent chapters.

BASIC CONSIDERATIONS

The most simplistic definition of a commercial bank would state that it accepts deposits and puts them to work to generate profits. Deposits, then, are the basic raw material, and in this regard a bank is equivalent to a manufacturer who converts the goods furnished by suppliers and derives profits from the sale of the finished product. However, there is an essential difference that results from the relationship of banks to their customers.

Those who supply raw material to manufacturers never expect to recover it; those who provide banks with money insist on that right of recovery. Every deposit, even if it is considered to create an asset because it can be put to profitable use, remains a liability, since at some time, in some manner, it must be returned to the customer.

Therefore, the considerations of liquidity, safety, and income directly

---

[21]*Federal Reserve Bulletin,* (September 1982):A17.

affect the credit function at commercial banks. At all times, a bank must attempt to meet the legitimate credit needs of its community and its customers, especially those corporations that have long-standing relationships and account for much of the bank's deposit base, and must simultaneously be in a position to honor all orders from depositors for payment or withdrawal of funds. The bank's options are severely limited if it cannot meet these twin goals on any given day. It may be forced to liquidate part of its investments, perhaps at a loss; or it may resort to borrowings to obtain the working funds it needs. As a last resort, it may be forced to call in some of its outstanding loans, to the extreme detriment of customer relationships.

During periods of high economic activity, the rate of deposit turnover and the demand for credit often escalate at the same time, creating intense pressures on the banking system. When this occurs while the deposit base is shifting from a demand to a time orientation, the problem increases in magnitude. Banks today must not only seek to attract and retain deposits in order to function; they must also derive maximum yield from their loans and investments to offset the rising costs of purchased funds. Yet the quest for yield, especially in lending, can easily lead to a deterioration of the loan portfolio if the bank relaxes its criteria and accepts borrowers who would otherwise be turned away.

Because of the interrelationship of loans and deposits, the ratio between them is often used as a yardstick to determine the extent to which banks are called on to employ available funds. Although much has been written regarding the increased demand for credit in 1978, 1979, and particularly 1980, when interest rates reached a record peak, the year 1974 remains of even greater interest, since it offers a classic example of responses by banks to the problem of funds managing. Table 5.1 traces the historical pattern of ratios of loans to deposits over a 25 year period.

During 1974, requests for credit grew in number and size, and lending at each of the nation's nine largest commercial banks increased by at least 21% over the prior year; at year-end, four of those banks showed loan-to-deposit ratios of 80% or more. In referring to 1974, one bank Chairman admitted, "We were guilty of excesses. We got caught up in giving analysts a thrill a minute."[22] It became evident that the banks, in their desire to meet as many credit requests as possible, and to increase profits by accommodating every borrower, neglected many of the fundamentals of

[22]"The Great Banking Retreat," *Business Week* (April 21, 1975):78.

Table 5.1. Loan to Deposit Ratios

Year	New York City Banks	All Commercial Banks
1950	37.9	33.7
1960	54.7	51.2
1970	70.2	65.2
1974	78.5	72.3

Source: Edward W. Reed, Richard V. Cotter, Edward K. Gill, and Richard K. Smith, *Commercial Banking* (Englewood Cliffs, N.J.: Prentice-Hall, 1976), p. 120. For comparison purposes, it may be noted that the ratio for all commercial banks in July 1982 was 80.6%: *Federal Reserve Bulletin* (September 1982):A15–A17.

credit. Paul Nadler's comments were particularly critical: "Every bank was on a drunken kick—buy your money, liability management, diversify, high multiples."[23]

The result was the charging-off of $2 billion in loans for the year, including $382 million that was charged off by the five largest banks alone.[24] In addition to that immediate consequence, long-term problems were created. Some condominium loans made in Puerto Rico and some financing extended to real estate investment trusts remained in workout status for five years after the actual lending took place. The W. T. Grant Company was the nation's largest retailer when it filed under Chapter XI of the National Bankruptcy Act; it owed $291 million to three major New York City banks at the time, and its bankruptcy required years to adjudicate.[25]

In retrospect, it is difficult to realize why the banks embarked on this course of credit expansion at a time when so many warning signals were clearly visible. An OPEC embargo on oil shipments to America existed from October 1973 to March 1974, causing major economic problems. Unemployment rose rapidly, housing starts decreased from an annual rate of two million units in 1973 to 1.3 million in 1974, and the term "double-digit inflation" was introduced into our vocabulary. The banking community was severely shaken by the news of the closing of Bankhaus Herstatt in West Germany, and the failures of the United States National

[23]In "The Great Banking Retreat," *Business Week* (April 21, 1975):78.
[24]Ibid.
[25]James A. Largay, III and Clyde P. Stickney, "Cash Flows, Ratio Analysis, and the W. T. Grant Bankruptcy," *Financial Analysts Journal* (July–August 1980):3.

Bank (a billion-dollar institution in San Diego) and the Franklin National Bank in New York. The federal government let it be known that there had been a meaningful increase in the official "watch list" that identified problem banks. These events combined to create a lessening of confidence in the banking system.

The year 1974 has been emphasized here in a very negative sense, because it was a year in which basic credit considerations seem to have been bypassed in favor of expanded profits. At its conclusion, the hope was expressed that it had served as part of a learning process for bankers who would be forced to reappraise their lending policies and return to more prudent operations. While that hoped-for emphasis on quality in credit analysis, portfolio administration, and funds management may have resulted at many banks, more recent experience indicates that even further reassessment of credit policies and practices may be needed. The Penn Square National Bank, International Harvester, Manville, Braniff, and Revere failures of 1982 can be cited as proof that the learning process is a continuous one.

THE LENDING PROCESS

If the millennium ever arrives and banking attains its utopia, a simple, foolproof set of standard guidelines will have been developed to remove every element of risk from the credit function. Unfortunately, no such ready formula has ever been developed. Except in those relatively few cases in which a loan is fully secured by cash collateral (e.g., a passbook or CD) or some form of immediately marketable, guaranteed security (e.g., United States governments), risk will always be present. An unforeseen event may convert what appeared to be an acceptable credit situation into a charge-off. Business recessions occur, manufacturers find that public taste has changed and that their products no longer sell, new competition—often from abroad—drives the profits of established businesses down, and even units of local governments often overextend themselves.

The objective of the lending process, properly implemented, is not to attempt to achieve zero losses, but rather to accept the fact that losses will sometimes occur and to take every prudent step to reduce that possibility. There is no magic formula guaranteeing a good loan, but there are certain procedures that will help assess the degree of risk, keep it to a minimum, and bolster public confidence.[26]

In this context, another aspect of the dynamics of change in commercial banking may be noted. It was traditional for a bank relationship manager— the account officer assigned responsibility for all phases of a customer relationship—to "grow up" with the client by spending many years in the same role. The relationship manager literally lived with the company through its growth and progress, and was intimately familiar with all the details of its profit structure. Today, there is a high degree of turnover among account officers at major banks; changes in assignment are frequent, and the lending officer is forced to rely on financial data supplied by the company, rather than on close personal knowledge.

The lending process logically begins with a clear understanding of the loan's purpose. Why is the customer requesting this accommodation? Is it consistent with bank policy? Does the purpose make the loan subject to government regulation, as in the case of loans secured by listed stock as collateral and made to buy or pay for other listed securities? Is there any indication that this same purpose will be used again in a future loan request, as in the case of a corporate borrower who requests repeated infusions of bank credit to meet working capital requirements?

The banker who is presented with a business loan request should determine *who* is assuming the bulk of the business risk involved. If the firm's equity—that is, invested funds— is very low in relation to its debt structure, then the banks are being asked to provide its financing, rather than its stockholders. The banker must also make every effort to evaluate the management team that is in charge of the company. Are they apparently conditioned to deal with adversity? If not, a problem that arises during the life of the proposed loan may be disastrous. Does the management team appear to be closely attuned to its market? Had this question been applied to American automobile manufacturers at a time when imports of smaller, more fuel-efficient cars were beginning to flood the United States market, the results might have been very different. What type of experience, over the course of how many years, has the management team had? Is there too much concentration on short-term profits at the expense of long-range planning?

Perhaps the most important step in the lending process is the effort to identify the specific source of repayment. If the company projects repay-

---

[26]Tracy G. Herrick, *Bank Analyst's Handbook* (New York: Wiley, 1978), p. 146.

ment from normal operating profits, there should be evidence of an ability to generate those profits. The clearer this identification, the more likely it is that the loan will not develop into a workout situation.

In some cases, the attempt to identify a source of repayment is neglected on the grounds that collateral is being tendered. This is a completely unsound credit practice. Good collateral lends strength to a request for credit, but of itself should not provide the basis for approval. Deterioration of collateral may occur, as in the case of listed securities that are subject to stock market fluctuations. Forced sales of collateral often yield less than the outstanding loan amount, and frequently serve as evidence that the loan was weak at the outset.[27] Most importantly, the lending bank is not in the basic business of repossessing and selling collateral. Loans should be collectible from the borrower's inflow of income and profits, and a bank should not rely on collateral alone.

Because unsecured loans make up by far the largest portion of a bank's portfolio, constant and thorough attention must be paid to the area of credit analysis. Gathering as much financial data as possible regarding a corporate borrower is an integral part of identifying the projected source of repayment. The bank's own credit files may serve as a starting point. They provide a history of the customer's relationship with the bank and include correspondence, reports of interviews, financial statements, and data on previous loans, account balances, and account profitability. Investigations may be conducted with the company's other banks, trade suppliers, and possibly competitors. Audited financial reports should be obtained wherever possible. Such critical ratios as debt to total assets, debt to net worth, current assets to current liabilities, and past-due receivables to total receivables should be calculated.[28]

Implementing bank policy is also an integral part of the lending process. Based on considerations of liquidity, safety, and income, and in keeping with regulatory constraints and money market conditions, the bank's directors and senior managers establish the guidelines for lending officers to follow. Merger or acquisition loans, for example, may be deemed to be contrary to policy. Certain loans that contribute to community well-being may be encouraged as part of the program of social responsibility. As a policy matter, the level of compensating balances expected from

[27]Crosse and Hempel, *Management Policies for Commercial Banks,* p. 170.
[28]Charles F. Mansfield, Jr., "The Function of Credit Analysis in a U.S. Commercial Bank," *Journal of Commercial Bank Lending* (September 1979):24.

corporate borrowers may be adjusted. If internal audits and management information systems disclose that many demand loans[29] are being allowed to remain on the bank's books indefinitely, a new policy may be implemented to require each such borrower to remain out of the bank's debt for an annual 30-day period. Factors in the money market may dictate acceptance or rejection of requests for long-term credit. These and all other policies are not to be considered as straitjackets applied to loan officers. There should be some degree of flexibility, but any exceptions or changes should be consistent with the overall planning process.

Interest Rates

A further area of bank policy entails setting the interest rates that may be appropriate at various times. In retail banking, the ability of management to set these rates was often restricted by state laws, as in the case of installment loans, home mortgage loans, and credit-card outstandings. In wholesale banking, interest rates may be more readily adjusted as money market conditions change.

Essentially, money is a supply-and-demand commodity; its *availability* sets the price that must be paid for it. In addition, the cost of money is affected by the factor of *safety;* the perceived degree of risk in a loan affects the interest rate placed on it. Another factor affecting interest rates is *time.* Loans made for longer periods generally carry higher rates, on the premise that there is an expanded time frame during which problems might occur.

The term *profit margin* has particular relevance here, in view of the fact that commercial banks must now depend heavily on purchased funds in order to carry out their credit function. The spread between the cost of such funds and the yield obtained through lending or investing them is critical to profitability. In 1981, net interest margins for the 391 largest bank holding companies averaged 3.12 percent, due to increased competition in loan pricing and a continued shift toward the use of higher-cost funds to support assets.[30]

---

[29]Demand loans are made without a fixed maturity date; they are callable by the bank or repayable by the borrower at any time. Interest rates on demand loans may be revised whenever necessary.

[30]Anthony G. Cornyn and Thomas L. Zearley, "Financial Developments of Bank Holding Companies in 1981," *Federal Reserve Bulletin* (June 1982):336.

Traditionally, banks established a *prime rate* to be charged to their most creditworthy major corporate borrowers. This rate reflected not only the company's credit standing, but also the bank's recognition of a long and valued account relationship. The concept has undergone significant changes in recent years. In the first place, there has been criticism of the fact that a major corporation pays interest at the prime rate—from which interest rates to customers of lesser stature are determined—while the latter category is penalized through higher rates. This criticism rests on the assumption that the former group can readily recover borrowing costs through increases in product prices, while smaller borrowers find this more difficult to do. The result has been a "two-tier" prime rate system, in which large corporate borrowers have one rate and customers of lesser size have another, lower rate.[31]

The second change has involved a growing degree of recognition of the fact that the prime rate, while widely publicized in the media, is a rate often ignored in the realities of the daily operations of commercial banks. An institution that is determined to attract a customer's borrowing activity frequently offers a rate below the quoted prime, and expects to recover through an enhanced relationship with the borrower.

Interest rates that truly mirror money market conditions and are applied impartially are generally accepted by the borrowing public as a "sign of the times" and do not necessarily inhibit borrowing, especially in times of tight money. There is evidence to support the belief that customers do not necessarily complain about high interest rates *per se;* rather, they take exception to the idea that other borrowers receive preferential treatment and that some form of rate discrimination is therefore in effect.[32]

The introduction by some banks of "floating prime rates," tied directly to money market instruments and revised regularly, has been a positive step in convincing the borrowing public that banks themselves do not directly establish the cost of money. Citibank, N. A., in New York, and First National Bank in Chicago, have been the pioneers in implementing this system, and their announcements of prime rate changes, in accordance with a publicized formula, are watched closely as important indicators of money market trends.

The prime rate charged by major banks on short-term commercial loans has fluctuated to a previously unheard-of extent in recent years, reaching

[31]Mayer, *The Bankers,* pp. 422–423.
[32]Crosse and Hempel, *Management Policies for Commercial Banks,* p. 198.

a peak of 21.5 percent in late 1980, dropping to 20.5 percent in mid-1981, and falling steadily through 1982. Because of the difficulty in adjusting interest rates on loans rapidly enough to keep pace with changing rates in the money market, including their own costs of funds, there has been a general trend away from the banks' long-term fixed-rate loans toward more flexible arrangements. As the primary mortgage lenders, thrift institutions have joined in this effort to achieve greater parity between the current costs of money and the rates charged for its use. Variations of renegotiable-rate and variable-rate loans have been introduced by both types of lenders.[33]

In addition, commercial banks have implemented a type of loan in which they match their activities in the futures market to loan pricing. If a bank feels that it can fix the price of its CD rollovers, hedged by trading in futures, at 12 percent for a period of time, it will then price loans at 14 or 15 percent; in effect, it has "locked in" the cost of its future funding, and charged the borrower accordingly. Nine major banks report use of this new format.[34]

Loan Classification

To meet the reporting requirements of government agencies, and for their own management information and internal control purposes, commercial banks have used various methods to categorize all their wholesale loan portfolios. Some common examples include classification by maturity, industry, form of collateral, and type of borrower.

In classifying loans according to maturity, the basic division is between time and demand loans. The former may then be subdivided into short-term (i.e., less than one year) and long-term. Ninety-day loans are the most common single type, reflecting the fact that liquidity needs compel banks to emphasize short-term lending.

By monitoring loans made to specific industries, management can avoid the risk entailed in any undue concentration. When domestic or global events affect a particular industry, it is essential that the bank know its

---

[33]Lawrence Motley and Dan Huyser, "Community Bank Update," *Bank Marketing* (April 1981):8.
[34]John Morris, "Banks Make Loans Based on Hedged Costs of Funds," *American Banker* (October 17, 1982):35.

credit exposure in that industry, so that appropriate policy decisions can be made.

Secured loans can be subdivided to show the type of collateral accepted in each case. Again, modern management information systems can disclose any undue concentration, such as the dollar amount of loans secured by shares of a particular stock.

Aside from those commercial banks that are heavily involved in agricultural lending, a typical classification of a loan portfolio would include the outstandings in commercial and industrial loans; real estate loans (subdivided into short-term construction loans and long-term mortgage loans); interbank loans and participations (i.e., loans to a single borrower that are shared by two or more banks); and installment loans to consumers. As of July 1982, all commercial banks reported total loans of $1,024 billion, including $386.7 billion in commercial and industrial loans and $297.5 billion in various types of real estate loans.[35]

Interbank lending consists largely of dealings in federal funds. As noted earlier, national banks need not report these as direct borrowings; however, management may wish to list them as such, to show the extent to which they supply needed funds. By obtaining federal funds from other banks, the borrowing institution can avoid or reduce direct borrowings from the Fed itself.

Participations may result from the fact that a loan request exceeds one bank's legal lending limit, from that bank's practical desire to diversify its credits, or from the borrower's decision to divide a loan among several banks at which accounts have been maintained. Correspondent banks are frequently asked to participate in credits, and a larger bank assists its smaller correspondent by assuming that portion of the requested credit that is in excess of the latter's legal limit. The previously cited case of the W. T. Grant Company provides a classic example of this type of loan. In addition to the $97 million loaned by each of three major New York City banks, 133 other lenders participated in the total credit of $700 million.[36]

Real estate loans increased steadily in amount and importance during the 1970s, as a thriving economy seemed to require more apartment houses, shopping centers, office buildings, and single-family homes. The basic

[35]*Federal Reserve Bulletin* (September 1982):A15.
[36]Largay and Stickney, "Cash Flows, Rates Analysis, and the W. T. Grant Bankruptcy," p. 3.

category includes short-term construction loans, which are made to provide developers with the funds needed to complete a project, along with permanent mortgage financing. Construction loans are generally made only when the developer is able to demonstrate that he has already obtained long-term financing; they are usually paid directly from proceeds of the final mortgage. Much of the overexpansion of the real estate industry in the 1970s was fueled by Real Estate Investment Trusts (REITs), which, in turn, obtained financing from commercial banks. When many of the condominiums, office buildings, and other REIT projects proved unable to generate sufficient cash flow to permit repayment of the loans, the REITs were forced to default on their own obligations and, in some cases, had no choice but to declare bankruptcy. During 1974, commercial banks loaned $5 billion to REITs, much of which was not recovered.[37]

BANK INVESTMENTS

The management of funds at a commercial bank operates on a strict priority basis. Liquidity needs must be satisfied first so that provision is made for possible withdrawal of deposits and expansion of the loan portfolio. Only then can management turn its attention to those investment possibilities that are legally permitted and can be a source of income.

In some cases, bank investments are made in order to provide additional secondary reserves. For example, United States Treasury bills carry no credit risk, and are both short term and immediately marketable. They contribute to liquidity and simultaneously generate income.

Other investments must be made to meet regulatory constraints and customers' special requirements. For example, some state laws call for banks to hold state or federal obligations amounting to 110 percent of all state deposits. In other cases, the required amount is not as large, but the same principle prevails: public funds, deposited with banks, must be backed up by guaranteed federal or state obligations, so that no loss of those funds can ever take place.[38]

A third category includes obligations issued by local communities. In

---

[37]"The Federal Reserve: Doctor to Sick Companies," *Forbes* (February 1, 1975):24.
[38]Reed et al., *Commercial Banking*, p. 325.

buying these, the bank assumes a higher degree of credit and market risk, but it also gains the significant benefit of exemption from federal tax on the income, and an enhancement of its image as a good citizen in the community. By buying the municipality's debt issues, the bank helps finance local projects and gives public recognition to the fact that its own growth is closely tied to that of the geographic area it serves. Local governments naturally tend to place their deposits with those banks that invest in their debt issues.

Legal Considerations

The Banking Acts that were passed by Congress in 1933 and 1935 to reorganize and strengthen the industry imposed several constraints on the banks' investment functions. Banks were thereafter prohibited from any investment in common stocks for their own portfolios. Their holdings of the obligations of any issuer except the federal government were limited to 10 percent of capital and surplus, thus forcing diversification. The Glass-Steagall Act of 1933 allowed commercial banks to underwrite general obligation bonds of a municipality when the full taxing power of the issuer was pledged to guarantee repayment. These are commonly known as "full faith and credit" issues, and commercial banks often act as the underwriters. However, the Glass-Steagall Act also separated commercial from investment banking by prohibiting any bank underwriting of revenue bonds, which are secured by the income from bridges, tunnels, highways, and other fee-earning municipal facilities.

To an increasing extent in recent years, banks have lobbied for repeal of this section of the Act. Revenue bonds traditionally account for some 60 percent of all municipal financing, and this percentage can be expected to increase as voters insist on less direct taxation and increased user payment. Commercial banks have taken the position that they can render a direct, substantial benefit to municipal financing programs if they are legally allowed to compete with securities firms in underwriting revenue bonds.

Investment Planning

A bank's portfolio is technically divided into two parts: investment securities, which are held for the bank's own account, and trading account securities, which are held in order to create and provide a market in federal government and municipal obligations.[39]

As part of its overall program of funds management, a bank may shift the composition of its portfolio on a daily basis, according to its liquidity needs and money market conditions. Because it must make every effort to accommodate customers in times of an increased demand for credit, it may sell off some of its investment holdings, even if sales are made at a loss, and use the proceeds for loan purposes.

During World War II, commercial banks were not faced with heavy loan demand from corporate customers; therefore, they built up substantial portfolios of United States government obligations. From 1941 to 1945, those holdings grew from $22 billion to $91 billion.[40] In the immediate postwar years, the banks continued to place most of their investment attention on the same obligations, the price of which was directly supported by the government itself. The Accord of 1951 brought about a change in strategy. Banks began to look more favorably on municipal bonds as investments, and the federal tax exemption these offered became far more important as the deposit structure changed and interest expense rose.

From 1959 to 1964, total deposits at commercial banks grew by some $80 billion, three-quarters of which was in time and savings deposits; during the same time frame, they increased their investments by $23 billion, but the percentage of United States governments in their portfolios declined from 75 to 62.[41] By 1974, the 331 major banks that are used for Federal Reserve reporting purposes had restructured their portfolios to such an extent that they held $49 billion in municipals and only $24 billion in United States governments.[42]

Contemporary topics of discussion among bankers relate the shift in portfolio structure to the basic questions of risk and social responsibility. Does a bank's obligation to provide maximum safety for the funds entrusted to it by depositors supersede its obligation to support a community that is in obvious financial difficulty? Should the same credit criteria be applied equally to corporations and municipalities? Does a bank's civic responsibility require that it lend to its own community, and at preferential

---

[39]Herrick, *Bank Analyst's Handbook,* p. 90.
[40]Reed et al., *Commercial Banking,* p. 343.
[41]Leland S. Prussia, Jr., "Bank Investment Portfolio Management," in Herbert V. Prochnow and Herbert V. Prochnow, Jr. (Eds.), *The Changing World of Banking* (New York, N.Y.: Harper & Row, 1974), p. 155.
[42]M. A. Schapiro & Co., Inc., *Bank Stock Quarterly,* (May 1974):3.

rates? Is a bank justified in demanding repayment of debt by a municipality when its own future profits and growth presumably are tied to that same municipality?

These questions pose challenges to the ingenuity, tact, and good judgment of bank management. Conflicts will inevitably arise. Civic activists will point out that no municipality has actually defaulted on any debt issue since the Depression. Yet depositors will always want assurance that their funds are being invested with all due consideration for safety and prudence. The fiscal crises experienced by New York City in 1975, Cleveland in 1978, and Chicago in 1979 may sound a warning signal, prompting banks to take new approaches to the subject of investing in municipals. These may dictate that municipalities disclose their operations in more detail, adopt more uniform accounting practices, accept the thesis that they are expected to identify specific sources of repayment whenever they borrow in any manner, and possibly give the investing banks more voice in future municipal budgeting.

6 Uses of Funds: Retail Banking I

Throughout the first 160 years of their history, American commercial banks as a group generally rejected the average individual wage earner as a customer, and concentrated on the aspects of wholesale business as outlined in the preceding chapter. However, one aspect of the dynamics of change in banking identifies the major shift in direction that has occurred in the years since World War II. There is evidence of a massive, ongoing effort by many banks to reverse the traditional posture and to become "Full Service" institutions by doing everything possible to attract and retain consumer deposits, payment activity, and loans—the three cornerstones of banking.

New services are being developed, new marketing programs introduced, and new types of quasi-account and account relationships offered to meet the needs and wants of the retail customer. The working person, who so often found the doors of commercial banks closed to him or her, is now regarded as a prime target for cultivation, and finds that every type of automated and electronic facility is available. By making banking more convenient and attractive—to the extent that they can do so, vying with competitors who do not operate under the same sets of regulatory constraints—banks have developed a new responsiveness to the consumer in the postwar years.

Wholesale business will never be neglected, but there are numerous examples of this trend toward retail cultivation. The word *retail* itself suggests a network of bank branches serving a mass rather than a restricted market, and intense lobbying by banks has resulted in considerable relaxing of many of the state laws that formerly prohibited or limited branching. Wherever this has occurred, new branches have proliferated.

The number of banks remained basically unchanged from 1950 to 1970, but the number of branches grew from 19,000 to 34,000; the number more than doubled during the decade of the 1960s alone.[1] In New York State, whose laws were liberalized twice, the statistics graphically demonstrate this trend:

Year	Number of Banks	Number of Branches[2]
1950	635	1390
1970	283	3067
1977	239	3414

During a ten-year period beginning in 1972, Iowa (1972), Arkansas (1973), and Minnesota (1980) became "limited branching" states, eliminating their former prohibitions on branch banking; and New Jersey (1973), New York (1977), and New Hampshire and Florida (1979) moved from limited to statewide branching.[3] In 1982, Pennsylvania similarly liberalized its branching statutes. Wherever legally possible, banks attempted to follow the population, capitalizing on the growth of the suburbs and the movement out of the central cities of so many industries, with their thousands of workers.

RETAIL MARKETING AND COMPETITION

The dynamics of change in overall banking philosophy may also be seen in the abandoning of traditional resistance toward actual marketing of bank services. The former viewpoint, which held that any potential users knew the bank and the bankers and would automatically come to them when some financial need arose, is no longer viable. Individuals are repeatedly

[1]R. Gene Conatser, "Retail Banking," in Herbert V. Prochnow and Herbert V. Prochnow, Jr. Eds., *The Changing World of Banking* (New York: Harper & Row, 1974), p. 189.
[2]New York State Bankers Association, personal communication.
[3]Donald T. Savage, "Developments in Banking Structure, 1970–81," *Federal Reserve Bulletin* (February 1982):79.

told today that they can do their banking at home, can apply for installment loans by telephone, can obtain a personal line of credit, can open new types of actual or quasi-accounts, can use bank cards for an infinite variety of goods and services, can pay bills by phone, or can buy various forms of relatively small-denomination, nonnegotiable savings certificates. The consumer's future security can be addressed through Keogh and IRA (Individual Retirement Account) plans. Personal investment management and counseling may be made available.

Largely as a result of their efforts to market retail services, America's commercial banks spent ten times as much on all forms of advertising in 1971 as in 1950.[4] All the facilities that are now readily available to individuals easily lend themselves to every form of mass communication: radio and television commercials, bus and subway advertisements, urban and suburban newspaper and magazine publicity, billboards, and throw away handouts. Banks that formerly used only low-key "tombstone" advertising, and that to a very limited extent, now employ any or all of these vehicles. An official of the First National Bank of Boston has identified marketing—that is, the integrated process of learning customer needs and wants, developing and managing the appropriate products and services, and packaging, pricing, and advertising them—as a new discipline for bankers and one that is still in the experimental stage. His senior counterparts at Bank One in Ohio and Wells Fargo Bank in California have cited the developmental process that is still going on in the industry.[5]

Walter Wriston[6] has pointed out a strong element of irony in today's retail banking: many financially oriented organizations that were always among the major customers of commercial banks have now become their aggressive competitors for consumer services. A vacuum in these services never exists for any length of time. An actual, perceived, or created consumer need, if left unsatisfied by the banks, will quickly be addressed by others. In today's society, there are more individuals who have higher incomes, are better educated, are more sophisticated as to service and yield opportunities, and represent more desirable candidates for bank solicitation than at any time in the past. The Chairman of the American Express Company has described them as part of a "basis-point society,"

---

[4]"Now Banks Are Turning to the Hard Sell," *Business Week* (June 24, 1972):78.
[5]Thomas Watterson, "New Services, Competition Spur Fresh Bank Marketing," *The Christian Science Monitor* (October 15, 1982):17.
[6]In "Consumer Banking," *Business Week* (April 23, 1979):62.

sensitive to interest-rate variations, and potential users of as many as 28 financially oriented services.[7] A major topic of current discussion involves the attempt to quantify and qualify ways in which this growing market can be served as banks endeavor to meet the competition. That competition includes the following arbitrary and sometimes overlapping categories:

1. Brokerage firms
2. Credit unions
3. Finance companies
4. Financial conglomerates
5. Thrift institutions

The continuing decrease in commercial banking's share of the total financial marketplace may be largely attributed to the successes these competitors have achieved. All of them have recognized the basic truth that "money is a commodity and can be marketed as such"[8] and their service approaches to consumer banking can be listed here.

BROKERAGE FIRMS

Bache Halsey Stuart Shields (the Bache Group), now part of the Prudential Insurance Company, offers a "Command Account" tied to a VISA debit card. Users have access to check and debit-card processing and, through a link to Citicorp, can order travelers' checks for home delivery. They can also enroll in a buying service that provides for catalogue shopping and telephone ordering.

Dean Witter Reynolds, acquired by Sears Roebuck in 1981, offers customers a money market fund with VISA, deposit, and check-writing services through Bank One (Columbus, Ohio). It attracted 17,000 consumers in 1981, and now has access to the 40 million cardholders of Sears as

---

[7]"Robinson of American Express Urges Banks to Specialize," *American Banker* (October 7, 1981):4.
[8]Watterson, "New Services, Competition Spur Fresh Bank Marketing."

additional potential users.[9] The overall operations of Sears will be discussed further in this chapter under the "Financial Conglomerates" caption.

E. F. Hutton, Inc. has introduced an "Asset Management" account, in which the minimum investment is $10,000. An American Express Gold Card is provided to subscribers. Hutton has 275 offices, with over 600,000 customers.[10]

Money market funds were introduced in 1972 and were an immediate success, chiefly because they gave the relatively small investor access to a combination of banking and investment services with interest rates that banks could not offer. *Merrill Lynch* was and is the major brokerage firm in this field. Its CMA (Cash Management Account) has attracted 620,000 customers, who have invested $13 billion.[11] The CMA customer receives overnight investment of funds at market rates, a VISA card, check-issuing facilities, and overdraft or direct loan privileges up to the value of the securities held in the account. The minimum investment is $20,000 in cash and/or securities. Bank One handles the VISA and check processing. Merrill Lynch has announced its intention to compete further with the banks by entering the field of commercial lending, and has formed a cadre of former bank officers to manage this new venture.

Shearson Loeb Rhoades became Shearson/American Express when it was acquired by the latter company in 1981. It will integrate its "Financial Management Account" with the American Express Gold Card, and has publicly announced its intention of pursuing the "up-scale" portion of the consumer market—the same segment that is most attractive to banks. Again, the overall operations of American Express, impacting as they do on retail banking, warrant further treatment in this chapter under the "Financial Conglomerates" heading.

Each of these brokerage firms has developed a "package" for the consumer that includes both high-yield investment opportunities and one or more services that traditionally were supplied only by banks. The total assets of money market funds consistently exceeded $225 billion during the second half of 1982.[12]

[9]Robert Trigaux, "Brokerages Hurrying to Unveil Their Versions of Merrill's CMA," *American Banker* (February 26,1982):1.

[10]Robert Trigaux, "E. F. Hutton Cash Management Plan to Use Amexco Gold Card," *American Banker* (July 30, 1981):3.

[11]Lee Smith, "Merrill Lynch's Latest Bombshell for Bankers," *Fortune* (April 19, 1982):67.

[12]*Donoghue's Money Fund Report* various issues.

CREDIT UNIONS

The importance of the nation's 22,000 credit unions as financial intermediaries was mentioned in Chapter 4. These institutions enjoy the benefits
of exemption from federal taxes on their income, and often use office help
and ancillary facilities donated by the companies or organizations with
whose employees they deal. Credit unions now include some 25% of all
American households among their membership. In addition to paying
members higher rates of interest on savings and charging them lower rates
on loans, they now offer credit cards, CDs, 30-year home mortgage loans,
and "share drafts" for bill payments.[13] During 1981, their deposit growth
was 6.1 percent, as compared with increases of 4.4 percent for commercial
banks, 2.4 percent for Savings and Loans, and 2.1 percent for mutual
savings banks.[14] In a 1980 study of consumer borrowing habits, conducted
among 1,500 households, 31 percent of the respondents identified credit
unions as their source of funds.[15]

FINANCE COMPANIES

Incurring debt may have caused some form of stigma in the minds of past
generations of Americans, who made purchases only when they had ac-
cumulated the necessary cash. No such reservations about borrowing exist
in today's social structure. "Buy now, pay later" has become a familiar
phrase to millions of Americans—a far cry from Benjamin Franklin's axiom
that it was better to "go to bed supperless than run in debt for breakfast."
The average consumer no longer displays any reluctance to incur additional
debt, even if his or her resources have already been strained, nor is there
evidence of a reluctance among lenders to continue fueling this expansion.
During 1981, monthly increases in outstanding consumer debt were typically $2 billion to $3 billion;[16] and at year-end, *per capita* personal in-

---

[13]"Consumer Banking," *Business Week* (April 23, 1979):62.
[14]Lisa J. McCue, "Credit Union Deposits Up 6.1 Percent," *American Banker* (April 26,
1982):3.
[15]"Survey of Consumer Credit," *The Practical Banker* (September 1980):6.
[16]*Federal Reserve Bulletin,* various issues.

Table 6.1. Consumer Installment Credit
August 1982

Holders	Outstandings[a]	Percent of Total
Commercial banks	$147.3	44.3%
Finance companies	93.2	27.9
Credit unions	46.2	13.7
Retailers	26.8	8.0
Thrift institutions	15.7	4.7
Gasoline companies	4.7	1.4
Total	$333.9	100.0%

Source: Federal Reserve Bulletin (October 1982):A42.
[a]In billions of dollars.

debtedness (including home mortgages) was $6,737 versus a 1975 figure of $3,613.[17] The increase in personal bankruptcies to a 1981 figure of 457,000 has been attributed to the ready availability of every type of consumer credit. Industry sources estimated losses of $2 billion on consumer loans in 1980.[18]

In an inflationary era, it appears likely that personal debt will continue to grow as consumers borrow today in anticipation of repaying with next year's "cheaper" dollars. Items that once were considered luxuries are now seen as necessities, and borrowing makes them available. Paul Nadler[19] adds the thought that individual debt is often incurred out of fear that inflation will drive prices still higher, therefore, borrowing to buy can now be rationalized.

As shown in Table 6.1, finance companies, whether "captive" (i.e., lending instrumentalities of a parent corporation) or stand-alone, are the second largest lenders in the retail area exclusive of home mortgages, and therefore the major competitors of banks in the retail lending field.

A more detailed breakdown of outstandings discloses the following reported receivables of the six largest finance companies at year-end 1981, in billions of dollars:

[17]"The American Way of Debt," Time (May 31, 1982):46.
[18]Robert A. Bennett, "Banks and Retailers Report High Losses on Consumer Loans," The New York Times, (February 13, 1981):D1.
[19]In "Banking in Transition," The Bankers Magazine (September–October 1978):26.

General Motors Acceptance Corporation	$40.0
Ford Motor Credit Corporation	17.1
General Electric Credit Corporation	10.5
Sears Roebuck Acceptance Corporation	6.9
C.I.T. Financial Corporation	5.6
Household Finance Company	4.4
	$84.5[20]

The $84.5 billion owed to these six organizations gives rise to speculation about the portion of this debt that commercial banks might have assumed had they been able to overcome the inherent advantages (i.e., absence of reserve requirements and Federal Reserve regulation and examination, and unrestricted nationwide operations) enjoyed by nonbank lenders.

There is an interesting parallel between the management planning of the third largest finance company, General Electric Credit Corporation (GECC), and that of some commercial banks. In both cases, the basic strategies of the organization have been changed to reflect market segmentation, which targets specific profit areas. Instead of merely financing its parent corporation's consumer sales and thus remaining dependent on retail business, GECC has transformed itself into an across-the-board lender, making eight- and nine-figure commercial loans, offering lease financing, and arranging syndications.[21] The analogy to the recent reorganization of Bankers Trust Company is striking.

FINANCIAL CONGLOMERATES

In traditional American retailing, a consumer purchased aspirin or cough medicine at a corner drug store and bought food at a neighborhood grocery. Today, that consumer finds it possible to buy lawn chairs, portable radios, or motor oil at a newly diversified "drug store," and obtains cosmetics and prescription medicines, as well as groceries, at the supermarket. The era of specialized, restricted lines of business has largely disappeared. So it is with commercial banking. In the years following World War II, when

[20]"100 Largest Finance Companies," *American Banker* (June 10, 1982):19.
[21]"General Electric Credit," *Business Week* (August 30, 1982):54.

the emphasis on solicitation and cultivation of consumer business began, commercial banks still enjoyed a high degree of exclusivity. Competitive pressures simply did not exist as they do today. However, what was once the banking industry has now become the financial services industry, and the sophisticated consumer now looks to institutions other than banks to provide the solutions to financial needs and wants.

Banking has always relied on a favorable spread between the cost of its funds and the yield derived from their use. As long as low-cost savings accounts and interest-free checking accounts provided a ready supply of money in retail banking, profits were virtually guaranteed. Federal Reserve ceilings on interest rates inhibited competition for the small saver's money.

When money market rates began to exceed those ceilings and brokerage firms began pooling consumers' investments in money market funds, the situation changed dramatically. Disintermediation occurred as the core deposits of "cheap" money moved to new, more attractive areas.[22] Walter Wriston commented in a Congressional hearing that it had required only 24 months for Merrill Lynch's money market funds to exceed Citibank's total domestic deposits, which had been built up over the course of 160 years.[23] A new type of non-bank institution, the "financial supermarket," has sprung up, and many of America's major conglomerates have been among the prime movers in its genesis and growth. The current operations and publicized future plans of some of these competitors warrant attention here.

Prior to its acquisition of Shearson Loeb Rhoades, *American Express Company* was a leader in the credit card, money order, and travelers' check fields; it also owned an international banking subsidiary with assets of over $7 billion. It operates a nationwide, on-line network of terminals and owns a satellite and cable communications system, an EFTS consulting and research firm, and a data processing subsidiary.[24] Shearson/American Express now combines brokerage, check-writing, mortgage, card, cash management, insurance, and money-market services.[25] Its Treasurer has specifically identified "up-scale" consumers as its prime market;

---

[22]Michael Wines, "The Financial Supermarket Is Here," *National Journal* (November 21, 1981):2059.
[23]Carol J. Loomis, "The Fight for Financial Turf," *Fortune* (December 28, 1981):62.
[24]C. Westbrook Murphy and Tomas W. Brunner, "Will Anyone Try to Block Amexco?" *American Banker* (April 23, 1981):1.
[25]John D. Mangels, "Competition Moving in on Bank Market," *American Banker* (June 23, 1982):17.

plans call for the full integration of its money market fund with its securities accounts and lines of credit based on the latter, and/or on the customer's real estate equity.[26] Through its ownership of Warner-Amex, Inc., whose cable television facilities have 1.1 million subscribers, the company has the ability to offer consumers a shop-at-home service, with purchases charged to the American Express card. This service can also be extended through the 1,100 travel offices and 260 Shearson branches.[27]

Beneficial Corporation, as mentioned earlier, is no longer merely a consumer finance company; it owns a commercial bank in Delaware and a $2 billion savings and loan in Texas, and has been granted deposit-taking authority in 26 states. It plans to extend this deposit function and a revolving credit system through its 2,000 domestic offices.[28] Parenthetically, it may be noted that federal law prohibits banks from accepting deposits across state lines. Beneficial also owns a multi-billion-dollar insurance group and a mail-order merchandising firm.[29]

Gulf + Western Corporation is a fully diversified conglomerate that owns Paramount Pictures, Madison Square Garden, Simon & Schuster (books), BeautyRest (bedding), No Nonsense (panty hose), and a sugar-farming company in the Dominican Republic. However, its financial service activities now represent a major source of corporate profits. It acquired Fidelity National Bank (Concord, CA) and two factoring companies, together with another firm that develops and manages real estate and underwrites a complete line of insurance. These operations supplement Gulf + Western's ownership of the former Associates Corporation of North America, which had loan receivables of $2.8 billion at July 31, 1982. During the fiscal year ended on that date, Gulf + Western subsidiaries extended commercial loans totaling $4.7 billion.[30]

Household International Corporation, like Beneficial, has moved from pure consumer lending into the full-scale arena of financial services. It owns both a commercial bank and a savings and loan association in California. Its President has stated the corporate objective: "Our particular

[26]Robert A. Bennett, "A Bank by Any Other Name," *The New York Times* (December 27, 1981):3-1.

[27]Wines, "The Financial Supermarket Is Here."

[28]M. W. Caspersen, "Whither the Finance Company in a Dynamic Environment?" *American Banker* (May 6, 1982):7.

[29]Wines, "The Financial Supermarket Is Here,":2056.

[30]Gulf + Western Industries, Inc., 1982 *Annual Report,* p. 6.

goal is to become a consumer bank. We will offer a broad range of financial services, loans, demand and time deposits, insurance services, and income tax services."[31]

A single thought repeatedly surfaces in every discussion of consumer banking: the new "money hybrid" is rapidly materializing. It combines real estate, insurance, credit and debit card functions, securities brokerage, and investments with many formerly traditional banking services. *Merrill Lynch,* the world's largest brokerage firm, has been in the forefront of those who would create this type of integrated financial institution. The Chairman of Bank of America has made this point: "We've already got the nationwide banking of the future. It's called Merrill Lynch."[32]

Merrill Lynch's total line of business today includes securities trading and underwriting; offering checking accounts, loans, and VISA cards; accepting the equivalent of deposits in its money market funds; making mortgage loans and insuring and servicing mortgages; and relocating corporate executives. It is the prototype of the "new breed" of organization that leads consumers, in increasing numbers, to ask whether they actually need a commercial bank at all.

National Steel Corporation sought relief from the problems of its basic industry by entering the financial services field, which it did not perceive as capital- or labor-intensive, affected by foreign competition, and vulnerable to environmental issues and problems.[33] In 1979 and 1981, it successively acquired Citizens S&L (with 85 branches in California and assets of $2.9 billion), West Side Federal S&L (with $2.5 billion in assets in New York), and Washington S&L (with assets of $1.3 billion in Florida). The 138 offices of this organization, now known as First Nationwide, will offer savings and checking accounts, insurance and trust services, mortgage financing, and estate and financial planning,[34] and can be expected to take full advantage of the newly expanded powers of thrift institutions under federal laws.[35]

There is no better way to evaluate *Sears, Roebuck and Company* as a

---

[31]Bennett, "Bankers and Retailers Report High Losses on Consumer Loans."

[32]In "The Savings Revolution," *Time* (June 8, 1981):59.

[33]Subrata Chakravarty, "Blast Furnace Banker," *Forbes* (October 26, 1981):95.

[34]Thomas C. Hayes, "First Nationwide: A New Era," *The New York Times* (November 19, 1981):D1.

[35]Lydia Chavez, "National Steel's Financial Arm," *The New York Times* (January 4, 1982):D1.

competitor in the area of retail banking than to quote directly from the objectives as publicly stated by its Chairman and President, Edward Telling:

> Our goal is to become the largest consumer-oriented financial service entity. . . .[36]
>
> Eventually all outlets in the Sears family of companies can have the capacity to accept and disburse funds. . . .[37]
>
> Someday every Sears outlet will be a bank, making second mortgages, selling to consumers in their homes via electronic buy-and-bank services, and more. . . .[38]
>
> Sears will have a truly national financial card, capable of handling practically all household financial transactions.[39]

Before its 1981 acquisitions, Sears' financial empire included Allstate Insurance (property, casualty, and life) with over $6 billion in revenues; Allstate S&L with over 100 branches in California and $3 billion in assets; and Allstate Enterprise Mortgage Corporation, which services $1.4 billion in mortgages. Sears has over 40 million cardholders, 25 million of whom are active; it operates 851 stores with total revenues of $18 billion.[40]

During 1981, Sears acquired the nation's fifth-largest brokerage firm (Dean Witter Reynolds) and the largest real estate broker (Coldwell Banker & Company). The 42,000 subscribers to Dean Witter's "Active Assets" account were then enabled to cash personal checks for amounts up to $250 at any Sears store.[41] In 1982, Sears opened "financial service centers" at eight of its stores in California, Georgia, Illinois, Virginia, and Texas. The products and services of the various Sears entities are marketed through these centers.[42] Sears has also introduced a money market fund with a minimum investment of $1,000 and checking-account privileges, and received 1,500 inquiries from prospective investors within two days

[36]In Winston Williams, "A Money Fund Next for Sears," *The New York Times* (September 2, 1981):D1.

[37]In John Morris, "Sears Promises to Have a Bank at Every Outlet," *American Banker* (February 26, 1982):1.

[38]In Laura Gross, "Sears Outlets Cashing Checks for Dean Witter Customers," *American Banker* (June 17, 1982):1.

[39]In Morris, "Sears Promises to Have a Bank at Every Outlet."

[40]"The New Sears," *Business Week* (November 16, 1981):140.

[41]Gross, "Sears Outlets Cashing Checks for Dean Witter Customers."

[42]Leonard Sloane, "Financial Retailing at Sears," *The New York Times* (October 7, 1982):D1.

Table 6.2

	Bank	American Express	Merrill Lynch	Sears
Domestic Commercial Banking	x			
Global Commercial Banking	x	x	x	
Securities Brokerage		x	x	x
Investment Management	x	x	x	x
Corporate Underwriting		x	x	x
Property & Casualty Insurance		x		x
Real Estate Brokerage			x	x
Mortgage Banking	x	x	x	x
Mortgage Insurance			x	x
Credit/Debit Cards	x	x	x	x
S&L Operations				x
Life & Health Insurance		x	x	x

Source: Carol J. Loomis, "The Fight for Financial Turf," *Fortune,* December 28, 1981, p. 57.

following its start.[43] The potential for synergy among all these Sears services and units is virtually limitless.[44]

Table 6.2 compares the range of financial services offered by a typical major commercial bank in New York City with that offered by three of these financial conglomerates, who are actively working to provide the "retail banking" of the future.

THRIFT INSTITUTIONS

At no time in their history have America's thrift institutions experienced periods of crisis like those that accompanied the increases in money market interest rates in 1980 and 1981. Because they were funding long-term, fixed-rate mortgage loans—the principal source of their earnings—with

[43]"Sears Pleased with Money Fund Response," *American Banker* (February 26, 1982):1.
[44]Winston Williams, "Sears Strategy: Beating the Banks," *The New York Times* (October 9, 1981):D4.

short-term deposits purchased at far higher rates, they encountered negative spreads and suffered record losses. Over 80% of the nation's savings and loan associations reported net operating deficits totaling $5 billion for 1981. The mutual savings banks' aggregate losses for the same year were proportionately greater ($1.4 billion). Three hundred mergers in the S&L industry, and nine among savings banks, were arranged by federal authorities in 1981, at a cost to the government of over $200 million.[45] Money market rates decreased in 1982, lowering the cost of funds to banks; yet the 92 state-chartered savings banks in New York State reported aggregate losses of $302 million in the second quarter and $332 million in the third quarter.[46]

The importance of thrift institutions to the overall economy, the housing industry, and consumers (whose weakened confidence could result in a widespread "run" on all financial institutions) is such that both the Monetary Control Act of 1980 and the Garn-St. Germain Act of 1982 contained provisions to assist them by giving them additional powers. For example, the former allowed federally charted S&Ls to operate remote service units; lend to customers with no geographic restrictions; offer loans, lines of credit, and credit cards to consumers; extend unlimited mortgage credit; and invest in consumer loans, commercial paper, and corporate debt issues up to a total of 20 percent of assets. The same legislation allowed federally chartered savings banks to accept demand deposits from corporate borrowers and to invest up to 5 percent of assets in commercial loans.[47] No savings banks with federal charters existed at the time the Act was passed; however, several states promptly enacted laws to create parity, and, in other cases, individual savings banks applied for conversion to federal charters.[48] In addressing the 1982 Convention of the American Bankers Association, the Comptroller of the Currency noted that the Garn Act had given S&Ls authority to offer commercial loans, leasing services, and nonresidential loans for real estate.[49] In 1981, a study conducted by the Federal Reserve Bank of Atlanta among sixty S&Ls demonstrated that they clearly saw themselves as the future providers of consumer-oriented

[45]Ann M. Reilly, "Derailing Bank Deregulation," *Dun's Business Month* (July 1982):30.
[46]Robert A. Bennett, "Heavy Losses Continue at State Savings Banks," *The New York Times* (November 20, 1982):29.
[47]"Quick Summary of New Omnibus Banking Law," *ABA Banking Journal* (May 1980):21.
[48]Laura L. Mulcahy, "Mutuals Invade Commercial Loan Area," *American Banker* (July 12, 1982):1.
[49]"Conover Looks at 1983," *American Banker* (October 25, 1982):4.

financial services,[50] and competition from the overall thrift industry can be expected to grow as more institutions broaden the range of their retail activity.

Under the terms of the Monetary Control Act of 1980, the Depository Institutions Deregulation Committee (DIDC) was established and given responsibility for arranging the orderly phase-out of all interest-rate ceilings. The Garn-St. Germain Act, Section 327, further directed DIDC to develop and authorize a new type of insured deposit account, to be made available to all depositors within 60 days without a regulated interest rate.[51] The account was specifically intended to enable commercial and savings banks and S&Ls to compete directly with money market funds. Immediately after the Act was signed into law by President Reagan on October 15, 1982, Richard Pratt, Chairman of the Federal Home Loan Bank Board and a member of DIDC, predicted that a dramatic shift of money back from the funds to banks and S&Ls would take place,[52] and the Chairman of one of the nation's largest S&Ls foresaw the most significant movement of funds in the history of his industry, given the freedom from withdrawal penalties, the insurance, and the check-writing privileges that the new account offered.[53]

On November 15, 1982, the DIDC publicized the detailed terms of the account. The following criteria were established:

The minimum deposit is $2,500.

Withdrawals payable to the account owner are unlimited; those payable to other parties, or transfers to other accounts, are limited to six per month.

The minimum deposit must be maintained in order to be free from interest-rate controls; if the average balance falls below $2,500 over a one-month period, the NOW account ceiling rate (5¼ percent as of November 1982) applies.

Financial institutions may guarantee a specific rate of interest for one

[50]William N. Cox, "Bank-Thrift Competition in the New Environment," *American Bankers* (August 6, 1981):4.
[51]Depository Institutions Deregulation Committee, 12 CFR Part 1204 (Docket D–0026) (October 15, 1982).
[52]Kenneth B. Noble, "Bankers Study New Accounts," *The New York Times* (October 18, 1982):D1.
[53]Daniel F. Cuff, "The New High-Rate Bank Account," *The New York Times* (October 17, 1982):F14.

month or less, at their option, and may establish minimum amounts for each withdrawal or transfer.[54]

BANKS AS RETAIL LENDERS

At the start of this chapter, a categorical statement was made regarding the commercial banks' historical posture in the overall area of retail banking. Two examples of that posture may be explored here regarding the credit function.

The unsecured, monthly-payment installment loan, granted to a typical wage earner, literally did not exist among commercial banks until the mid-1920s. At year-end 1945, these loans accounted for only 7.5 percent of total bank portfolios. By 1971, that percentage had tripled.[55] In mid-1982, the percentage had been reduced to 14.1;[56] nevertheless, commercial banks remain the largest lenders in the retail field.

Entry into that field can be an extremely costly effort for a bank. To supplement the work of the loan interviewers, specialized accounting, collection, and credit investigation units must be established; if the volume warrants it, a special approval committee is needed, and many banks have developed credit-scoring plans to assist in the decision-making process. These plans assign point values to such factors as length of present employment, income, home ownership and equity, and current fixed-debt payments. The bank that enters the installment loan field must also mount an advertising campaign to publicize that fact.

The consumerism that prevails in our society today is reflected in many of the federal and state regulations affecting installment lending. Annual percentage rates (APR) must be clearly stated so that the borrower is aware of what the loan is actually costing. Documents must be written in simple, clearly understandable language. Any reasons for declining a loan must be disclosed, and any detrimental credit information must be made available if requested. Collection practices must conform to certain stand-

---

[54]Kenneth B. Noble, "No Interest Limits Set as U.S. Allows New Bank Account," *The New York Times* (November 16, 1982):A1, and Jay Rosenstein, " 'Money Market' Account Has $2,500 Minimum, No Ceiling," *American Banker* (November 16, 1982):1.

[55]Howard D. Crosse and George H. Hempel, *Management Policies for Commercial Banks,* 2nd Ed. (Englewood Cliffs, N.J: Prentice-Hall, 1973), p. 176.

[56]*Federal Reserve Bulletin* (October 1982):A42.

ards. Federal Reserve Regulation B was amended to require that banks give full weight to an applicant's pension, alimony, or other income.[57] In a two-income family, the bank is required to consider the wife's earnings on a fully equivalent basis, as opposed to the former bank policy that disregarded them on the grounds that she was likely to cease working for family reasons. The Equal Opportunity Act of 1976 prohibits discrimination based on sex, race, marital status, color, religion, age or national origin.

A bank's investment in consumer lending is almost invariably justified by the results. Installment loans are usually discounted—a major advantage for the lender, because the full interest for the entire life of the loan is collected at the time the loan is made. Historical losses have generally been low. In addition to its direct contribution to bank income, the installment loan department may be a source of other new business for the institution if the borrower opens a personal account, rents a safe deposit box, or becomes a user of other services.

The fundamental change in the commercial banks' deposit structure in recent years, coupled with the usury laws that established loan interest ceilings in many states and increases in money market rates, created a host of new problems for major bank lenders. Costs of funding the installment loan department rose steadily, as core retail deposits shifted to an interest-earning basis, and new deposits had to be acquired at record prices.

One technique for avoiding this problem has been introduced at those banks that have discarded the traditional method of structuring loan repayment. They have offered variable-rate, fixed-payment loans, on which the bank adjusts the interest rate according to money market conditions, while the dollar amount due each month remains constant. The maturity of the loan is extended or reduced with each rate change. While this loan is burdensome from the accounting standpoint, it transfers rate risk from the lender to the borrower, and helps to overcome a bank's reluctance to "lock in" one-, two-, or three-year rates in a volatile market.[58] One commercial bank reports success in offering automobile loans on this basis.[59]

For many years, individual states have had usury laws governing interest

[57]Federal Reserve Bank of New York, "Amendment to Regulation B," Circular 8564 (April 1979).

[58]Lawrence Motley and Dan Huyser, "The Advantages of Fixed-Payment, Variable-Rate Installment Loans," *Bank Marketing* (April 1981):8–10.

[59]Barbara Rudolph, "People Like to Do Business with Folks They Know," *Forbes* (October 26, 1981):142.

rates on various types of retail credit, for example, installment loans and home mortgages. For example, Citibank, N.A., as a major lender in the installment-loan field in New York, found itself severely restricted by this type of legislation, and therefore established a complete facility in South Dakota. By booking loans and bank card outstandings from that location, it has begun enjoying the benefits of total freedom from rate ceilings.[60] South Dakota, California, and Arizona are among the states that have repealed their usury laws on retail lending.

Consumers today are besieged by various forms of bank solicitation, encouraging them to take advantage of the availability of personal credit. Social and philosophical questions arise as to the overall effects of this promotion. By making it possible for their borrowers to buy appliances, automobiles, and other goods, the banks have undoubtedly contributed to both the growth in the GNP and the overall standard of living. At the same time, the banks may have given consumers a false sense of security by creating the impression that debt can be expanded indefinitely, or that repayment is not a matter of serious concern. The actions of the commercial banks in 1974 have been cited in this regard.

During the "credit crunch" of that year, every type of loan in the typical commercial bank's portfolio showed dramatic growth. Installment loans contributed significantly to this increase. The banks made no real effort to curtail credit expansion, nor did the Fed impose controls on them.[61] Delinquencies on installment loans rose sharply, yet at the same time some banks were "urging—almost begging—families to sign up for open lines of credit."[62] The point was made then, and is equally relevant today, that a bank displaying no restraint in lending cannot expect consumers to display restraint in borrowing.

MORTGAGE LENDING

The deposit structure of American commercial banks began to assume its present shape in the early twentieth century, when a ruling from the Office

---

[60]"Retail Banking: It's Terrible, It's Wonderful," *ABA Banking Journal* (June 1980):90.
[61]Because of its failure to act, the Fed was criticized for fueling inflation. See Martin Mayer, *The Bankers* (New York: David McKay Co., 1974), p. 344.
[62]Ibid.

of the Comptroller of the Currency (1903) held that national banks could accept demand deposits, and the Federal Reserve Act (1913) extended the authority of member banks to offer mortgage loans.[63] The latter legislation provided banks with a profitable vehicle in which to place less volatile funds.

The general increase in retail banking since the end of World War II has affected the mortgage market, as well as the installment loan area. As of June 30, 1982, total mortgage debt on 1- to 4-family homes was $1.1 trillion, of which commercial banks held $173 billion. This figure was exceeded only by the $428 billion owed to savings and loan associations, the major source of this type of credit.[64] In addition to direct loans to home buyers, commercial banks are also active in the warehousing of mortgages; that is, they provide interim financing until the creditors sell the obligations in a secondary market.

Housing starts in the United States totaled 1.6 million in 1979, 1.2 million in 1980, and 986,000 in 1981; for the first eight months of 1982, the average (annualized rate) was 893,000.[65] The steady decrease obviously reflects mortgage interest rates, which were 17 percent in mid-1981.[66] The chronic problem of negative spreads, caused by long-term fixed-rate loans and resulting in lenders' unwillingness to make those loans, has been addressed by government regulators, who have authorized a variety of new financing arrangements. These can be grouped under the generic caption of Adjustable-Rate Mortgages (ARMs). Examples include Renegotiable-Rate Mortgages (RRMs), granted for three to five years, but automatically renewable at revised rates;[67] Graduated-Payment Mortgages (GPMs), on which monthly payments start at a lower level and increase as the borrower's income and the property value grow; and Variable-Rate Mortgages (VRMs), which allow for mutually agreed-upon rate changes. The effect of the latter is to increase monthly payments, lengthen the maturity, or both.[68]

In March 1981, the Comptroller of the Currency authorized national

[63]Weldon Welfling, *Mutual Savings Banks* (Cleveland: The Press of Case Western Reserve University, 1968), p. 7.

[64]*Federal Reserve Bulletin* (October 1982):A41.

[65]*Federal Reserve Bulletin* (October 1982):A50.

[66]"Housing's Storm," *Business Week* (September 7, 1981):62.

[67]Adam Smith (George Goodman), "Houses and Houses of Cards," *The New York Times* (February 22, 1981):F3.

[68]J. Cliff Dodson, "Alternate-Rate Mortgages: a Must for the 1980s," *ABA Banking Journal* (April 1981):98–99.

banks to offer ARMs on which the rate could change as much as one percent each six months; in April of that year, the Federal Home Loan Bank Board gave similar authority to federally chartered S&Ls, but allowed them to make rate changes monthly, without limit.[69]

One further area of discussion, regarding commercial banks as mortgage lenders, reflects both the willingness of consumers to incur additional debt and the corresponding willingness of many banks to find ways to accommodate them. Both borrowers and lenders appear to have forgotten the lessons of the Great Depression, when losses on second mortgages were heavy, and are becoming increasingly involved in that type of credit, despite an alarming growth in the number of foreclosures. In mid-1981, the estimated total for second-mortgage loans stood at $40 billion, and such major banks as Manufacturers Hanover, Crocker, Chemical, and Security Pacific were active in the field. Both Crocker and Bank of America were offering or planning personal revolving lines of credit of $50,000, secured by second mortgages on the borrowers' homes.[70]

The requirements for disclosure by all depository institutions of their mortgage-loan activities are contained in the Home Mortgage Disclosure Act of 1975, as amended in 1980 (U.S. Code, Title 12, Sections 2801–2811). They are required to compile and publicize data regarding the number and dollar amount of home-purchase and home-improvement loans they have made, broken down by Standard Metropolitan Statistical Areas (SMSAs).[71]

PERSONAL BANK ACCOUNTS

Until the immediate postwar years, checking accounts at commercial banks were reserved for business firms, institutions, government agencies, and the more affluent individuals who could maintain appropriate balances. The introduction of the so-called special checking account, requiring no minimum balance but carrying monthly maintenance and per-check

[69]Gretchen Chell, "Bank Board Eases Rules for S&Ls to Adjust Mortgage Rates," *The Money Manager* (April 27, 1981):3.
[70]Michael Kolbenschlag, "Nothing to Lose But Your House," *Forbes* (July 20, 1981):47–50.
[71]Board of Governors of the Federal Reserve System, "Regulation C: Home Mortgage Disclosure," 12 CFR 203 (August 4, 1981).

charges, was a manifestation of the banks' new approach to the retail market. While the name "special" may have fallen into disuse, this type of account continues and is offered by commercial banks throughout the country. The largest banks have hundreds of thousands of these, and frequently offer them as part of combination plans that tie them to other bank services.

In one example, the "combination" relationship links a personal checking account to a passbook or statement savings[72] account, with transfer privileges in either direction. In a survey conducted in 1981, 72 percent of the respondents expressed a desire for a bank relationship that would provide these features.[73]

A new, more liberal approach to the question of overdrafts is also part of the banks' postwar effort to market personal checking accounts. "Insufficient funds" remains as the chief reason for dishonored checks; yet many commercial banks have reversed their traditional policy; instead of automatically rejecting these items, they establish a personal line of credit for the customer, so that checks can be issued without having a balance to cover them. Interest on the overdrafts is usually charged on a daily basis. This system not only spares the customer the trauma of returned checks, but saves the bank at least part of the expenses connected with coupon books and related paperwork that are inherent in actual installment lending.[74]

The availability of these "combination" accounts and services may help to explain the fact that, despite disintermediation and the opportunities that exist for other investments, Americans still held $299 billion in low-yielding passbook accounts as of late 1981.[75]

The Economic Recovery Tax Act of 1981 revised the federal regulations regarding Individual Retirement Accounts (IRAs) by making millions of Americans eligible for these tax-sheltered accounts, even if they were already covered by an employer's qualified pension plan. Intense competition immediately developed among commercial banks, thrifts, brokerage firms, and insurance companies; for example, Merrill Lynch attracted $700 million, and Prudential Insurance Company $200 million, in

[72]The statement savings account eliminates the anachronistic passbook by posting all transactions on a computerized statement.

[73]Peter Mears, Frederick Siegel, and Robert Osborn, "How to Find Out What Customers Want from Their Bank," *The Bankers Magazine* (July–August 1981):70.

[74]H. J. Maidenberg, "The Dangers in an Overdraft Account," *The New York Times* (February 7, 1982):D1.

[75]Robert A. Bennett, "Passbook Rates: Too Low?" *The New York Times* (November 25, 1981):D1.

new IRAs during the first four months of 1982.[76] Effective December 1, 1981, the DIDC authorized all depository institutions to offer time deposits of 18 months or more, without interest-rate ceilings, for use in IRAs or Keogh (i.e., self-employed retirement) plans.[77]

For many years, commercial banks have used repurchase agreements ("repos") as a means of attracting funds. These are contractual agreements in which the owner of an asset (typically an obligation of the United States government) sells it to another party and commits to buy it back on a specified date at a stated price. Under this system, a bank debits the buyer's account for the sale or receives a check drawn on another institution.[78] Repos were frequently offered on an overnight basis to corporate and governmental investors; more recently, banks and S&Ls have been aggressively marketing them in small denominations to individuals, for periods of 89 days or less, as part of the liability-management effort in retail banking.[79] Their advertising specified that a repo was not a deposit and was not insured. If consumers ignored those caveats, or believed that they were making fully secured or guaranteed loans to their banks,[80] they became more aware of the risks involved with the failure in 1982 of a bank (in which customers held $353,000 in repos) and an S&L (with $67 million in repos).[81] Banks which actively market retail repos to attract customers must therefore now deal with a new, more cautious attitude.

Before the Garn-St. Germain Act directed DIDC to authorize a new account, competitive with money market funds, many banks had developed yet another innovation through the so-called "Sweep" account. Details varied among competing institutions, but the basic concept provided that computer technology would be used to monitor customers' NOW or checking balances each day and to place all funds above a specified minimum into money market funds or investments.[82] Union Planters National

---

[76]David O. Tyson, "Prudential Sees 250,000 IRAs by June," *American Banker* (May 13, 1982):1.

[77]*Federal Reserve Bulletin* (October 1982):A8.

[78]Robert R. Dince and James A. Verbrugge, "The Rush to Retail Repos," *The Bankers Magazine* (March–April 1981):77.

[79]Richard J. Bayer, "Retail Repos," *The Magazine of BANK ADMINISTRATION* (October 1981):43.

[80]Jane Bryant Quinn, "How Safe Are Those 'Repo' Investments?" *Gannett Westchester Newspapers* (October 17, 1982):BB6.

[81]Michael Quint, "Repo Backing Is Under Cloud," *The New York Times* (September 29, 1982):D1.

[82]John W. McGonigle, "Banks Have Legal Guidelines for Offering Sweep Accounts," *American Banker* (May 3, 1982):4.

Bank (Memphis) introduced a prototype in 1982; the first $2,000 of a customer's balance earned interest at the NOW rate, and all excess funds were automatically invested.[83]

Each of these vehicles illustrates the fundamental problem of retail and commercial banking today, in general. To attract or retain consumer deposits, banks have no choice but to offer various forms of relationships that accelerate the decline in interest-free balances and the increase in interest expense. The alternative, of course, is to remain static and to risk the loss of those balances to unregulated competitors. However, the basic philosophy holds that an interest-paying account remains more desirable than no account at all, as long as effective asset/liability management enables the bank to maintain a viable spread on its funds.[84]

[83]"Union Planters Offering Checking Account with Money Market Rates," *American Banker* (July 6, 1982):2.
[84]"Banks Blend with the Funds," *Business Week* (May 24, 1982):143.

7 Uses of Funds: Retail Banking II

When commercial banks began to address the retail field during the 1950s, the first requirement that had to be met involved a change in the approach to personal selling. The word *salesman* was still shunned by the bankers at that time. However, during the 1960s, this reluctance to conduct actual consumer marketing was slowly replaced by a recognition of the need for advertising, promotions, and greater convenience for the customer.[1] Competitive pressures, especially from non-banks, escalated during the 1970s and forced further reappraisal of the retail marketing function. For the 1980s, additional refinement is needed. New technology and new consumer services, including those in the trust and personal consultative fields, must be developed, pre-tested, priced, and effectively brought to the attention of prospects.[2] The statement of a corporate executive epitomizes the new consumer attitude: "I need a bank where I can lay down my income and expense figures and then have its people tell me how to maximize my usage."[3]

For many years, banks have marketed a family of specialized services to their wholesale customers under the generic term, *cash management*. This product line will be discussed in Chapter 10. However, the point must be made here that cash management is no longer exclusively within

[1]Michael P. Sullivan, "Bank Marketing Strategy," *The Bankers Magazine* (July–August 1981):28–30.
[2]Peter Mears, Frederick Siegel, and Robert Osborn, "How to Find Out What Customers Want from Their Banks," *The Bankers Magazine* (July–August 1981):70.
[3]Donald R. German, "One-on-One Banking," *The Bankers Magazine* (July–August 1981):74.

the province of corporations, units of government, institutions, and correspondent banks. Consumers today, in increasing numbers, are their own cash managers, and expect their banks to provide retail services comparable to those which corporate financial officers have utilized. John Fisher, Senior Vice President of Banc One Corporation (Columbus, Ohio), states the theme very succinctly: "Consumers now are demanding what the corporate account has always had: cash management."[4]

The innovative and progressive banks recognize that if they do not broaden their horizons in retail banking to the extent that they are legally permitted to do so, even more of their business will move to unregulated competitors. It is a traumatic experience for the traditionalist in banking to learn in 1982 that the Kroger Company, a major supermarket chain with 1,200 outlets in 21 states, has entered into a joint venture with a financial holding company and is selling IRAs, insurance, and mutual and money market funds through those stores. Kroger's Chairman and President, in announcing this, said simply: "It is service that customers want, and we are in business to serve consumers."[5]

The major challenge to retail bankers today involves the effort to sell against this type of competition. One effective technique is through "cross-marketing." Given that multiple-service users are less likely to change suppliers,[6] more attention must be paid to existing customers. For example, each monthly statement sent to a depositor can be accompanied by promotional material for other services. A borrower in the installment loan department automatically becomes a candidate for an account, and may gain a preferential interest rate by authorizing the bank to charge monthly payments directly to an account. Whenever a personal account is opened, the bank may develop a profile sheet to give its marketing staff an indication of other services for which the new customer is a likely prospect. Existing bank customers always generate much of the new business, and by stressing the "Full Service" concept to its depositors, an institution can cement its deposit relationship in many ways.

---

[4]Margaret Yao, "Next on Horizon for Check, Card Users: Access to Home Equity, Life Insurance," *The Wall Street Journal* (October 13, 1981):40.
[5]"Ohio Supermarket Is Selling Insurance and Mutual Funds," *The New York Times* (September 28, 1982):D3.
[6]Thomas J. Stanley, "Product Positioning for the Home Terminal," *The Bankers Magazine* (May–June 1982):62.

BRANCH BANKING

When commercial banks turned their attention to the consumer market in the years following World War II, their new emphasis on retail services necessarily led to the notion that branch banking would have to expand for the convenience of customers. As noted earlier, many banks that had previously been wholesale-oriented expanded into branch banking by merger, and wherever it was legally possible under state laws, they steadily increased their branch networks. However, this basic philosophy has recently come under intense questioning.

The overall concept of profit planning includes the creation of individual profit centers, each of which can be assessed according to its contribution to the overall success of the bank. In the case of branches, bottom-line figures can be developed for each. If the deposits generated through a branch exceed its loans, it is a supplier of funds to the rest of the institution's "pool," and is given credit for the excess at prevailing rates. If its loans exceed its deposits, it is a net user of funds and must obtain them from the bank "pool" and be charged accordingly. If the bank is restructured internally so that corporate accounts are taken out of the branches and centralized, branch budgets must be revised.

As rental, equipment, and labor costs increase, many banks have begun to ask whether full-scale "brick and mortar" branches are actually needed to meet the needs of retail customers, and whether the number of existing branches should be reduced. Based on earnings projections, market segmentation may persuade a bank that the present range of retail services and/or the size of the target population should be curtailed. In this event, the network of branches may no longer be appropriate to meet organizational profit objectives. Those banks that are now focusing only on "upscale" individuals exemplify this revised policy. Morgan Guaranty, for example, has instituted a monthly fee of $60 on all personal accounts with balances of less than $5,000.[7] In this case, the bank did not need to reduce the size of its branch system because it operated at only a handful of prime locations; however, it chose to reduce the scope of its potential retail market through direct pricing.

In other cases, bank management may determine that the solution to

---

[7] "The Savings Revolution," *Time* (June 8, 1981):61.

rising costs lies in a change in the manner of delivering consumer services. There has been a tremendous increase in the number of automated facilities (to be discussed fully in Chapter 8) that operate on an around-the-clock basis throughout the year. Bank patrons of all ages, led by younger customers who are more amenable to change and more accustomed to electronic technology, have become convinced of the ease and convenience of dealing with automated teller machines, of which over 26,000 are now in place in all types of financial institutions.[8] Citibank, N.A., has installed over 450 of these machines in New York City; they handle almost one-third of the bank's total consumer activity, at half the cost of human-teller transactions.[9] Automated teller machines represent a costly initial outlay of funds, but over a long range of time, they contribute significantly to the overall reduction of the expenses connected with retail banking.

Loan-production offices, storefront locations, or check-cashing installations may also be used to replace the imposing, expensive branches that proliferated during the years of the retail banking explosion.

As interest expense and operating costs rise, it is incumbent upon bank management to reassess its thinking about the advisability of maintaining some of the branches that no longer make adequate contributions to overall earnings. Perhaps two or three branches were optimistically opened in the same geographic area and can now be combined. Perhaps the potential business in a community was overestimated, and new evidence shows that it is no longer profitable for the bank to compete there. Perhaps significant demographic changes have occurred in an area, and there is no longer a sufficient number of customers to make the branch worthwhile. If a reorganization, as mentioned earlier, has transferred corporate and institutional accounts away from branches, the end result may be a decision to close some of them. For those that remain, management may consider the feasibility of confining their services to those segments of the retail market that carry high profit potential. In other words, the bank determines that it is no longer advisable to attempt to be "all things to all people." Finally, the opening of thrift-institution branches or nonbank facilities in a community may have gained so many customers that competition by the commercial bank is no longer feasible.

In 1974, a member of the Federal Reserve Board of Governors asked

[8]Thomas Watterson, "New Services, Competition Spur Fresh Bank Marketing," *The Christian Science Monitor* (October 15, 1982):18.
[9]"The Savings Revolution," p. 61.

rhetorically, "Once a man can cash a check at a local supermarket, what does he need a branch for?"[10] His question, which obviously anticipated the entry of Sears, Kroger, and others into the field, has even more relevance today.

However, a word of caution must be interjected here on the subject of branch closings. Community activists may use the concept of social responsibility as their rationale for demanding that a branch be kept open, even if it is unprofitable. Bank spokespersons must be both forthright and tactful in explaining why such branches actually constitute luxuries that are no longer affordable.

BANKING AT HOME

For many years, bankers used the catch-all word "convenience" as the justification for establishing large numbers of full-scale branches. The ever-rising rates that must now be paid to attract and retain core deposits, the heavier competition from many sources, and increased labor and occupancy costs combine to mandate a change in management thinking. The banking institution that prospers is the one that best estimates customer needs and wants, and best judges the extent to which new technology and ideas will be accepted. The need to serve customers in a convenient and attractive way, while simultaneously meeting organizational profit objectives, has led to a dramatic development: the large-scale introduction of systems that allow banking at home.[11] There is a marked increase in the number of two-income families who place a premium on convenience and time; a service that allows them to conduct much of their banking business without leaving home has become more and more popular.[12]

The generic term *videotex* has been coined to describe the transmission of text and graphic data to a mass market, usually by displaying one page at a time through a screen. The emphasis that has been placed on videotex is a logical step forward in a progressive trend in retail banking. The consumer has successively been introduced to networks of branches, bank

[10]Martin Mayer, *The Bankers* (New York: David McKay Co., 1974), p. 180.
[11]Derek Bamber, "One Day Your Bank Will Be Your Home," *Euromoney* (May 1981):20.
[12]Charles E. Bartling, "Positioning Your Bank for In-Home Banking," *Bank Marketing* (April 1981):14.

cards, ATMs, and other applications of electronic funds transfer systems (EFTS). Videotex logically extends this progression; in its most sophisticated form, it provides the customer with an interactive communications service that furnishes information at home through a terminal, and accepts his or her instructions in return.[13]

A conservative estimate by the American Telephone and Telegraph Company in 1981 indicated that 7 percent of all United States households would have videotex terminals by 1990; however, another estimate, prepared by a California consulting firm, multiplied that estimate fivefold.[14] Major market applications of videotex are evolving in other parts of the world, often with the backing of the local government.[15] About 500,000 microcomputers were purchased in America in 1980;[16] their users automatically appear as prime targets for videotex marketing by banks.

A Senior Vice President of Chemical Bank, one of the leaders in the videotex movement, has said that

> One has only to look at the incursion into banking of a Merrill Lynch or a Shearson/American Express . . . to recognize that banking at the end of this decade will be very different than it is today. The basic realities dictate our finding new, better, more competitive, and more cost-effective ways to serve our customers. We are quickly moving past the point where banking can continue to be done at burgeoning cost, with mountains of paper, armies of people, and a branch on every corner.[17]

In 1977, Dow Jones, Inc. introduced the forerunner of today's videotexsystems: a news retrieval service that now has over 33,000 users.[18] Throughout 1980, 1981, and 1982, commercial banks built on that foundation and introduced a series of videotex-related systems. The significant milestones include the following:

United American Bank (Knoxville, Tennessee) operates a system enabling customers to access accounts and view statement printouts on a

[13]Sarah Ordover, "Videotex Brings Banking into the Home," *American Banker* (October 6, 1981):20.
[14]"The Home Information Revolution," *Business Week* (June 29, 1981):76.
[15]Ibid., p. 83.
[16]John A. Farnsworth, "Attitudes Toward Computers May Effect In-Home Banking," *American Banker* (October 6, 1981):15.
[17]Ibid.
[18]Marjolijn van der Velde, "Home Banking: Where It Stands Today," *The Magazine of BANK ADMINISTRATION* (September 1982):18.

TV screen. They can also instruct the bank to pay bills for them, using this system.[19]

Customers of Bank One (Columbus, Ohio) can use a similar system.[20]

In July 1981, the Chase Manhattan Bank announced a bank-at-home service, offering the above features but also allowing the user to enter and store in the terminal up to 20 bills, to be paid by the bank at future dates.[21]

Participants in San Diego's Interactive Data Exchange can use an electronic retrieval system that gives them access to local and national news, a shop-at-home service, and educational programs, and also enables them to handle banking transactions.[22]

San Diego is also the site of a system shared by three commercial banks and two savings and loans. Users can receive account information, initiate transfers, request bank cards, obtain information on bank services, and pay bills.[23]

Citytrust (Bridgeport, Connecticut) has introduced a home computer system, using a TV screen and a hand-held control. Customers can verify account balances, make transfers of funds, apply for loans, and order payments. Information services can also be provided, and the bank's President foresees the eventual inclusion in the system of real estate listings and travel reservations.[24]

In September 1982, Shawmut Bank (Boston) and New York's Chemical Bank simultaneously announced the start of their respective systems for at-home banking. In the Chemical Bank system, an Atari computer is furnished by the bank; Shawmut requires use of the customer's personal computer, which is linked to an information-services firm.[25]

Chemical Bank also plans to license its "Pronto" system to other banks. The service has been pilot-tested in 200 New York City households. Users can schedule and review card payments, arrange automatic payment of

[19]Bartling, "Positioning Your Bank for In-Home Banking."

[20]Ibid.

[21]Robert Trigaux, "Chase to Offer Bank-at-Home to Broad Market," *American Banker* (July 9, 1981):1.

[22]Ordover, "Videotex Brings Banking into the Home."

[23]Ibid.

[24]Megan Gallagher, "Citytrust Turns to Home Banking," *Gannett Westchester Newspapers* (June 21, 1982):C10.

[25]David O. Tyson, "Chemical Unveils Pronto System," *American Banker* (September 9, 1982):1.

loans or other recurring expenses, and pay bills electronically to 250 participating landlords, utilities, and stores.[26]

A Senior Vice President of Banc One Corporation has predicted the eventual development of a national processing system, in which a financial-services supplier will connect with VISA and MasterCard networks and the automated clearing houses, which in turn will be linked to all banks, credit unions, and savings and loans in an area. If creditors supply data on customers' bills to the banks via computer tape, users of the service can view those bills on the TV screen; their instructions for payments can also be made directly through computer tapes.[27]

The marketing of a particular bank's system of banking at home can be expected to stress certain major benefits for the consumer. The home terminal may be marketed as an information vehicle, an educational or entertainment system, a household management tool, or a combination of these. It can become a major shopping, investment, and time-saving device, and the convenience it offers today and for the future may well substitute for the convenience that was formerly offered through the "brick-and-mortar" branch systems.[28]

BANK CARDS

In the face of the tremendous acceptance attained by bank cards in recent years, it is perhaps difficult to appreciate that they constitute a relatively recent development in commercial banking. Yet, with the exception of some minor efforts made by banks in the 1950s to emulate the success that gasoline companies, Diners Club, airlines, and hotel chains had achieved in the credit card field, there was no concerted effort until the mid-1960s.

The rationale for the banks' entry into the field at that time becomes apparent if viewed in the context of the economic climate that prevailed.

[26]"Home Banking Moves Off the Drawing Board," *Business Week* (September 20, 1982):39.
[27]John F. Fisher, "Vast Future Seen for In-Home Banking Industry," *American Banker* (October 6, 1981):10.
[28]Stanley, "Product Positioning for the Home Terminal," p. 62.

Large sums of money were leaving them in favor of other, more attractive investment media. Those deposits that remained were shifting toward a time basis, creating new expenses. Banks felt compelled to develop new forms of high-yield business and new retail inducements. The improvements in computer technology at that time made it possible for them to process huge volumes of paper at relatively low cost.

The credit card, as it was then known, appeared to offer a most attractive profit potential. Increased deposit activity would result from processing the sales slips turned over to banks by merchants. Cardholders would pay interest on their outstandings, and a discount on each deposited sales slip would generate additional direct income. When cards were used to obtain cash advances, an immediate interest charge could be levied. Although commercial banks, by federal law, could not branch across state lines, they could issue cards on a nationwide basis, thus attracting new customers.

Today, two major bank cards dominate the field. Table 7.1 illustrates the extent to which MasterCard and VISA have become integral parts of the life style of millions of individuals throughout the world.

According to all indications, bank cards possess still further opportunities for growth and profitability. Several thousand banks still do not issue cards and therefore may join either system or both. Issuers of travel and entertainment cards may withdraw from the market, and thus yield new customers to bank cards. Present cardholders may increase their usage as they find new areas of acceptance. The bank card is the key to many electronic funds transfer systems (EFTS) applications, including automated

Table 7.1. Bank Card Statistics As of December 31, 1981

	MasterCard	VISA
Cardholders	$78.7 million	$93.6 million
Merchant Outlets	3.7 million	3.4 million
Banking Offices	210.0 thousand	122.0 thousand
Annual Dollar Volume of Transactions	$ 43 billion	$ 52 billion

Source: Robert Trigaux, "Last Year Was One of Consolidation, Limited Victories for Bank Cards," *American Banker* (June 9, 1982):1.

Note: All figures are worldwide.

teller facilities, and customers' perception of this fact has steadily increased.[29]

Two major nationwide marketing efforts were initiated in 1979. Citibank, N. A. sent out 27 million solicitation letters for VISA cards; Continental Illinois (Chicago) offered consumers up to $3.5 billion in credit through a campaign to attract new customers for both cards.[30] The fact that both banks disregarded state boundaries is seen by some observers as a step toward eventual interstate banking. A cardholder who has been granted a personal line of credit, and can obtain cash by using a card issued by a bank many miles away, may no longer feel that a local account is needed. The same card can be used for local purchases, as well as those made in other parts of the country or world. This potential creates a fear for many independent bankers in small communities that the consumer system will eventually be monopolized by large institutions in the nation's money-market centers.

The sheer convenience of the bank card is the most important factor in its present acceptance and potential for further growth. To some extent, as an Executive Vice President of Bank of America points out, it has replaced the installment loan by putting the user in charge of his own finances and letting him or her decide when and how much to borrow, without going through the application process each time.[31]

Historical Development

For banks that are entering the card field, there is a critical dilemma that must be resolved. In the early 1960s, some of the institutions that confronted this problem chose a course of action that proved disastrous.

The dilemma lies in the fact that merchants can be induced to join a card plan only if they are convinced that the cards are already in the hands of an army of cardholders who are anxious to begin using them. At the same time, individuals realize that the cards have no value unless merchants are ready to accept them. A management decision must be made about the best manner of addressing this question.

In one well-documented instance, a number of major banks in the same

---

[29]Peter J. Brennan, "Bank Cards Are Here to Stay," *ABA Banking Journal* (September 1980):85.
[30]"Consumer Banking," *Business Week* (April 23, 1979):82–83.
[31]Kenneth V. Larkin, in Brennan, "Bank Cards Are Here to Stay."

large city simultaneously reached a decision to begin offering cards, and chose to do so by flooding the population with their new form of "plastic money." They purchased mailing lists from several sources, and conducted unsolicited mailings of cards to every name on every list. No attempt was made to weed out duplications or to verify the accuracy of addresses; no credit investigations were conducted, and no limit was placed on the dollar usage of any card. Mass mailings of the new cards took place at the peak of the city's Christmas mail rush.

This program resulted in the receipt of many cards by a single individual, widespread thefts of cards from the mail and their repeated uses by the thieves, and uncontrolled use of the cards by many recipients in buying quantities of merchandise, sometimes with the collaboration of unscrupulous merchants who were guaranteed payment by the card-issuing banks. Direct losses of over $7 million were sustained by the banks within six months.[32]

The early history of the card program contains other examples of problems and losses experienced by some major banks. A New York institution admitted losses of $8.4 million in two years resulting directly from card operations, while a California bank conceded that it had lost $7 million in three years.[33] These reports served to convince other banks not to enter the card field at all.[34] More recently, rising costs of funds, coupled with the problem of state usury laws that limit the interest which can be charged on cardholders' outstandings, have led other banks to divest themselves of their existing card operations.[35]

However, there has not been any widespread abandonment of the card as an integral part of retail banking. Rather, there has been a systematic effort by the banks to learn from the problems that were experienced in the early years, and to install corrective mechanisms. This effort has been supplemented by considerable legislative action, affecting many phases of bank-card operations.

Following the well-publicized move of its card function by Citibank, N. A. to South Dakota, several states acted to change their usury laws.

---

[32] A detailed history may be found in Mayer, *The Bankers,* pp. 347–348 and in Harold Taylor, "The Chicago Bank Credit Card Fiasco," *The Bankers Magazine* (Winter 1968):49–52.
[33] Irwin Ross, "The Credit Card's Painful Coming of Age," *Fortune* (October 1971): 108–111.
[34] R. Gene Conatser, "Retail Banking," in Herbert V. Prochnow and Herbert V. Prochnow, Jr., Eds., *The Changing World of Banking* (New York: Harper & Row, 1974) p. 199.
[35] Brennan, "Bank Cards Are Here to Stay," p. 79.

This liberalization enabled banks in those states to charge interest rates more in keeping with the rising costs of their consumer deposits.

As a policy matter, most banks today establish criteria for the issuance of any new card and restrict its use to a specified dollar limit. Strict security measures have been imposed on the operations units, from which cards are mailed out and where records of outstandings and payments are maintained. In many cases, banks will not mail new or renewed cards, but will require that the cardholder visit the bank and sign for the card. Merchants can obtain prompt answers through computer installations when they inquire about a cardholder's status. Both VISA and MasterCard have established nationwide networks for credit verification, and some banks have included a cardholder's photograph on the card itself.

Legislators have also acted to protect consumers against the loss of their cards and subsequent unauthorized use. A cardholder who promptly reports theft or loss of a card cannot be held responsible for its use. All unsolicited mailing of actual cards is prohibited.

As in installment lending, expansion of the bank card field has created fears that consumers are actually being encouraged to go even more deeply into debt and to embark on programs of excessive purchases without giving thought to the method and timing of repayment.[36]

It is no longer appropriate to use the term *credit card*; in increasing proportions, banks now offer a *debit* card, through which purchases are charged to a cardholder's account. The generic term *bank card* can be used to describe all forms of card usage.

Bank cards—and it must be noted that the Monetary Control Act gave thrift institutions authority to issue "plastic money"—have given the public a new, widely accepted tool to be used for obtaining needed or wanted goods and services, whether or not they have accelerated and facilitated impulse buying.[37] They have become a permanent fixture in retail banking, and Russell Hogg, President of MasterCard International, predicts that they will become an even more integral part of the American consumer's finances. He views them as "the chief interface vehicle between the bank and the consumer."[38]

A major bank in Philadelphia, reporting that it has increased its market

---

[36]Peter J. Gray, "The Case for Credit Cards," *The Bankers Magazine* (July–August 1978):27.
[37]R. Michael Rice, "The Growing Consumer Debt Burden," *Bankers Monthly Magazine* (April 15, 1979):35.
[38]"Russell Hogg (MasterCard) and Charles Russell (VISA) Discuss Bank Cards," *The Bankers Magazine*, (May–June 1981):63.

share of households in a highly competitive urban area from 15 to 18 percent in five years, emphasizes the role of the bank card in its success. The bank has implemented ATMs at many of its locations, each of which requires use of the card. It offers users a single consolidated statement, showing every transaction for the period, including all bank-card usage and current outstandings. By coupling these retail services with bank-by-phone capability, and by converting some of its former branches into "mini-branches," this institution has met the challenges of contemporary retail banking and made its total program profitable.[39]

SELF-SERVICE BANKING

The most readily identifiable trend in retail banking today involves an effort to allow customers to conduct their banking business at the time and location of their choice, often without any interaction with bank personnel. There are three major self-service areas: banking at home, point-of-sale devices, and customer-operated facilities. The entry of banks into these three areas is, in turn, driven by three critical factors.

First, the cost structure of retail banking now demands new ways of conducting business. Costs for both personnel and property have increased at an annual rate of 7 percent, making greater efficiency mandatory if the retail program is to generate profits. Consumer balances in increasing proportions have shifted to some form of interest-bearing account, driving up expenses. The Federal Reserve's new program of explicit pricing compels banks to charge customers for services that were traditionally offered "free" because of compensating balances. Bank cards, traditionally offered without an annual fee, must implement new systems of cost recovery; 50 to 55 percent of the banks that issue cards have now introduced direct annual charges.[40]

Second, the introduction of new technology has made new services not only feasible but economically attractive. Prices for the equipment needed for self-service banking have decreased substantially.

Finally, the retail market has changed, and banks must respond to that

[39]Richard S. D'Agostino and Harold Y. Jones, "Retail Banking: The Girard Approach," *The Magazine of BANK ADMINISTRATION* (June 1979):28.
[40]"Russell Hogg (MasterCard) and Charles Russell (VISA) Discuss Bank Cards,":60–61.

change. One recent study comprises 48 percent of all United States households; it estimates that the individuals who were demographically surveyed will display far more sophistication toward, and acceptance of, electronic devices.[41] The manner in which banking services can be offered to them in future years is part of the new world of banking—a world largely dependent on all that the acronym EFTS implies. Although many previous references have been made to the interrelationship of EFTS with retail banking, the broad topic of electronic technology warrants a detailed treatment of its own, to be found in Chapter 8.

[41]Marc J. Frankel, "Self-Service: An Emerging Trend in Retail Banking," *Chase Directions* (New York: The Chase Manhattan Bank, N.A., Fall 1979), p. 2.

8 Electronic Funds Transfer Systems

Early in the twentieth century, American telephone companies increased their marketing efforts, stressing all the advantages of telephone service for every type of user. Their campaigns were so successful that an entirely new technology had to be developed to handle the volume of calls. The manual format, in which an operator personally placed each call, gave way to the dial telephone, and the latter in turn has undergone many enhancements needed to support customer usage.

Similarly, the nation's brokerage firms, as they became aware of the increased level of American family income in the postwar years, introduced a succession of advertising campaigns to attract new investors. The stockholder base of many corporations consequently grew, as did the volume of market transactions each day. The brokerage firms found themselves swamped with a "back office" volume beyond their capacity as a result of the promotional campaigns they themselves had conducted. "Fails" (transactions in which purchased securities were not properly delivered) became so common that many firms had to be liquidated.

In each of these cases, an industry sold its services to the public, only to find that it could not cope with the transaction volume generated by its own efforts. Both situations may have influenced the thinking of bankers during the 1960s.

Banking has always been a paper-intensive field, with the check as its most widely used document. The normal annual growth in check volume in the years prior to World War II was handled with no great difficulty, and in the immediate postwar period, this increase did not create any serious concerns. The assumption was that the banking system had enough flexibility and capacity to adjust automatically to customer demands.

The growth of the postwar economy gradually brought about a change in thinking. Check usage grew at an unprecedented rate. Businesses expanded and required more checks to pay suppliers and employees. Retail marketing efforts brought a new type of customer into commercial banking; the checking account was no longer a vehicle used only by the affluent. The average consumer—more sophisticated, better educated, and with a higher level of income than his predecessors—came to recognize the advantages of checks as payment instruments.

As check usage steadily increased, fears were expressed regarding the banking industry's ability to cope with the volume. The introduction of the magnetic ink character recognition (MICR) system, opening the door to a new world of check processing through high-speed technology, allayed these fears for only a short time. Predictions of imminent calamities in the system began to be heard. Bankers wondered if their industry might suffer the same fate as the brokerage firms and find itself submerged in a sea of paper, with consequent delays, errors, and increases in processing costs. A study conducted in 1970 for the American Bankers Association projected annual increases of 7 percent in check volume for the remainder of that decade.[1] One authority in the data processing field claimed to have invented the phrase *checkless society* to indicate the direction in which he felt the banks would have to move; that is, they would have to find a substitute for the checks as payment media.[2]

The prediction of the annual growth rate in check volume proved substantially correct. Check usage in 1948 had been 5 billion; by 1970 it had reached a figure of 18.5 billion; in 1974 it was 24.3 billion,[3] and the 1981 volume was estimated at 35 billion.[4] Although several prominent bankers expressed confidence during the 1970s that the industry could, in fact, cope with the steady increase, pressures for change continued and new approaches to the payment system were sought.[5]

[1]Wray O. Candilis, *The Future of Commercial Banking* (New York: Praeger, 1975), p. 117.
[2]Dale Reistad, speech delivered at the Bill Payment Workshop, New York (December 1977).
[3]William Ford, "Number of Checks Written Expected to Peak by 1990," *American Banker* (March 25, 1981):8.
[4]"Electronic Banking," *Business Week* (January 18, 1982):70.
[5]David Van L. Taylor, "Banking Technology More Paradox than Panacea," *American Banker* (May 22, 1979):7.

Costs of overall check processing have always been an important consideration in this area. A study conducted in Atlanta in 1972 showed that checks cashed or deposited at the drawee bank, and therefore processed completely in-house, created per-item costs of $0.103; checks that had to be routed to other banks cost $0.137 each.[6] Years of inflation, and escalating labor costs, have had such a severe impact that the average cost of processing a check has now been estimated at $0.41.[7]

In retrospect, it now appears that in many cases commercial bankers, equipment designers, consultants, and systems experts were caught up in a syndrome of overreaction, in which each group vied with the others in projecting a totally new world of banking. A new society was envisioned on the assumption that all types of bank customers would enthusiastically adopt the latest technology. Checks would be eliminated, and visits to banks would be made unnecessary by the accessibility of electronic facilities in supermarkets, airports, and other key locations.

These prophesies have been only partially fulfilled. There are, indeed, many areas where electronic funds transfer system (EFTS) services have been introduced with considerable success, offering benefits to both the bank and the user. However, as a generalization, it appears that the early forecasts of universal adoption of EFTS were totally unrealistic. Instead of using "checkless society," today's bankers speak of a "less-check" system, in which checks will continue to be used, but in greatly reduced quantities. Evolution, rather than revolution, has taken place.

As a generic term, EFTS (or EFT) has become one of the most widely used acronyms in banking. Its origin lies in the initial letters of the four words, electronic funds transfer systems (or services). The reference is to the broad spectrum of automated technology that uses bookkeeping entries for the movement of funds among financial institutions.

The emphasis on EFTS has been so great that entire libraries are now dedicated to its reference material. It is undoubtedly one of the most significant areas of discussion in contemporary banking. Questions continually arise, and opinions are expressed, as to the extent to which EFTS is likely to gain acceptance, the effects of regulatory constraints and pending or potential legal action, and the degree to which non-bank financial institutions will participate.

---

[6]Alfred L. Hunt, *Corporate Cash Management and Electronic Fund Transfers* (New York: AMACOM, 1978), p. 139.
[7]"Electronic Banking," p. 74.

For purposes of this text, the focus is on four fundamental EFTS applications:

1. Systems that produce *credits* to accounts
2. Systems that generate *debits*
3. Systems that entail the use of *point-of-sale terminals*
4. Systems that entail use of *automated teller machines* (ATMs) or *customer-bank communications terminals* (CBCTs)

In each case, the known reactions and statistical results to date will be discussed. To provide a fully balanced presentation of this critical topic, both positive and negative viewpoints of potential users and actual customers are analyzed.

EFT CREDIT SYSTEMS

In April 1968, members of the local bank clearing house associations in Los Angeles and San Francisco determined that the future progress of EFTS required the establishing of automated facilities, analogous to their check-handling counterparts, but capable of processing magnetic tape. The Subcommittee on Paperless Entries (SCOPE) began operation of the first automated clearing houses (ACHs) in the two cities in October 1972.[8] Similar installations were established in Atlanta (1973), Minneapolis, (1974) and Boston (1974), and by 1980, 36 ACHs were serving all 48 contiguous states, with over 9,700 commercial banks as members.[9]

The magnetic tape submitted to ACHs includes all identifying data on each payment: dollar amount, names of the parties involved, and bank and customer account numbers. The ACHs then generate new tapes for all the financial institutions that participate in the system.[10] The Federal

[8]"California's Step Toward Checkless Banking," *Business Week* (September 9, 1972):56.
[9]Myron L. Kwast, "Cost Economies from ACH Use," *The Magazine of BANK ADMINISTRATION* (June 1980):48.
[10]Carl M. Gambs, "Automated Clearing Houses," *Economic Review* (Federal Reserve Bank of Kansas City, May 1978), p. 4.

Reserve System usually permits ACHs to use its computerized communications system to clear items.[11]

The ACH effort reflected the banks' concern over steadily increasing check volume, and by year-end 1977, over 9 million monthly payments were being processed at ACH installations.[12] By 1979, that volume had increased to 13 million.[13] Although these figures indicate that steady growth in EFT activity has taken place, it must also be disappointing to those who had predicted much greater acceptance of the system to note that their original projections have not been met. For example, SCOPE predicted a volume for 1977 of eight million monthly EFT transactions from the private sector alone, whereas an analysis of actual activity showed that 85 percent of the 1977 volume consisted of payments from the federal government.[14] In April 1979, government usage accounted for 83.9 percent of the total ACH volume.[15]

It made eminently good sense for Washington to assume a leading role in EFT credits. In the 20-year period from 1958 to 1978, civil service retirement payments tripled, railroad retirement payments doubled, veterans' payments increased 15 percent, and monthly check usage for Social Security rose from seven million to 32 million.[16]

Aside from the sheer growth in volume, the Treasury Department recognized the costs involved. An analysis conducted in the early 1970s indicated that in-house costs for each check issued were $0.18. The Department was also processing over one million claims per year, from individuals who denied having received checks as scheduled. On behalf of the Treasury's Fiscal Service Unit, Plumly summarized the official viewpoint:

> We had no palatable alternative to the development of a better means of coping with continually increasing workloads. At the same time, we needed a more positive payment delivery system. And lastly, it has become more and more difficult to attain higher productivity and reduce consumption of resources under the check disbursement system.[17]

[11]Stanley W. Anderson, *The Banker and EFT* (Washington, D.C.: American Bankers Association, 1982), p. 23.
[12]Gambs, "Automated Clearing Houses," p. 4.
[13]Kwast, "Cost Economies from ACH Use" p. 48.
[14]Gambs, "Automated Clearing Houses," p. 5.
[15]Kwast, "Cost Economies from ACH Use."
[16]Les Plumly, Paper presented at the First Annual Cash Managers Conference (New York, April 12, 1978), p. 2.
[17]Ibid.

In late 1973, the federal government announced the start of its first EFT system test, under which Air Force personnel were invited to begin receiving direct deposits of their wages and salaries at the banks or other financial institutions of their choice.[18] By 1980, over 79 percent of Air Force personnel on active duty were participating in the program.[19] The success of this test led other branches of the Armed Forces to begin implementing their own direct-deposit systems, all of which use the facilities of local ACHs.

In February 1976, the second stage of federal adoption of EFTS began with the direct depositing of 51,000 payments to Social Security beneficiaries. By year-end 1980, 10.3 million, or 31 percent, of all monthly Social Security payments were being made through direct deposit; a Treasury Department forecast at that time projected program participation of 55 percent by 1985, and 80 percent by 1990.[20]

The results of the program have been gratifying both to the government and to the financial institutions. Social Security recipients have expressed their satisfaction, the receiving institutions have reduced by 70 percent their processing costs for a Social Security payment, and recipients' balances have increased.[21] The federal government is exploring the possibility of directly depositing income tax refunds, federal payrolls, and all payments of principal and interest on government debt issues.[22]

To some observers, the success of this effort provides evidence that the new world of banking is here, and that the use of checks for purposes such as payroll will disappear. Acceptance of direct deposit by so many Social Security recipients gives rise to an assumption that other segments of the population will make the same choice.

However, in actual practice, this has not been the case. Private-sector use of direct deposit is woefully small by comparison with the government's use of it.[23] The Social Security beneficiary has certain characteristics that the wage earner lacks. Most such recipients have checking or

---

[18]Since the inception of EFTS, user participation has been optional. Most recently, Title IX of the Financial Institutions Regulatory Act of 1978 bans any compulsory use of EFTS.

[19]Robert O. Thompson, Paper presented at the 9th Annual Payment Systems Symposium (Atlanta, April 20–22, 1980), p. 7.

[20]Robert Trigaux, "Direct Deposit Benefits to Institutions Found Substantial," *American Banker* (April 13, 1981):1.

[21]Joan Hyman, "97% of Direct Deposit Users Confident of Program," *Bank Systems & Equipment* (May 1981):20.

[22]Thompson, Paper presented at the 9th Annual Payment Systems Symposium.

[23]George C. White, Jr., "Banks Should Encourage Customers to Use Direct Deposit," *American Banker* (March 26, 1981):4.

savings accounts, so that direct depositing is easy to arrange. They are vitally concerned that each monthly payment be received on time, since their standard of living is dependent on prompt availability of funds. They may have had problems with lost or stolen checks, may have experienced mail delays in receiving payments, or may have had difficulty cashing a Social Security check.

The office or factory worker does not fit this same profile and has not displayed any overwhelming desire for direct depositing of net pay. Management personnel, on the other hand, have demonstrated a willingness to adopt it. A list of corporations that have implemented direct deposit of payroll includes Allied Chemical, IBM, Aluminum Company of America, Dow Chemical, and American Motors, yet each of these has applied it only to managerial personnel, and at most is "exploring its application" to other categories of employees.[24] Considerable skepticism still prevails among workers who seem to feel that the system is simply another way in which corporations gain benefits for themselves at the employees' expense.[25]

Advantages of Direct Deposit

For the typical employee, direct deposit of pay offers as its chief advantages timeliness, convenience, and security. Individuals who accept it are given a guarantee by their financial institution that the net pay will be credited on the stipulated date, even if the necessary input tapes have not been received.

Direct deposit eliminates the possibility of stolen or lost payroll checks and the need for payees to spend time cashing checks. A further benefit exists for those employees who have used the services of private check-cashing firms; direct deposit avoids the fees charged by those organizations.

The potential benefits to the employer may not be as significant in every case. The time and expense of preparing actual payroll checks can be eliminated, but statements showing earnings, deductions, and year-to-date figures must still be prepared. Some companies have said that as long as

---

[24]"Improvements in Automated Clearing House Services," Federal Reserve Bank of New York, Circular 8572 (May 17, 1979).
[25]Hunt, *Corporate Cash Management and Electronic Fund Transfers*, pp. 150–151.

these reports must be generated, there is little additional cost to them in issuing checks.[26]

In addition to payroll activity, many firms have considered direct deposit for dividend and pension payments. In these instances, postage costs are a major factor, and the same circumstances that make the Social Security recipient a likely candidate apply here. General Motors, Allied Chemical, American Motors, and National Cash Register Corporation have reportedly been planning to use direct deposit for these purposes.[27]

The advent of explicit pricing for collecting checks through the Federal Reserve System, as mandated by the Monetary Control Act, gives payees an additional reason to consider direct deposit. As banks necessarily begin to pass along direct charges for Fed processing, check recipients will have an immediate rationale for moving toward electronic payments.[28] Banks themselves, given the vulnerability of paper-based systems to upward cost pressures, will likewise be motivated to market a better way of accepting deposits.[29]

Banks that effectively market direct deposit can anticipate these benefits:

1. Direct deposit can be made part of an attractive "package" of EFTS, tying it to automated teller machines, automatic transfers, and banking at home. The Wilmington Savings Fund Society reports a success ratio of over 80 percent in selling this type of integrated plan to its 45,000 retail accounts.[30]

2. Direct deposit can make a very significant contribution to a bank's program for cost reductions. For example, processing costs in 1981 for a deposited Social Security check at tellers' windows averaged $0.24, versus a cost of $0.07 through EFT.[31]

3. Direct deposit can be linked directly to a bank's program for cross-marketing. The new customers who open accounts to take advantage of direct deposit can automatically become candidates for other services, aside from those related to EFTS.[32]

---

[26]"Checkless Banking," *Business Week* (September 9, 1972): 56.
[27]Federal Reserve Bank of New York, Circular 8572 (May 17, 1979).
[28]White, Jr., "Banks Should Encourage Customers to Use Direct Deposit."
[29]Ford, "Number of Checks Written Expected to Peak by 1990," p. 22.
[30]Helene Duffy, in "After a Decade, Where Is EFT Headed?," *ABA Banking Journal* (May 1980):86.
[31]Trigaux, "Direct Deposit Benefits to Institutions Found Substantial."
[32]Barry Deutsch, "You Can't Sell the ACH, Only the Services It Can Provide," *American Banker* (July 15, 1981):4.

Opposition to Direct Deposit

For a variety of reasons, acceptance of direct deposit has never been as widespread as antitipated.[33] Despite bank guarantees, employees seem to fear that their net pay will not be available on the specified date and believe that rectifying any error will be far more difficult under EFTS.[34] Their past experiences may have conditioned them in this respect. Many Americans have been the victims of computer errors that caused incorrect bills, of repeated and erroneous notices of nonpayment, of deliveries of unordered goods, or of incorrect reports of unsatisfactory credit. The basic impersonality of computer systems, along with the problems and delays encountered in correcting mistakes have a negative affect on attempts to market EFT credits.

A study conducted in 1972 by COPE, the Atlanta Committee on Paperless Entries, identified 27 separate areas of consumer resistance to EFTS; loss of personal control was most frequently mentioned, and the study highlighted the fact that many workers want their net pay in cash or a check so that they gain both privacy and control.[35] Many wage earners believe that direct deposit of pay will make information regarding net pay (including overtime, bonuses, and incentive payments) available to other household members through credit advice slips or bank statements. This belief makes the concept unattractive to them.

Employees do not appear to consider check-cashing at banks a sufficient hardship to justify converting to direct deposit. This is especially true when state laws compel employers to allow paid time for cashing purposes. Other resistance to direct deposit comes from the 20 percent of American households operating on a cash basis, without checking accounts. These families generally purchase money orders for bill paying, and see no valid reason for changing their financial pattern.[36]

From the payer's viewpoint, an objection to direct deposit has been voiced by corporate financial officers who actively manage daily "float" (the time cycle required for the presenting and collecting of deposited or cashed checks) and who realize that payroll, dividend, and pension checks are mere entries in a disbursement register until they are actually presented to drawee banks and debited to accounts. The corporate treasurer who

---

[33] Alex W. Hart, in "After a Decade," p. 88.
[34] Candilis, *The Future of Commercial Banking*, p. 131.
[35] In *Bank Systems and Equipment*, (November 1972): p. 54.
[36] Gambs, "Automated Clearing Houses" p. 10.

keeps demand deposits to an absolute minimum has little interest in a system that entails immediate debiting—a process that takes place as soon as tape input is processed by an ACH.[37]

These objections and areas of resistance help to explain why, as of October 1982, the federal government's programs for direct deposit were generating 17 million monthly credits—approximately eight times the volume in the private sector.[38]

Opportunities for the Future

Payroll checks continue to represent the largest single portion of total volume. Given the resistance to direct deposit expressed by many blue-collar workers and mentioned above, it would appear that the marketing effort of banks might profitably be directed to other areas in which consumer acceptance may be greater. For example, there is little evidence of a concerted effort by banks to market direct deposit of their own dividend payments to their stockholders. Similarly, overall corporate dividend-disbursing activity does not appear to have been given a great deal of emphasis. Millions of American stockholders regularly receive dividend checks, and constitute a very attractive market.[39]

Programs for effective marketing of direct deposit of dividend payments can be aimed at both the recipients and the issuers, stressing the benefits both parties can gain. Here again, the corporate financial officer, who presently pays stockholders by check and therefore uses float to the company's advantage, must be convinced that the potential cost reductions through direct deposit more than offset any existing positive features. Explicit pricing for check collection through the Fed can be made part of the marketing approach.

Insurance companies of every type generate large volumes of checks in payment of annuities and pensions, other benefits, and medical and surgical claims. They therefore constitute an attractive potential market for direct deposit of these payments in lieu of issuing checks.

[37]Paul S. Nadler, "The Human Side of Electronic Banking," *Bankers Monthly Magazine* (May 15, 1978):12.
[38]National Automated Clearing House Association, personal communication, October 12, 1982.
[39]White, Jr., "Banks Should Encourage Customers to Use Direct Deposit."

EFT DEBIT SYSTEMS

In view of the reservations expressed by so many consumers regarding direct deposit, one might expect as much or more resistance to a system that automatically debits accounts. Surprisingly, variations of this EFT concept have been successfully marketed throughout the United States, often as a joint effort conducted by the banks with the recipients of large volumes of checks such as insurance companies. At year-end 1977, private debt transfers totaled 60,000 per month[40]; as of October 1982, over four million monthly debits were being processed.[41] Typically, these transactions represent payments of predetermined amounts to meet important obligations on recurring specified dates.[42]

The concept of debit transfers originated with a paper-based system, still widely used, under which a bank received prior authorization from a consumer to create a check or draft against his or her account. Insurance companies were the principal beneficiaries. Evolving technology then made it possible to introduce electronic debits, eliminating paper in many cases. In addition, many banks implemented systems of direct debits for customers' installment- and mortgage-loan payments.[43]

The EFT application to insurance payments was pioneered by the Equitable Life Assurance Society, in collaboration with the Chase Manhattan Bank in New York. Their joint program has received widespread publicity. The insurer periodically prepares magnetic tapes, containing all necessary data on those policyholders who have authorized account debiting at their individual banks. These tapes are delivered to Chase, which initially uses them to debit the accounts of its own depositors. Chase also prepares a single credit to Equitable for the dollar total of all payments on the tapes. The bank then forwards the remaining tape data through ACH facilities to over 1500 financial institutions throughout the country. Each of these then debits its own policyholder accounts. The success of this system has led other insurers to implement similar plans.[44]

[40]Gambs, "Automated Clearing House," p. 8.

[41]National Automated Clearing House Association, personal communication, October 12, 1982.

[42]Gambs, "Automated Clearing House," p. 8.

[43]George C. White, Jr., "Payment Systems Today—and Tomorrow," *The Bankers Magazine* (March–April 1980):29.

[44]George C. White, Jr., "Electronic GIRO Payments," *American Banker* (October 14, 1976):5.

The "Bill-Check" system offers another example of innovative technology in processing consumers' debits. It enables a bill payer to examine each invoice rendered by suppliers of goods and services, and to return part of that invoice to a bank as authorization for payment. Funds are then directly transferred from the consumer's account to the supplier's. When this proposal was first outlined in the Atlanta questionnaire prepared by COPE, 1,375 respondents gave it the highest degree of acceptance of all the services listed.[45]

An additional system, analogous to the "Bill-Check" plan, is the GIRO method of payment. It has been successfully implemented in several European countries, either through the local postal service or the banks. In essence, it is a system in which a bill payer instructs a bank to make direct payments of funds to the accounts of payees. It enables the consumer to gain the benefits of automatic transfer while retaining full control.

In the GIRO system, businesses use a standardized bill format containing a special data field. An Optical Character Recognition (OCR) typeface is used so that the bill can be read by automated equipment. The bank and account to which funds are to be transferred, the type of payment and dollar amount, and the payer's identification are encoded in this field. By examining and signing the bill, the payer authorizes the movement of funds to the payee's account.[46]

Advantages of EFT Debits

Under certain circumstances, EFT debits are now known to possess advantages that meke them more easily marketable than some other forms of funds transfers. They eliminate the direct costs of checks, the time and effort required to issue them, the postage expense, and the fear that a critical payment will be neglected and not made when due. Transaction costs under EFT are generally far lower than those levied by drawee banks as per-check charges. Such fixed, recurring payments as those made for loan amortization and insurance premiums readily lend themselves to the EFT debit system because the consumer has advance knowledge of the

[45]Candilis, *The Future of Commercial Banking,* p. 129.
[46]George C. White, Jr., "Electronic GIRO or Credit Transfer Payments," *United States Investor* (October 4, 1976):17.

amount owed and the timing of each payment. His or her basic and essential element of control is preserved. Banks must stress these benefits if growth in the system is to continue.[47]

For the insurance company, bank, public utility, or other recipient of a large volume of payments, EFT debits offer substantial benefits when compared with papar-based systems. If the payee has been receiving payments directly, the costs of opening mail, examining checks, and preparing timely deposits must be incurred. If, instead, the payee is using lock-box service, (by which incoming checks are received, examined, processed, and deposited) through one or more banks, compensating balances must be maintained or direct fees paid for the service.

EFT debits address this entire problem. They reduce the payee's direct and indirect expenses, and provide quicker availability of funds with greater assurance of actual payment since the risk of returned checks is minimized. Direct tape input for computer posting of accounts receivable is a by-product of the EFT debit system. Efforts by businesses to cooperate with banks in marketing the debit concept can be anticipated as the benefits become more widely known.[48]

Opposition to EFT Debits

Why has the EFT debit system grown much more rapidly than the credit system? The question becomes even more interesting if one considers the opposition manifested in the early stages of the program.

A 1972 study conducted by Louis Harris showed that two-thirds of the respondents were opposed to any form of automatic bill payment from their bank accounts,[49] and senior officers of Citibank in New York and Security Pacific National Bank in Los Angeles publicly stated that their banks' customers would probably have very strong reservations about the system.[50] Repeated surveys of the consumer marketplace identify fears of a loss of control over financial affairs resulting from EFTS,[51] and the

[47]Robert E. Knight, "Cautionary Notes on EFTS," *American Banker* (September 25, 1974):4.
[48]Gambs, "Automated Clearing House," p. 12.
[49]*The Second Study: The American Public's and Community Opinion Leaders' Views of Banks and Bankers in 1972* (Philadelphia: The Foundation for Full Service Banks, 1972), p. 123.
[50]"Obstacles to National EFTS," *American Banker* (September 25, 1974):4.
[51]Gambs, "Automated Clearing House," p. 11.

slow development of the SCOPE project has been attributed to the banks' failure to take this basic attitude into consideration.[52]

A study conducted by one of America's largest accounting firms identifies much of this opposition. In the survey, consumers mentioned reluctance to "do business with a machine," their fears that unauthorized debits might be posted, and their awareness of the float benefits inherent in the check system. In this respect, the survey reinforces the thought that today's consumers know how to utilize float to their advantage and, like their corporate financial counterparts, are reluctant to lose the benefit float can achieve.[53]

As Nadler[54] has pointed out, there is irony in the EFT debit program. In marketing checking accounts, commercial banks always cited the value of a paid check as positive proof of payment. Now the same banks are trying to convince customers that no such paper receipt is necessary, and that EFT debit advices will serve equally well. Uncertainty over this point causes customer resistance.

Despite all the evidence of consumer hostility or apathy, the growth in acceptance of EFT debits has been gratifying. It can be attributed to two fundamental causes. The first of these reflects the types of debits that account for much of the growth. The statistics cited earlier evince carefully restricted use; almost exclusively, the program succeeds when applied to payments that pertain to important obligations, do not vary in amount, and recur at regular intervals. On the other hand, consumers have been slwo to accept the EFT debit system in its broader aspects. If they feel that scrutinizing a bill carefully and timing its payment are important, they are likely to resist the program. Many recipients of bills rendered by card issuers, utilities, and department stores want to examine every invoice, especially if their past experience includes computer-related errors.

The second reason for the acceptance of the debit program can be traced to the many *constraints* that have been sequentially imposed on it. Regulation E (12 CFR 205) of the Federal Reserve System was amended on two occasions during 1979 to provide the consumer with more safeguards,[55]

[52]Mayer, *The Bankers,* p. 174.
[53]Peter D. Louderback, "Who's Afraid of EFT" *World* (Peat, Marwick, Mitchell & Co., Autumn 1977):47.
[54]In "The Human Side of Electronic Banking," p. 14.
[55]Federal Reserve Bank of New York, Circular 8619, (August 8, 1979) and Circular 8669, (October 29, 1979).

and further amendments were made in 1980[56] for the same reason. Regulation E specifies that "reasonable advance notice" must be given whenever the amount of a preauthorized debit is to vary beyond a predetermined range. The consumer has the right to stop payment, orally or in writing, on any preauthorized transfer up to three days before the payment is to be made. Section 4-404 of the Uniform Commercial Code has also been revised to treat stop payments on EFT debit transfers in the same way as those on checks and other instruments.[57]

In addition to the federal statutes, a 1981 survey conducted by the Conference of State Bank Supervisors disclosed that 34 states had various types of EFT laws on their books.[58]

The effect of these statutes has been to allay some of the fears and doubts originally expressed by consumers. Placing legislative restrictions on the debit system may also help convince users that the nation's financial institutions are not assuming full control over their payment procedures and invading their privacy.

The steady expansion of EFT-related technology has created a further subdivision of debit transfers, which may be described as Customer-Initiated Entries (CIE).[59] In this system, the consumer initiates a bill-paying transaction by instructing a depository institution to credit a payee at the same or another institution. The instructions may be communicated in writing, by telephone, or through an ATM.

POINT-OF-SALE TERMINALS

When the concept of a "checkless society" was first introduced, one of its precepts called for the widespread use of computer terminals activated by a bank card. Cardholders presumably would use these to pay for purchases by directly transferring funds to the payee's account. If the consumer insisted on paying by check, the terminal could be designed to provide a guarantee of payment to the merchant. Under the first option, the seller of goods or services would benefit from the immediate availability

---

[56]Federal Reserve System, *Electronic Fund Transfers* (May 10, 1980).
[57]Steven Pastore, "EFT and the Consumer," *The Bankers Magazine* (March–April 1979):39.
[58]"Electronic Transfer Laws Found in 68% of States," *American Banker* (July 29, 1981):12.
[59]Anderson, *The Banker and EFT*, p. 25.

of funds, and the consumer would be spared the inconvenience and expense of issuing a check. Under the second option, merchants would no longer have to cope with the chronic problem of bad checks. Point-of-sale (POS) terminals could also be designed to give the store complete inventory controls and sales records.

The evolution of the POS concept has taken three forms that are actually subsets of the original concept mentioned above. *Check guarantee* and *card authorization* systems serve the merchant market by decreasing risk and increasing operating efficiency. *In-store banking* systems use the supermarket as a replacement for the bank branch, and enable the consumer to conduct his or her banking business without physically visiting the institution's premises. *Direct debit* systems create electronic transfers of funds from the purchaser's account to the seller's; they may also perform the functions associated with in-store banking.[60]

That same evolution, however, is one that has been marked by failures and disappointments. During 1971 and 1972, City National Bank and Trust Company introduced the concept in Columbus, Ohio, using sixty terminals in thirty merchant locations. The Hempstead Bank in New York implemented a similar plan in 1971.[61] Neither of these programs proved successful. A savings and loan association discontinued its POS program (140 machines) after 18 months, and another institution cited operating costs and fraud as its rationale for closing down many of its POS installations.[62] These original systems failed largely because they were operated by individual financial institutions, and no single bank or savings and loan association proved capable of generating a volume of transactions large enough to cover its expenses. A second reason for failure lay in the fact that a computer infrastructure capable of processing a large volume of retail transactions was not in place at the time.[63]

In addition to being aware of these early failures, bankers who expected POS to become a major component of the predicted "checkless society" must have been discouraged by the results of a survey conducted in 1976. It showed that 30 percent of the 800 household respondents expressed an actual dislike of POS, while 18 percent were neutral on the subject, and

[60]Susan A. Anderson, "Taking a Second Look at Point-of Sale Banking," *American Banker* (June 2, 1981):17.
[61]Candilis, *The Future of Commercial Banking,* p. 126.
[62]Susan A. Anderson, "Taking a Second Look at Point-of-Sale Banking," p. 29.
[63]"Electronic Banking," p. 74.

only 6 percent favored it. Among the reasons given for opposition were fear of overspending, personal preference for paying by check or in cash, and the possibility of computer error.[64]

Perhaps the most innovative yet controversial POS use is that introduced in 1974 by Hinky Dinky, a supermarket chain in Nebraska. Terminals in the stores were directly connected with a computer at the First Federal Savings and Loan Association in Lincoln; clients of the latter were given encoded cards that could be presented to a Hinky Dinky clerk to activate the terminal. Shoppers had the option of paying for grocery purchases by direct transfers of funds to Hinky Dinky's account at the S&L, by depositing funds to their accounts at the S&L, or by making cash withdrawals. In the last-named case, the clerk would give the shopper currency and the terminal would perform the same function as an ATM.

The Hinky Dinky/First Federal program proved an immediate success. Within forty-five days, First Federal Savings and Loan showed a gain of $603,000 in deposits, of which almost one-half came from new customers. The traditional family trip to the supermarket could now be combined with deposit or withdrawal transactions that otherwise would have necessitated visits to a teller's window. Hinky Dinky gained through immediate crediting of funds to its account for purchased goods, reduced losses on checks, and expanded sales. The consumer found a convenience in this program that no commercial bank could match.[65]

Bankers were quick to challenge this development. The Nebraska Bankers Association and the state Attorney General brought litigation against both the supermarket and the S&L, charging them with illegal entry into the commercial banking business and infringement of banking functions. State courts ruled in favor of the defendants in both cases.[66]

In addition to its deposit expansion, First Federal found that it had achieved substantial cost reductions each time a deposit or withdrawal was made through the store terminals. Instead of transaction costs estimated at $1.67 at a teller's window, the S&L calculated the cost of a Hinky Dinky transaction at $0.82.[67] Since that time, financial institutions

---

[64]Olin S. Pugh and Franklin J. Ingram, "EFT and the Public," *The Bankers Magazine* (March–April 1978):47.
[65]"An S&L Puts the Teller in the Supermarket," *Business Week* (April 20, 1974):88.
[66]Alan Richman, "Court Upholds Hinky Dinky EFTS Service," *Bank Systems and Equipment* (September 1974):8.
[67]Louderback, "Who's Afraid of EFT?" p. 48.

in the POS field have been able to achieve steady decreases in processing costs through POS installations, and the 1982 figure is $0.40 per transaction.[68]

The court rulings in favor of the Hinky Dinky program gave strong impetus to the overall POS concept, and the Federal Home Loan Bank Board encouraged the S&Ls under its jurisdiction to implement similar projects. The nation's fourth largest S&L, California Federal, promptly began installation of 200 terminals in local supermarkets, and other thrift institutions followed in short order.[69]

A shared POS system, led by the First National Bank (Topeka) and involving three other local banks, was introduced in 1978; 36 merchants, who are required to have accounts with any of the participating banks, accept the proprietary Vantage Card issued by those institutions.[70] In 1979, a major breakthrough occurred when the J. C. Penney Company decided to accept VISA cards for POS transactions, and there have been several significant developments since that time.[71]

Rocky Mountain Bank Card combines POS and ATM features through 4,800 terminals at 500 retail outlets in the Denver area. Users may charge purchases to their accounts or handle other banking transactions through these terminals.[72]

Citizens Fidelity Bank (Louisville) operates 65 terminals in local stores. The system contains the same elements found in the Hinky Dinky program; users who make cash withdrawals are paid by the merchant, who is then immediately credited through electronic transfers of funds. The 1980 volume under this plan exceeded one million transactions.[73]

In the Des Moines area, a pilot program involving 105 financial institutions that belong to the Iowa Transfer System, Inc. was introduced through local supermarkets in 1981. However, the terminals can be used only for direct debiting of purchases to a user's account. Each of the 105 participating institutions has issued its own proprietary card for use in this program.[74]

[68]"Electronic Banking," p. 80.
[69]"Memphis S&L Goes on Line," *Bank Systems and Equipment* (February 1974):8.
[70]Bill Streeter, "Renewed Interest in POS Banking," *ABA Banking Journal* (September 1980):104.
[71]White, Jr., "Payment Systems Today," p. 31.
[72]"Electronic Banking," p. 76.
[73]Streeter, "Renewed Interest in POS Banking," p. 109.
[74]"Electronic Shopping Builds a Base," *Business Week* (October 26, 1981):125.

New York State law prohibits the sharing of automated facilities between commercial banks and thrift institutions; therefore Metroteller Systems, Inc., which is owned by the state's largest savings bank, has divided its operations between the two groups. In 1981, it operated at 159 locations across the state. Marine Midland Bank, N.A., and The Bank of New York were the major commercial participants, while Dime Savings Bank, with twenty-nine of its terminals in supermarkets, was the leading institution among the thrifts.[75]

Early in 1982, Allstate Savings and Loan Association (a Sears subsidiary) introduced a service enabling holders of its debit card to buy gasoline at service stations in California through self-service pumps that operated around-the-clock. All purchases were directly charged to an account at the S&L.[76]

A significant aspect of many of these systems is found in the *type* of card that is used to activate the POS terminal. In most cases, individual financial institutions have chosen to issue their own debit cards, instead of becoming part of the nationwide MasterCard and VISA programs. Bank spokespersons in various parts of the country have explained the rationale for this policy: "If everyone issues VISA and MasterCard debit cards, they all look the same . . . Banks want their own identity."[77] And, "It's important for local and regional financial institutions to have an alternative to national debit-card systems."[78]

The Outlook for POS

From the merchants' standpoint, POS terminals may eventually prove to be the most widely accepted examples of EFTS applications. Department stores, supermarkets, furniture stores, and many other retail outlets have already been identified as likely targets for POS installations, and one market study indicates that the number of terminals may increase to 10,000 by 1985, as contrasted with a figure of 1,000 in 1977.[79] However, as with

[75]Susan Anderson, "Taking a Second Look at Point-of-Sale Banking," p. 17.
[76]"Allstate S&L Pumps Up Debit Card Appeal with Gas Link," *American Banker* (February 17, 1982):7.
[77]Frank J. Schultz, in "Electronic Banking," p. 72.
[78]Robert A. Holzinger, in "Electronic Shopping Builds a Base," p. 126.
[79]Marc J. Frankel, "Self-Service: An Emerging Trend in Retail Banking," *Chase Directions* (New York: The Chase Manhattan Bank, N.A., Fall 1979):2.

other aspects of EFTS, it is the consumer who must make the ultimate decision as to the value of the system. Banks that wish to increase customer acceptance of POS must stress the fact that the benefits outweigh the perceived costs such as computer errors or unauthorized uses. The dollar amount of a purchase and the type of merchandise being bought may induce a customer to accept the system in one case and reject it in another. For example, the consumer who is making a small purchase and leaving the store with it is likely to use a card to pay for the item, whereas the buyer of a major appliance or furniture will be reluctant to give the merchant immediate use of the funds while the customer is waiting for home delivery. Sophisticated individuals today are well aware of the benefits of float, and this fact affects the potential acceptance of the debit card, even when a relatively small and basic purchase (e.g., gasoline) takes place.[80]

AUTOMATED TELLER MACHINES

Of all the applications of EFTS that have been introduced, by far the most successful is the one with which the consumer can most easily identify: the automated teller machine (ATM). The word *explosive* has been used advisedly to describe the growth of ATMs, as financial institutions—certainly including nonbank competitors—of every size and type have recognized the value of these machines in reaching their customers when and where those customers want to be reached.[81] At the same time, more consumers are now using more ATMs for more purposes, so that what was once the total number (8,000) of ATMs in place in 1977 is now less than the number of new ATMs added in a year (8,456 were shipped to financial institutions in 1981).[82] In March 1982, a survey disclosed that the average ATM now handles 7,200 monthly transactions.[83]

The ATM represents one application of EFTS in which the predictions

[80]"Allstate S&L Pumps Up Debit Card Appeal," p. 7.
[81]Raoul D. Edwards, "The ATM and the Delivery System," *United States Banker* (July 1981):50.
[82]Linda Zimmer, "ATMs: Time to Fine-Tune and to Plan," *The Magazine of BANK ADMINISTRATION* (May 1982):20.
[83]"Marine ATMs Pass One Million," *American Banker* (April 16, 1982):14.

of the original visionaries have come to fruition—probably because, with some personal reservations, consumers have found that it relates best to their wants and needs, and gives them the convenience of twenty-four-hour banking throughout the year. At the same time, the ATM has assisted many banks by providing them with significant benefits at a time when every possible technique for cost reduction must be explored.

In their infancy (the first ATM was installed in 1971 by Citizens and Southern National Bank in Atlanta)[84] these machines were far simpler, and were commonly referred to as "cash dispensing units." By using a bank card, the consumer could withdraw funds from an account at any time. This eliminated the two-fold problem of issuing a check and waiting to cash it in a long line at a bank.

From the banks' standpoint, ATMs similarly addressed a number of issues and problems at the same time. If these units could be operated at points remote from the banks' premises, they could replace some of the latter facilities and therefore help reduce operating costs for branches. Bank labor costs in 1979 were growing at an annual rate of 8 percent,[85] and overall costs of maintaining networks of branches were becoming prohibitive.[86] More recently, escalating interest costs on formerly "free" deposits have served to exacerbate the problem. Transaction costs through ATM are generally half those incurred through teller handling; for example, in 1981 Crocker National Bank reported costs of $0.26 and $0.55, respectively.[87]

In this context, it should be noted that one-fifth of the total nationwide volume in 1981 was represented by routine balance inquiries.[88] Michigan National Bank estimates its personnel costs at $10 to $15 for each such inquiry, and its President views the use of ATMs for these inquiries as highly relevant to the bank's programs for increased productivity with reduced expenses. He considers the bank's 1,000 ATMs at 365 locations as critical to its competitive posture and integral to its objectives.[89]

---

[84]Zimmer, "ATMs: Time to Fine-Tune and to Plan."
[85]Roger J. Abouchar, "EFT Is Inexorable," *American Banker* (May 22, 1979):4.
[86]Alan J. Weber, "Bankers Must Change Technology," *American Banker* (September 15, 1980):9.
[87]Leo P. Hardwick, "What Role Will the ATM Play?" *The Bankers Magazine* (May–June 1981):49.
[88]Zimmer, "ATMs: Time to Fine-Tune and to Plan."
[89]Stanford C. Stoddard, "Lobby ATMs Free Tellers of Routine Tasks," *American Banker* (June 15, 1982):13.

With each increase in customer acceptance, the economies of scale in ATMs become more obvious. At Crocker National Bank, for example, the cited reduction in transaction costs must be related to the fact that many of the bank's 650 units handle 11,000 transactions per month,[90] and in 1980, Citibank, N. A. reported that its 400 ATMs in the New York area were processing 68 percent of the bank's total cash withdrawals.[91]

ATMs may be regarded as offensive and/or defensive tools in a bank's efforts to attract and retain deposits. When installed at carefully selected sites, they can simultaneously prevent the attrition of funds and be a source of new business. As banks vie with one another and with their unregulated competitors (e.g., Sears), ATMs can provide a means of product and service differentiation, and can convey the message that the bank is endeavoring to make transaction handling easier, more convenient, and less expensive.[92] The nationwide statistics for 1981 indicate that at least 25 percent of ATM usage occurs when tellers *are* available, and that the average deposit and withdrawal were $264 and $37.[93]

Some banks have placed their ATMs "on line" by connecting them directly to a central computer, so that every transaction is immediately posted to an account. In other cases, the ATM merely produces a record of all activity, which is posted as of the close of business.

The original simple "cash dispensing unit" has generally been replaced by far more sophisticated equipment, thus justifying the title *automated teller*. These machines can be used not only to supply currency, but also to accept deposits, process loan payments, and initiate transfers. Those units having the capability to handle multiple types of transactions and linked directly to a bank's computer are often referred to as CBCTs (Customer-Bank Communications Terminals). In 1981, nationwide statistics indicated that 76 percent of ATM usage was represented by withdrawals, 19 percent by deposits, 4 percent by transfers between accounts, and 1 percent by payments.[94] Tests have also been conducted on the feasibility of using ATMs to dispense travelers' checks at banks, in direct competition

[90]Hardwick, "What Role Will the ATM Play?"
[91]Weber, "Bankers Must Change Technology."
[92]Marvin C. Johnson, " 'Institutional' ATM Placement: A Practical Approach." *The Bankers Magazine* (March–April 1980):40–41. See also Lonnie L. Sciambi and Wayne K. Nystrom, "Fundamentals of ATM Program Success,":34–36.
[93]Zimmer, "ATMs: Time to Fine-Tune and to Plan."
[94]Ibid.

with a similar terminal program already implemented by American Express.[95]

A study conducted in 1979 analyzed the demographics of existing users of ATMs and provided useful data for marketing purposes. Of the respondents who deposited funds through ATMs, 78.6 percent were younger than 35, and 57.2 percent had incomes of $10,500 or more. Of those who used ATMs to obtain cash, 60 percent were under 35, and 60 percent had incomes of $10,500 or more. These statistics again reinforce the theory that the younger segment of our society is now more affluent, as well as more receptive to those innovations providing readily perceived benefits.[96]

Shared Facilities

Start-up costs are quite high, often in the medium five-figure range, for any financial institution in an ATM program, including the cost of the equipment and all the support facilities it requires. This does not include expenses incurred in building facilities to house the unit. This factor led to the concept of ATMs that would be shared by several users. The National Committee on Electronic Funds Transfers recommended that legislation be enacted wherever necessary to permit such sharing; the New York State Bankers seconded the recommendation[97], and the amendments made in 1979 to Regulation E of the Federal Reserve System permitted two or more banks, or other financial institutions, to contract with one another for this purpose, subject to individual state legislation.[98]

A study of the application of this concept in Western Europe indicates that many countries in that area had already implemented it to a great extent. In 1981, shared networks of ATMs were in place in Austria, Great Britain, Denmark, West Germany, Italy, Norway, Sweden, Switzerland,

[95]"Citibank Tests Dispensing of Travelers' Checks at an ATM," *American Banker* (October 31, 1979):1.
[96]Jerry M. Hood, "Demographics of ATMs," *The Bankers Magazine* (November–December 1979):69.
[97]"Comments on the Recommendations of the NCEFT," (New York State Bankers Association, April 1978):31.
[98]Federal Reserve Bank of New York, "Electronic Funds Transfers," Circular 8669 (October 29, 1979).

and Greece; the common feature of all these facilities is found in an ability to dispense cash.[99]

In the United States, one of the earliest examples of sharing of ATM facilities is found in the system known as ACT. This network was originally established to serve the needs of credit unions in Michigan, but was subsequently expanded to include banks. Legislation in that state required all ATMs, other than those that were physically part of a bank branch, to be offered to other financial institutions for sharing. The ACT system derives its profits principally from the Detroit area.[100] A parallel operation in Michigan, the Mac Link network, is planned to include 207 ATMs shared by five financial institutions.[101] The Rocky Mountain Bank Card and statewide Iowa systems, mentioned earlier, and the TYME system in Wisconsin also exemplify the concept.[102]

In an apparent contradiction to the viewpoint that proprietary systems are preferred as a means of firmly establishing a bank's identity, 34% of the institutions responding to a 1981 survey conducted by TransData Corporation indicated that they planned to convert from proprietary to shared facilities in order to achieve cost savings.[103]

The New York State Banking Department prohibits sharing between commercial banks and thrifts; however, 23 savings banks and one savings and loan have joined in a system known as Thrift Transfer. Its ATMs, housed in storefront facilities, handle deposits and withdrawals, transfers, and loan payments. Each bank and savings and loan issues its own "PayCard" for use in this system.[104]

Texas is the site of a rapidly growing system developed by Mercantile Texas Corporation, which is the holding company for the state's fifth largest bank, with assets of $6 billion. The system is known as MPACT, and includes both commercial banks and savings and loans. Over one million cardholders can obtain cash or handle other transactions at 259 MPACT units throughout the state. As a result of an amendment to Texas law in 1980, off-premises ATMs may be placed in supermarkets, shopping

[99]Robert Trigaux, "Western Europe Votes for ATMs, Mostly as Shared National Systems," *American Banker* (October 29, 1981):1.

[100]Hardwick, "What Role Will the ATM Play?" p. 48.

[101]Ibid.

[102]Edwards, "The ATM and the Delivery System," p. 51.

[103]Robert Trigaux, "ATM Services Being Established at Highest Rate Ever," *American Banker* (June 17, 1981):10.

[104]Joan P. Hyman, "Thrift Transfer's Monthly ATM Volume Burgeoning," *Bank Systems & Equipment* (May 1981):49.

centers, and airports. MPACT has already positioned itself in these locations, and hopes eventually to attract more of the state's 1,500 commercial banks. The real significance of MPACT may lie in the fact that Texas is a unit banking state; that is, branch banking is not allowed. The shared network of ATMs provides the convenience of branches to the consumer, while observing the state's restrictive legislation.[105]

The growth of shared networks has given rise to many predictions about the eventual abolition of federal laws that prohibit interstate banking. If a shared ATM system crosses state lines and enables users to activate (through their cards) machines of their own bank as well as those of other members, then interstate accepting of deposits may occur, and a crack would appear in the federal dike. In 1981, a step in this direction was taken by the Federal Home Loan Bank Board, which gave blanket approval for any savings and loan association under its jurisdiction to establish 24-hour ATMs anywhere in the United States, without geographic limitations.[106]

During 1982, three major developments took place, each of which involved the sharing of ATM facilities by a group of commercial banks. Credit Systems, Inc., a data-processing firm in Kansas City, announced the formation of a network of 45 banks in Kansas, Illinois, Iowa, Missouri, and western Kentucky. All ATMs in the system will accept the cards issued by any of the participating banks.[107]

The system known as *Cirrus* embraces such major institutions as Mellon Bank (Pittsburgh), Manufacturers Hanover (New York), Bay Banks (Boston), First Interstate (California), and Sun Banks (Florida). Again, the cardholders in this system can access any ATM in the 35-state network for cash withdrawals. Sun Banks has extended the service to include machines that will be located in Publix supermarkets throughout the state.[108]

In April 1982, twenty-six commercial banks announced formation of the Plus System, Inc. The largest (Bank of America), third largest (Chase), and seventh largest (Continental Illinois) banks in the country were among the participants. Customers can make cash withdrawals using their cards at ATMs operated by any bank in the system, and also make transfers and cash advances. The banking officials who announced formation of the system predicted that more than 3,000 financial institutions would

[105]"Tapping a Cash Machine Bonanza," *Business Week* (October 12, 1981):136.
[106]"Savings Unit Automation," *The New York Times* (August 7, 1981):D5.
[107]"Electronic Networks Springing Up All Over," *American Banker* (March 19, 1982):2.
[108]"Sun Banks Will Launch ATM Access at Stores," *American Banker* (October 4, 1982):3.

eventually join it, thus making its services available to some 25 million consumers.[109]

REGULATORY CONSTRAINTS

At present, 60 percent of the American population lives in suburban areas—the same areas where shopping centers and supermarkets abound. May banks install ATMs in these stores to serve existing depositors and attract new ones? To the merchant or supermarket operator, the prospect is extremely appealing. Ideally, the machines would charge purchases directly to the customer's account, as at Hinky Dinky. Under a lesser scenario, the ATMs could supply cash and thus lessen check usage.[110] What is the legal status and actual definition of a unit that is geographically remote from the bank or banks that own or share it?

Each of these questions has been addressed by federal and/or state regulators, and the banker who seeks a unanimity of answers is doomed to frustrating disappointment. There is little agreement, even among judicial bodies. The reasons for this reflect a long-standing lack of uniformity in matters concerning the regulation of banking, even in so basic an area as defining the word *branch*.[111]

The McFadden Act (1927) is the fundamental law affecting the ability of national banks to open new branches. It provides that they may do so *only* to the extent that state-chartered banks have identical privileges; if state laws prohibit or restrict branch banking, national banks are bound equally by those statutes. Section 36(f) of the Act defines a branch as "any bank office, agency, or place of business where deposits are received, checks paid, or money lent."[112] By a six to two vote, the Supreme Court reinforced this Act in 1969, and stated that offering *any* of the three above-mentioned services at any location would constitute *prima facie* evidence of branch banking.[113]

---

[109]Robert A. Bennett, "Banks Will Link Cash Machines," *The New York Times* (April 8, 1982):D1.
[110]Almost 80 percent of supermarket sales of over $90 billion are paid for by check (Louderback, "Who's Afraid of EFT?" p. 47).
[111]"What is Branch Banking?" *Datamation* (February 1975):81.
[112]12 U.S.C., Section 36.
[113]396 U.S. 135.

In December 1974, James Smith, then Comptroller of the Currency, issued an interpretation of the National Bank Act, allowing all national banks to establish customer-bank communications terminals (CBCTs) without regard for state-imposed restrictions on branching. Since this was not a direct regulation but an interpretation of the Act, it became effective immediately upon publication. Since CBCTs had not been contemplated when federal laws on branching were originally passed, it was the Comptroller's opinion that CBCTs did not come under the statutes, and that national banks therefore could install those facilities anywhere.

The Comptroller's interpretation was an effort to place national banks on the same competitive basis as savings and loan associations and credit unions, which were not bound by McFadden. A subsequent Comptroller, expressing his agreement with his predecessor's action, spoke in support of Congressional revision of the Act.[114]

Predictably, a storm of controversy was touched off by the 1974 interpretation. Numerous challenges were brought by various groups, including associations of banks who claimed that the Comptroller had violated federal laws and brought litigation against him. The Commissioner of Financial Institutions in Michigan issued an immediate ruling contrary to the Comptroller's, and brought all CBCTs under state restrictions on branching.[115] A moratorium on all CBCT expansion was called for in a bill introduced in Congress. Two federal district courts, in adjudicating lawsuits brought against the Comptroller, ruled in his favor; four United States Courts of Appeals, in separate decisions, ruled to the contrary, and the Comptroller was ordered to rescind his interpretation.[116]

The controversy is by no means fully resolved. The decisions by the Courts of Appeals are taken to mean that terminals *are* subject to state laws on branching *if* the individual states classify them as branches. If so, CBCTs must meet the same capital requirements that the states impose on "brick-and-mortar" branches.[117] A survey of the current status of legislation on this subject discloses that 10 states consider remote units as equivalent to branches; 24 states do not do so, 15 states have not yet

[114]John G. Heimann with Richard B. Miller, "A Conversation with the Comptroller," *The Bankers Magazine* (January–February 1979):28–29.
[115]"Off-Premise Teller Ruled Branch in Michigan," *American Banker* (December 12, 1974):1.
[116]40 Federal Register 49077 (1975).
[117]John G. Heimann, in "Banking in Transition," *The Bankers Magazine* (September–October 1978):22.

issued definitive rulings, and New Mexico, a "limited branching" state, classifies them as branches if they are unmanned, but not as branches if they are staffed.[118]

Through this bewildering succession of judicial and regulatory rulings and interpretations, some of which reversed earlier decisions, the federal law remains fully operative prohibiting banks from doing a full banking business across state lines, including the accepting of deposits.[119] At the same time, the question of states' rights has consistently surfaced, and the authority of each state to regulate *all* forms of branching within its borders has been reinforced in every case. The traditional principle of separation of powers, such as between the federal and state governments, still prevails. A uniform banking policy throughout the nation, standardizing the entire EFTS program and enunciated by a single central authority, may not be appropriate to address the community needs in each of the 50 states, and any attempt by a federal regulatory agency to do so would certainly provoke a new series of lawsuits and a new area of controversy. Of greater importance at this time is the ability of commercial banks to act, to the extent permitted by state laws, to meet the competition of those institutions not bound by those same laws.

INTERBANK EFT NETWORKS

To facilitate the movement of funds from bank to bank, three specialized EFT systems have been developed and can be cited here as examples of the improved facilities for funds transfers that now exist.

CHIPS is the acronym for Clearing House Interbank Payments System. It was formed by the member banks in the New York City Clearing House in 1970, and is used only for direct interbank transfers, typically in very large amounts. Transactions are initiated in a rigid data format, and are settled through electronic debits and credits to accounts at the Federal Reserve Bank of New York.

SWIFT is the acronym for Society of Worldwide Interbank Financial Telecommunications. It does not handle funds settlements but does process

[118]Stanley Anderson *The Banker and EFT,* p. 117.
[119]Robert A. Bennett, "Banks Will Link Cash Machines."

instructions, using numerical data field codes, for third-party transfers, foreign exchange transactions, and letters of credit. It was implemented in 1977 by agreement among North American and European bank representatives.

In 1979, the Federal Reserve announced the start of an experimental program, aimed at expediting the clearing of large-dollar checks by using a variation of EFTS. If a vendor in Atlanta, for example, receives a check for $100,000 drawn on a bank in Minneapolis, and if the vendor deposits that check in an Atlanta bank, the latter converts the payment instructions to magnetic tape and follows the same procedure for all large checks on that day. The Atlanta Fed accepts incoming tapes from all the Atlanta banks, sorts the payment instructions by destination, and forwards all necessary data to the Federal Reserve Banks in each district. The latter then instruct the drawee banks in their areas to create debits to the makers' accounts.[120]

THE STATE OF THE ART

Paul Nadler[121] has described as "vastly exaggerated" the early forecasts of a "checkless society" and the projections of quick, widespread acceptance of all forms of EFTS. A great deal of progress has indeed been made in many areas of EFTS implementation, but much unforeseen resistance has also been encountered. It is now apparent that the prophets ignored a basic truth: consumers and users, and not new technology, drive the market.

The potential benefits to many categories of EFTS users still exist. Corporations can no doubt gain quicker availability of funds, more accurate and complete data on payments received and disbursed, and savings in postage and handling costs. Yet questions of float reduction and reciprocity arise. Corporate treasurers may be willing to adopt a system that allows them to receive funds more quickly, but will not consider one that draws down their bank balances with equal speed. They must also wonder if

[120]Federal Reserve Bank of New York, "Electronic Presentment of Checks," Circular 8573 (May 17, 1979).
[121]In "Banking: The Next Ten Years," *The Bankers Magazine* (July–August 1978):56.

their counterparts at other firms will handle transactions involving their own companies in the same way.

There is no doubt that employees can benefit through direct deposit of payroll funds. Check-cashing costs and problems can be completely or partially eliminated, along with losses and thefts of salary checks. Yet many employees continue to insist on check or cash payments. They do not consider check cashing a problem and fear a loss of personal privacy. Their employers, who would also stand to gain substantially through direct deposit of payroll, cite the loss of float or the lack of demonstrated bottom-line benefits as the main reasons for opposing it.

There is no doubt that bill-paying through EFTS can, in certain cases, be advantageous to both remitters and recipients. Yet consumers have again expressed strong reservations. The fear is pervasive that a "big brother" is gathering and reporting their financial transactions through a computer.[122] Other individuals have mentioned their fears of computer malfunction, fears that a payment will not be processed in a timely manner, and fears of not having receipts to document each transaction, even though such documentation is legally required.[123]

There is no doubt that ATMs offer the maximum convenience to bank customers. They are accessible at all times, and eliminate at least part of the volume that causes long lines at tellers' windows. Under proper security conditions, "push-button" banking should have far more appeal than issuing and cashing checks. Yet thousands of consumers still refuse to accept the idea. The study by Pugh and Ingram disclosed fears that unauthorized persons might have access to accounts, that robberies would take place after the user had obtained cash from an ATM, and that computer errors would occur; hence, 42 % of the respondents felt ATMs were "not needed."[124]

As the original cash dispensing machine evolved into a unit capable of handling many other types of transactions, volume *has* significantly increased, but the successes have not taken place as quickly or as extensively as in the original scenario. If commercial banks had been granted the same latitude enjoyed by their competitors, the results might well have been very different; but the plethora of rulings, decisions, and state laws on the subject has served only to create a climate in which savings and loan

---

[122]Nadler, "The Human Side of Electronic Banking," p. 14.
[123]Candilis, *The Future of Commercial Banking,* p. 129.
[124]Pugh and Ingram, "EFT and the Public," p. 45.

associations, credit unions, and nonbanks such as Sears operate at a real advantage.

If the total experience of commercial banks with all forms of private-sector EFTS (excluding the federal government's programs) were analyzed, one basic theme could be developed: the future of EFTS depends not on new technology (for that is already in place), but on concerted efforts by banks and bankers to educate the public regarding the potential benefits of the system. Executive Vice President John Lee of the New York Clearing House Association has called for a two-way communication process, in which the banks will listen to consumer views about what is actually needed and wanted, and in which consumers will listen to bankers' views and explanations. The message must be conveyed that EFTS programs have not been designed purely for the banks' profit purposes.[125]

Consumer acceptance of EFTS can be achieved only through an educational program that dispels the fears and reservations so frequently expressed by so many categories of potential users. A "less-check" rather than a "checkless" society *is* possible, but it cannot be force-fed to a public that does not fully understand it and in many cases sees no good reason for helping it arrive.[126]

[125]"The Automated Clearing House Network," *Banking* (March 1979):84. This article also presents the views of Federal Reserve and industry experts on many EFTS-related topics.
[126]Nadler, in "Banking in Transition," *The Bankers Magazine* (September–October 1978):28.

9 Multinational Banking

During his unsuccessful campaign for the United States presidency in 1940, Wendell Willkie espoused the concept of "One World," and published a book under that title. His basic thinking was that nations were actually interdependent, and that the actions of any major power inevitably affected all the others, regardless of the geographical distances separating them. Willkie's ideas surprised and alienated many Americans, whose attitudes were generally far more parochial and narrow.

In 1940, America's Gross National Product had largely recovered from the Great Depression, and the average individual's standard of living was far better than that of his or her counterparts in foreign countries. Hence the prevailing feeling was that the United States need not become involved with other nations and could very well exist alone, untroubled by the problems of others and indifferent to any marketing opportunities the latter might offer. This feeling was articulated on the floor of Congress by leaders of the isolationist movement, and was implicit in the actions of banking and business leaders who chose to operate outside the United States only on a limited basis.

Willkie's notion of the interdependence of all nations, and his prediction of vastly expanded foreign trade for America, supply a prelude to one of the major changes in our banking history. Traditional barriers and philosophical objections vanished as American banks began to move into every corner of the world where they were legally allowed. Foreign banks subsequently followed the same course of action, and became a steadily more important factor in our overall financial picture. Were he still alive, Willkie might be gratified to see his prophecy realized in the tremendous volume of transactions now processed every day under the generic heading of international banking.

The end of World War II was followed by the gradual rebuilding of the shattered economies of many countries, accompanied by a natural increase in demand for many products by the populations of those countries. Their own manufacturers' facilities had, in many cases, been destroyed during the war; therefore, they turned to America to supply the goods they needed. American corporations, identifying these new markets, intensified their efforts to introduce their products throughout the world. American chemical products were sold to German farmers, American foodstuffs appeared on the shelves of British and French grocery stores, and American cash registers and computers were sold to merchants and industrialists in many countries.

Many of those same American corporations found that they could obtain relatively inexpensive labor and raw materials outside the United States. Others needed imports of essential goods to manufacture their products. Foreign distribution points, factories, and import offices were opened to handle all phases of trade, and the names of America's industrial giants became as well known in Europe and the Far East as in the United States.

While foreign trade has increased tremendously in the years since World War II, its basic nature has changed in that the United States has become a net importer of goods, rather than an exporter. As foreign merchandise flows into the United States in steadily increasing proportions, our deficit in the "Balance of Payments"—that is, the excess of imports over exports—grows. Table 9.1 discloses the figures for the years 1979, 1980, and 1981.

FOREIGN OPERATIONS OF UNITED STATES BANKS

The expansion of American business abroad led many of our commercial banks to perceive the wisdom of acting in the same fashion as their major corporate clients in identifying new market opportunities outside the United States and establishing overseas facilities. In steadily increasing numbers throughout the postwar years, they abandoned their former parochialism and isolationism, and adopted a policy of following their customers into every part of the world where their entry was legally permitted.

Table 9.1.   U.S. Foreign Trade (in Billions of Dollars)

	U.S. Exports	U.S. Imports	Deficit
1979	$181.9	$209.5	($27.6)
1980	220.1	244.9	(24.2)
1981	233.7	261.3	(27.6)

Source: Federal Reserve Bulletin (September 1982):A55.

Wherever a corporation from the "Fortune 500" list was functioning, an American commercial bank sought the approval of the local government to open a branch or otherwise establish a presence.

Before this change took place, American banks had generally conducted all their foreign business through networks of correspondent banks. In 1947, only seven American banks had opened foreign branches.[1] By 1970, sixty-one American banks had foreign offices, with $50 billion in assets, and by 1978, there were 155 such banks, with foreign-office assets of $260 billion.[2] At year-end 1981, 156 Fed member-banks operated 800 overseas branches,[3] and in mid-1982, total assets of foreign branches of United States banks were $458.6 billion.[4]

In the 20 years following the end of World War II, short-term loans by United States banks to foreign borrowers increased almost 900 percent.[5] Since that time, steady increases in all types of global banking account for the fact that the ten largest United States commercial banks derived 50.5, 50.5, 45.5, 42.6, and 46.7 percent of their total earnings from international operations in the five years from 1976 through 1980.[6]

The most important traditional components of the foreign banking business—loans to the private sector, letters of credit, money transfers, collections of drafts and other instruments, foreign exchange, and trust receipt financing—have been supplemented by new services, including

---

[1]Martin Mayer, *The Bankers* (New York: David McKay Co., 1974), p. 437.
[2]Barbara Negris, "Insured Commercial Bank Income in 1978," *Federal Reserve Bulletin* (September 1978):701.
[3]Board of Governors of the Federal Reserve System, *68th Annual Report* (1981):187.
[4]*Federal Reserve Bulletin* (September 1982):A56.
[5]Frederick Heldring, "The International Banking Function of U.S. Commercial Banks," in Herbert V. Prochnow and Herbert V. Prochnow, Jr., Eds., *The Changing World of Banking* (New York: Harper & Row, 1974), p. 347.
[6]Thomas H. Hanley, Jeffrey L. Cohn, and Raymond C. Stewart, *U.S. Multinational Banking* (New York: Salomon Brothers, July 1981), p. 2.

global cash management, and by increasingly large loans made directly to governments. This fact, coupled with the sheer increase in the volume of transactions, accounts for the steady growth in earnings. The annual volume of international bond issues multiplied sixfold from 1973 to 1981, with much of the growth attributed to those countries whose annual deficits resulted largely from the world-wide increase in oil prices.[7]

If there is a single development to which much of the growth in global banking can be attributed in recent years, it is that same causative factor: the quantum leap in revenues for the OPEC nations resulting from the price increases they implemented in 1973 and 1979.[8] This is also testimony to the "One World" concept, for every action taken by the cartel of oil-producing countries is felt throughout the rest of the world.

In addition, Japan, Germany, and many smaller countries depend heavily on foreign trade. The emergence of new nations throughout the postwar period and the expansion of currency trading have combined to create opportunities for banks to provide their services to a far broader range of customers.

American banks today participate in syndicates that extend large foreign credits. They penetrate the Iron Curtain by opening branches in countries that for years were sealed off from the Western world. They establish local facilities to provide installment loans and savings and checking accounts to consumers. Their foreign subsidiaries engage in various types of leasing. They have assumed a leading role as direct lenders to foreign governments. Their networks of "offshore" banking centers provide them with tax and operating-cost advantages, and permit them to function under the prevailing liberal regulations of certain governments.

EUROCURRENCIES

The entire concept of funds management has taken on new dimensions through the Eurodollar and other types of Eurocurrencies. Eurodollars are dollars on deposit in banks outside the United States; they represent the same currency and have the same monetary value as "domestic" dollars. The only essential difference is their geographic location. Similarly,

---

[7]Dwight B. Crane and Samuel L. Hayes III, "The New Competition in World Banking," *Harvard Business Review* (July–August 1982):90.
[8]Ibid.

Eurocurrency deposits are those denominated in a currency other than that of the country in which they are on deposit—hence Eurosterling, Eurofrancs, and so on.

The prefix *Euro-* may be misleading. Although Eurocurrencies are primarily deposited with European banks, they may equally be found in Singapore or Nassau because those locations have become important trading centers. A Eurobond market also exists and is concerned primarily with long-term placements of funds.

There are three general sources of Eurodollar deposits. They originate from the transfer of dollars out of the United States in payment for imports or through capital movements. They also result from purchases of dollars in the foreign exchange market for delivery abroad. In a third instance, they arise from increases in the total monetary base resulting from the creation and redepositing of funds through bank loans. The reasons for the growth of Eurodollars may be understood through an analogy comparing the position of the American dollar in world trade in recent years with that of the bank notes that proliferated in the United States before 1863.

In theory, the bank notes were redeemable in specie if presented to the issuer; similarly, dollars had value in terms of their potential convertibility to gold. In actual practice, of course, an issuing bank never had enough specie to permit conversion of all its notes at one time, and the United States did not have enough gold to redeem all outstanding dollars. The essential element in each case is simply a faith in the soundness of the paper money.

If a major American corporation earns $10 million on European sales and deposits the funds in a London branch of a United States bank, the money becomes loanable by that bank in any part of the world, but is not subject to the reserve requirements that would apply if it were on deposit in New York. This freedom from reserves lowers the bank's costs of funds; hence it can pay higher interest rates to depositors and can lend the funds out at a lower rate. There was a further benefit for the depositor: Eurodollars were not subject to the provisions of Federal Reserve Regulation Q, and so the American prohibition on payments of interest on demand deposits did not apply.[9]

The origins of the Eurodollar market can be traced to the Cold War between the United States and the Soviet Union. As relations between

[9]Peter K. Oppenheim, *International Banking,* 3rd Ed. (Washington: American Bankers Association, 1979), p. 143.

the two powers deteriorated in the 1950s, countries in Eastern Europe feared that their deposits in American banks might be blocked. Branches of European banks in London began accepting these deposits, and offered to maintain them in dollars instead of in the local currency. In the 1960s, when the United States followed the action of Great Britain by forbidding companies to export dollars to build foreign plants, Eurodollars became a source of corporate funds. In 1966, the negotiable certificate of deposit was introduced in London, and during that same year American banks became the largest borrowers of Eurodollars in order to fund their loans. When OPEC announced its price increases in 1973 and 1974, its members deposited a substantial part of their newly-earned dollars in banks outside the United States. The continued American deficit in balance of payments led to devaluation of the dollar in 1971 and again in 1973, suspending the convertibility of the dollar into gold at any price. Therefore, the holders of dollars sought ways of putting them to profitable use in lieu of actual conversion, further fueling the Eurodollar expansion.[10]

The operation of a network of foreign branches obviously permits a bank to serve the needs of its multinational customers anywhere in the world. The Eurodollar is a major component in this flexibility, since it is readily available and provides the mechanism through which OPEC nations recycle their wealth to other countries.

Largely because of the growth of the Eurodollar market, funds management today has become largely dependent on global communications. If the current status of deposits at each foreign branch is known to the head office and all the other branches, funds can readily be moved and one branch can borrow from another, instead of using the open market at a higher rate.

RISK AND RELATED FACTORS

The keystone of international operations at major banks is the financing of foreign trade, chiefly through loans in the private sector and letters of credit or other instruments of foreign trade. The extension of credit to

[10]Mayer, *The Bankers*, p. 451.

foreign correspondent banks is second in importance. The third area involves direct lending to foreign governments; this facet of international banking is creating the greatest concern at the present time.

Global lending must necessarily take into account that dimension of risk which is absent in domestic banking: the economic stability of the country in which loans are being made. The risk factors in making loans to the government of, or a firm in, a particular nation include political and economic conditions demanding careful analysis. Several contemporary and recent situations are relevant to this discussion.

As part of their expression of concern over the social responsibility of banks, stockholders have subjected some of America's largest financial institutions to questions about the desirability and extent of loans made in countries where repeated violations of civil rights are said to have occurred. It is the contention that the banks should play no part in helping companies to function in such countries, and as a gesture of protest, institutional and individual stockholders have sold their shares in some major commercial banks. In rebuttal, the banks have pointed out that their credit facilities are not provided to support the governments in certain countries, and that they have not taken a position in support of the policies of those governments. Rather, they state that they have simply assessed the borrowing customer's creditworthiness, and have approved loans without using local politics as the determining criterion.

A second contemporary topic reflects the banks' concern over possible revolutions in foreign countries where loan and investment exposure exists. There is substantial historical evidence of losses incurred by banks as a direct result of changes in government. A new regime in a country may arbitrarily decide to nationalize the banks and industries, and to repudiate all outstanding government obligations. This was the pattern followed by Castro in Cuba; all loans incurred by the previous government were cancelled, and all American banking offices were expropriated.[11] In 1979, a change in the government of Iran resulted in the blocking of all assets of non-Iranian banks in that country.[12] American banks must take this fundamental political risk into consideration whenever they lend abroad.

The third area of concern is both the most recent and the most potentially serious regarding the global economy. During the joint annual meetings of the World Bank and the International Monetary Fund in September

---

[11]Heldring, ''The International Banking Function of U.S. Commercial Banks,'' p. 351.
[12]''The Banks Squabble Over Iran's Assets,'' *Business Week* (December 3, 1979):110.

1982, figures came to light showing that as many as 35 countries, from Argentina to Zaire, were facing extreme financial difficulties, and that the hundreds of billions of dollars in loans they had received were in real danger of becoming uncollectible.[13] For example, the total public and private debt of Mexico was listed at $80 billion, of which $25 billion was owed to American banks. When there were indications in August 1982 that Mexico was on the verge of default, a consortium of American and foreign banks provided emergency financing of $1.85 billion to the government. Of that amount, $925 million came from the United States Treasury Department and the Federal Reserve.[14] A group of banks with large loans in Mexico agreed to freeze all scheduled repayment of principal, but could not solve the problem of scheduled interest payments on those loans.[15] In 1982, the total external debt of Argentina was estimated at $38 billion, while that of Poland was believed to be $27 billion.[16] In terms that have not been heard since the Great Depression, bankers have spoken frankly of the possibility of a global credit collapse. "Rescheduling" has become the widely used stopgap measure to avert such a collapse.

There has been extensive criticism of American banks for their apparent combination of optimism and naivete in extending credit to the so-called less-developed countries (LDCs), despite many adverse indicators.[17] In 1979, the total external debts of LDCs exceeded $205 billion, according to the Organization for Economic Cooperation and Development, and were escalating at an annual rate of 15 percent.[18] During that same year, Henry Reuss, then Chairman of the House Banking Committee, publicly criticized the banks for continuing to lend to LDCs.[19] Zaire was then cited as a prototype, since its debt was $3.5 billion and its economy was evidently deteriorating; yet by 1982, the external obligations of that nation had reached $5.5 billion.[20] As news of the problems of Zaire and many other countries surfaced during 1982, there was a general increase in the cautiousness of American banks in extending further credits to and in foreign countries. At the same time, however, it was evident that very substantial

[13]Harry Anderson, "Running Short of Cash," *Newsweek* (December 20, 1982):66.
[14]*Federal Reserve Bulletin* (September 1982):538.
[15]George Russell, "We Are in an Emergency," *Time* (December 20, 1982):31–34.
[16]Harry Anderson, "A Crisis of Confidence," *Newsweek* (September 20, 1982):57.
[17]Benjamin Weiner, "The Banks Should Have Known Better," *The New York Times* (December 19, 1982):3–2.
[18]"Default Threatens Those LDC Loans Again," *Business Week* (July 2, 1979):79.
[19]"A Threat to Global Growth," *Time* (July 2, 1979):54–55.
[20]Anderson, "A Crisis of Confidence," p. 57.

annual funding would be needed for the World Bank and the International Monetary Fund, and the United States would logically be expected to make its contribution to that funding, in the hope of averting actual defaults.[21]

Analysis of Country Risk

Although the domestic operations of United States banks are, almost without exception, subject to control by one or more federal agencies, the same does not hold true in their foreign operations. For example, a bank is limited in the unsecured amount it can lend to any one borrower in the United States, but no such limit exists on the amount it can lend in the public and private sectors of a foreign country. Even for loans to foreign governments, more than one agency may borrow, thus creating a total debt far beyond the amount that a major American corporation could borrow from one bank.

Some years ago, the Federal Reserve suggested a more thorough and systematic approach to supervising international banking, and the office of the Comptroller of the Currency introduced a risk report that identified concentrations of lending in particular countries.[22]

To minimize risk in the foreign loan portfolio, various types of specialized analysis may be used. They include detailed approaches to the international, sociocultural, political, and economic factors that exist in a country, and can be used to develop a rating scale that classifies risk.[23] They can also be refined to offer guidelines for both short- and long-term lending, interest rates, and the limits that seem appropriate for both private- and public-sector loans.[24]

In developing a profile for a particular country, the following are among the key factors to evaluate:

1. Measures of Political Stability. The national governing structure, the main political/ethnic/tribal religious blocs of governmental support, the

[21]Muriel Siebert, "Despite Strains, the System Works," *The New York Times* (December 19, 1982):3–2.

[22]"A New Supervisory Approach to Foreign Lending," Federal Reserve Bank of New York, *Quarterly Review* (Spring 1978):1–6.

[23]Tracy G. Herrick, *Bank Analyst's Handbook* (New York: Wiley, 1978), pp. 242–243.

[24]Christopher M. Korth, "Developing a Country-Risk Analysis System," *The Journal of Commercial Bank Lending* (December 1979):56–57.

number and strength of anti-governmental groups, the issues raised by those groups in opposition to the government, and the "swing groups" who can determine the outcome.

2. National Issues, Goals, and Instruments.   The socioeconomic issues of a domestic, foreign, or structural (i.e., urban-rural balance, distribution of income, development of infrastructure) nature; the goals of the government as stated in national plans; and the measures and programs initiated to implement those goals.

3. Country Vulnerabilities and Strengths.   The characteristics of the country that will aid or inhibit achievement of national goals, and the internal and external strong points and areas of weakness.

FOREIGN EXCHANGE OPERATIONS

A Senior Vice President of the New York Fed has described foreign exchange trading as "probably one of the most widely discussed and yet least understood subjects of our times."[25] His reference is to an area where billions of dollars change hands each day, and in which banks and customers function under intense pressures and assume high risks. Heightened tensions among nations, changes in government leaders, rumors, political sensitivities, and economic predictions affect each day's operations. Still fresh in the minds of many bankers is 1974, a year in which the Franklin National Bank and Bankhaus Herstatt collapsed, and Union Bank (Switzerland) and Lloyds Bank (England) admitted losses of tens of millions of dollars—all caused entirely or in part by foreign exchange trades.[26] Yet the possibility of substantial profits is as ever-present as the risk factor.

As of January 1982, the Federal Reserve had reciprocal currency arrangements totaling $30 billion with the central banks of 14 countries and the Bank for International Settlements.[27] In Europe during 1981, members .

---

[25]Scott E. Pardee, "How Well Are the Exchange Markets Functioning?" Federal Reserve Bank of New York, *Quarterly Review* (Spring 1979):49.
[26]Mayer, *The Bankers*, pp. 476–477.
[27]*Federal Reserve Bulletin* (March 1982):143.

of the European Monetary System sought to keep their currencies within agreed limits, but official intervention was needed to maintain the arrangement whenever strong pressures existed on those limits. Foreign central banks also intervened in large amounts to moderate movements against the dollar.[28] However, commercial banks cannot depend on intervention by their own or a foreign government to insure the profitability of their foreign exchange trading. Prudence and maximum use of forecasting techniques and other data are indispensable in this field, and the onus remains on the banks to protect themselves as completely as possible.

EDGE ACT FACILITIES

In 1919, Congress passed the Edge Act as an amendment to the Federal Reserve Act, and the provisions of the former in time were incorporated into the latter under Regulation K. However, it was only in the years following World War II that American banks began to take full advantage of the Act, and since that time it has enabled them to broaden the scope of their international operations in many ways.

The Edge Act allows commercial banks to cross state lines to open specialized offices that are not permitted to handle any purely domestic business. These offices can assist customers with all types of foreign business. Because so much of our foreign trade originates in such cities as San Francisco, Miami, Houston, and Chicago, these have become the favored locations for Edge Act offices. The Act also allows banks to form subsidiaries that can acquire minority or controlling interests in foreign banks, and to establish overseas operations for investment and mortgage banking, leasing, factoring, and consumer financing.

A most important addition to the Edge Act facilities of American banks, and to their activities in the Eurodollar market, took place in December 1981, when the Federal Reserve permitted the establishment of the first international banking facilities (IBFs). The purpose was to allow these new facilities to conduct a deposit and loan business with foreign residents, including foreign banks, without being subject to reserve requirements or

[28]Federal Reserve Bank of New York, *Annual Report* (1981), p. 23.

interest-rate ceilings.[29] IBFs were not allowed to accept deposits from or lend to American companies, nor were they permitted to issue negotiable CDs. IBFs are, in effect, "free banking zones," through which transactions with foreign residents can be handled in a regulatory environment broadly similar to that of the Eurodollar market—most recently estimated at $900 billion, net of interbank deposits.[30] By September 1982, almost 400 banking institutions had established IBFs with total assets exceeding $150 billion, of which those in New York accounted for over 75%.[31]

THE FOREIGN BANKS

There is a striking and exact corollary between the pattern of international growth in American industry and banking, and that which has been displayed by foreign businesses and banks. As noted earlier, many of America's major corporations recognized the potential of the overseas markets in the years after World War II, and the products of IBM, General Foods, Procter and Gamble, Eastman Kodak, and National Cash Register were made available throughout the free world. As these corporations became global in their operations, American banks emulated them and established strong presences abroad. While preserving their traditional correspondent relationships with foreign banks, they also embarked on a program of overseas branch expansion. New service areas were also devised and implemented to serve the needs of global customers.

Mirroring these developments, an identical evolutionary sequence took place in the opposite direction. Corporations from many foreign countries came first, as exports became vitally necessary to the economic recovery of countries that had experienced the ravages of World War II. America came to represent one of the most fertile markets for foreign merchandise, and in steadily growing proportions, the United States balance-of-payments deficit grew as the nation became a net importer rather than an exporter of goods. Japan, West Germany, Italy, France, and other nations supplied the electronic goods, steel, apparel, and automobiles that American con-

[29]Sydney J. Key, "International Banking Facilities," *Federal Reserve Bulletin* (October 1982):566.
[30]Robert A. Bennett, "America's Debut in Offshore Banking," *The New York Times* (November 22, 1981):3-1.
[31]Key, "International Banking Facilities."

sumers wanted. The low costs of labor and raw materials outside the United States enabled foreign goods to be sold at prices below those charged by domestic manufacturers. The OPEC cartel only exacerbated an already difficult situation.

The growth of foreign trade in the United States was followed by an influx of foreign banks. Just as the American banks had increased their penetration of overseas markets after major industrial firms had taken the lead, so their counterpart banks from other countries expanded their own global operations and became steadily more important in the American economic picture. They accomplished this not only through a concerted effort to deal effectively with their own corporate customers in the United States, but also by capitalizing on several significant competitive advantages.

Those advantages included an ability to cross state lines with a variety of deposit-taking entities when American banks were legally prohibited from doing so; an ability to acquire American banks, often in situations where potential United States acquirers would have no such opportunity because of anti-trust statutes; a freedom from the reserve requirements and deposit-insurance requirements, to which American banks are subject; and the ability to diversify into areas (e.g., securities activities) from which American banks are barred.[32]

Interviews with officials of foreign banks have disclosed their motives for entering the American marketplace, aside from the above-mentioned advantages. The banks, in addition to following their own customers to the United States, were also frequently motivated by a desire to diversify as an offset to the limited growth prospects in their home countries and the need for access to dollar funding.[33]

The growth of foreign banks in the United States has been explosive. From 1972 through 1980, their total assets grew from $24 billion to $172 billion.[34] In 1972, 60 foreign banks operated 111 United States offices of one type or another, whereas by year-end 1979, the figures were 315 and 702, respectively.[35] During a single year (1978), 90 foreign banks opened

[32]Paul Horvitz, Peter Merrill, and Bernard Shull, "Foreign Bankers Cite Reasons for Move to United States," *American Banker* (March 20, 1981):12.
[33]J. Randall Woolridge and Klaus D. Wiegel, "Foreign Banking Growth in the United States," *The Bankers Magazine* (January–February 1981):31.
[34]"Which Have the Edge: U.S. Banks Abroad or Foreign Banks Here?" *ABA Banking Journal* (August 1981):80.
[35]"Banking in the United States: a Guide for Foreign Bankers," (New York: Peat, Marwick, Mitchell & Co., 1980), p. i.

Table 9.2

State	Branches	Agencies	R.O.[a]	Sub[b]	Total
New York	75	60	135	26	296
California	1	76	21	18	116
Illinois	31	0	21	2	54
Texas	0	0	30	0	30
All Others	23	25	8	0	56
Totals	130	161	215	46	552

Source: U.S. Comptroller of the Currency, in Franz J. Lutolf, "Foreign Bank Expansion in the U.S.," *American Banker* (July 29, 1981):43.
[a]Representative Offices
[b]Subsidiaries

one or more offices in the United States; twenty-four of these established a presence here for the first time.[36]

Foreign banks operate in the United States in any of four different ways. They may establish full-scale, separately chartered subsidiaries to conduct a general banking business, or they may open representative offices, agencies, or branches. There are important legal differences among these. Representative offices cannot accept deposits, extend loans, or perform other banking functions; they serve merely as liaison points between their institutions' head offices and the customers in a specific geographic area. Agencies and branches may conduct full-scale lending operations, but agencies cannot accept deposits. Branches may issue domestic certificates of deposit; agencies cannot do so. Table 9.2 shows the breakdown among these types of foreign bank facilities as of July 1981.

The competitive advantage that has made much of the foreign banks' growth possible lies in their ability to open branches and agencies in more than one state "with relative ease."[37] This privilege has been denied to domestic banks since the McFadden Act was passed in 1927. The freedom enjoyed by the foreign banks in this respect, coupled with the fact that their facilities were supervised only by the licensing state and were not subject to reserve requirements, created a problem that the Congress con-

[36]Anthony F. Mattera, "90 Foreign Banks Established U. S. Offices in 1978," *American Banker* (March 23, 1979):2.
[37]Sydney J. Key and James M. Brundy, "Implementation of the International Banking Act," *Federal Reserve Bulletin* (October 1979):787.

sidered for many years before the International Banking Act was passed in 1978. For example, Barclays Bank in 1982 had branch or representative offices in fourteen American cities, subsidiaries in New York and California, and a finance company with 364 offices operating in thirty-five states.[38]

Foreign banks have been increasingly successful in securing a large share of the commercial and industrial loan market in the United States. In 1981, their credits under this heading amounted to some 15 percent of the total market.[39]

The extent to which foreign banks have succeeded in penetrating the American market in many ways, other than through extending loans, reflects the innate ties they have to the corporations with which they have close relationships at home. Just as a major United States firm operating in Venezuela is likely to do business with the Caracas branch of the American bank to which it is most closely tied, a Japanese bank in San Francisco enjoys a natural marketing advantage in soliciting business from the subsidiary of a corporation headquartered in Tokyo. In dealing with domestic firms, foreign banks have also stressed the fact that they can exert influence in their home countries, and thus assist in the overseas expansion plans of those companies.[40]

THE INTERNATIONAL BANKING ACT

In growing numbers and with increased vehemence, American bankers protested the very significant competitive advantages enjoyed by foreign banks in the United States. The International Banking Act (IBA) to some extent reflects those protests; but the point must be stressed that there was no attempt to exclude foreign banks, curtail their right to function, or place them at a competitive disadvantage. Rather, the IBA has been described by Key and Brundy[41] as "part of a general policy of national

---

[38]Crane and Hayes, "The New Competition in World Banking," p. 91.
[39]Franz J. Lutolf, "Foreign Bank Expansion in the U.S., *American Banker* (July 29, 1981): 43.
[40]"Foreign Banking in America," *Institutional Investor* (September 1977):103.
[41]"Implementation of the International Banking Act," p. 787.

treatment in order to promote competitive equality between domestic and foreign banking institutions in the United States.''

As in the case of EFT services, banks found themselves unable to do what their competitors could do, because of the geographic and statutory limitations of our laws. The policy of ''national treatment'' attempts to give foreign institutions the same powers, and subject them to the same obligations, as their domestic counterparts in host countries.

A bank headquartered in Hong Kong, London, or Amsterdam can cross state lines and/or acquire a major American bank; domestic commercial banks can do neither. By 1978, there were twenty-seven foreign banks operating in the United States with branches, agencies, or subsidiaries in more than one state. In some cases, individual states extended privileges to foreign banks that they denied to domestic institutions; for example, Illinois and Florida historically enforced unit banking laws and did not allow American banks to open branches, yet they permitted foreign banks to do so.

The IBA (and its amendments, enacted in 1980) establishes certain restrictions on the interstate operation of branches, agencies, subsidiaries, and commercial-lending companies associated with foreign banks. Each foreign bank was required to designate a ''home state'' in the United States, and its deposit-taking activities are limited to that state. However, foreign banks that were operating as of July 27, 1978 were ''grandfathered,'' and thus were allowed to continue interstate banking.[42] It allowed a foreign bank to establish a federal branch or agency with the approval of the Comptroller of the Currency, thereby placing that bank on the same basis as a domestic national bank. If the foreign bank has consolidated worldwide assets of $1 billion or more, the Act authorizes the Fed to impose reserve requirements on it. United States offices of foreign banks accepting retail deposits of less than $100,000 must join FDIC, and foreign banks were allowed to establish their own Edge Act offices.[43]

The year 1979 was marked by announcements of large-scale acquisitions of American banks by foreign institutions. One member of the New York Clearing House, National Bank of North America, was purchased by the second largest bank in the United Kingdom, the National Westminster. America's twenty-fifth largest bank, Union Bank (Los Angeles), was

[42]Federal Reserve Bank of New York, ''Interstate Banking Activities of Foreign Banks,'' Circular 8930 (October 9, 1980).
[43]For a full discussion of the provisions of the IBA, see ''Banking in the United States: A Guide for Foreign Bankers,'' 89–98.

bought by Standard Chartered Bank of London, and La Salle National Bank (Chicago) was acquired by Algemene Bank Nederland, a $25 billion institution located in Amsterdam. In the largest of all the acquisitions, Hong Kong and Shanghai Banking Corporation, with total assets of $18.9 billion, bought Marine Midland Bank, N.A. (New York), which at that time ranked twelfth among all American commercial banks, with assets of $14.3 billion.

The decision of Bankers Trust Company to sell many of its branches, as cited earlier, indicated that the Bank of Montreal would be the purchaser. When that transaction did not materialize as planned, three other foreign banks—Bank Leumi Trust Company, National Bank of North America (now owned by National Westminster), and Barclays Bank of New York[44]—bought fifty-five of the branches.[45]

Acquisitions by foreign banks during 1981 were even larger in their individual scope. Midland Bank (England), with total deposits of $55 billion, acquired a majority interest in Crocker National Corporation, whose major subsidiary was the Crocker National Bank, with assets of $19 billion. A group of investors representing Saudi Arabia, the United Arab Emirates, and Kuwait acquired Financial General Bankshares, a multistate bank holding company, with 12 banks located in New York, Maryland, Tennessee, Virginia, and the District of Columbia. Banca Commerciale Italiana acquired LITCO Bancorporation, a bank holding company owning all the shares of the $1.1 billion Long Island Trust Company (New York).[46]

These acquisitions highlight the fact that foreign banks have frequently been allowed to do what domestic banks were barred from doing. If a major American bank had attempted an acquisition of similar magnitude within its own state, a conflict with anti-trust laws would have immediately been identified, and the Department of Justice would undoubtedly have made every effort to prevent it. If, instead, the proposed acquisition involved a bank holding company in another state, the Bank Holding Company Act would be invoked to forestall it.

The issue of reciprocity cannot be ignored in this discussion of foreign

[44]Barclays Bank of New York (with thirty-two branch offices in the New York area) and Barclays Bank of California (with forty-seven offices) are subsidiaries of Barclays Bank International.

[45]Robert A Bennett, "Bankers Trust Sells 55 Branches," *The New York Times* (June 30, 1979):D1.

[46]Details of these three acquisitions may be found in the Statement to Congress of Henry C. Wallich in the *Federal Reserve Bulletin* (October 1982):621-624.

bank operations in the United States. American bankers have not directly sought to exclude foreign banks, to prevent them from doing business in the United States, or to block the abovementioned acquisitions—possibly because any such action would carry with it the possibility of retaliation by a foreign country. The banker who expresses resentment over the acquisition of an American bank by a British buyer must, at the same time, recognize the liberality that has been shown by British banking authorities in allowing American bank branches to proliferate in the United Kingdom. The same principle applies to other nations. Parity is the key issue. In his Statement to Congress, Henry Wallich, Member of the Federal Reserve Board of Governors, summarized the principle that foreign banks and their owners are to be treated on the same basis as their domestic counterparts,[47] and it is to be hoped that the same principle will be applied in the banking legislation seen in those countries which have allowed branching by American institutions.

[47]*Federal Reserve Bulletin* (October 1982):623.

10 Specialized Service Areas

Under the concept of "Full Service" banking, many commercial banks in the United States have expanded their horizons and, often with the help of computer technology, have moved into specialized areas of customized arrangements that defy classification under other headings. Two of these warrant special attention. One is traditional, the other relatively new. The *trust services* field dates back to the early days of American banking. The family of *cash management* services began to develop in the 1950s, and has shown impressive and steady growth. Both figure prominently in the profit planning of many of our major banks.

TRUST SERVICES

The fact that so many of the nation's oldest and largest financial institutions include the word *trust* as part of their legal names offers a clue to the history of fiduciary services in America. Many trust companies were organized in the early nineteenth century, often in connection with insurance companies, and operated under state charters to provide various investment services. The equities of those who turned their assets over to these trust companies resembled shares in an investment fund. However, by 1850, trust companies in many cases had assumed a different role, and were accepting demand and time deposits and making short-term loans.

This led to resentment among commercial bankers, who found, then as now, that their competition was coming from entities that were not subject to the same constraints as their own institutions. The trust companies also enjoyed tax advantages at that time, and were able to offer higher interest rates on deposits.[1]

To counter this competition, many state-chartered banks sought and obtained trust powers. At the same time, the word *trust* frequently took on pejorative connotations, referring to the corporate "pools" or cartels formed to control the production and distribution of petroleum, iron, steel, and other goods and services. The Standard Oil Company trust (1879) served as a prototype. Monopolistic practices engaged in by some of these trusts led to federal laws (the Clayton and Sherman Antitrust Acts) aimed against them.

State-chartered banks found it desirable and profitable to combine trust and commercial banking functions. This synthesis, a forerunner of the "Full Service" approach, led to Section 11(K) of the Federal Reserve Act of 1913, which allowed national banks to apply for permission to offer trust services. At the same time, the Act specified that such banks would also be subject to the laws of the individual states applying to the trust field.[2]

Since that time, the fiduciary functions of commercial banks have increased tremendously in scope and importance. Over 4,050 banks now offer personal trust or corporate trust services, or a combination of both.[3] They act both as agents and as trustees. In the former capacity, they perform services under a contractual agreement, while legal title to property remains with a principal; as trustees, they actually take title to the property in question. They act as administrators and executors in settling estates; provide safekeeping, custody, managing agent, and escrow services; act as registrars, transfer agents, paying and dividend disbursing agents, and as trustees under indentures; manage employee benefit (pension and profit-sharing) trusts; and provide personal financial counseling and estate planning. In all these trust services, banks stress the inherent advantages they possess. For example, a commercial bank is characterized

---

[1]Margaret G. Myers, *A Financial History of the United States* (New York: Columbia University Press, 1970), p. 249.

[2]American Bankers Association, *The Commercial Banking Industry* (Englewood Cliffs, N.J.: Prentice-Hall, 1962), pp. 297–298.

[3]Ronald L. Blevins, John M. Clarke, James J. Mitchell III, Jack W. Zalaha, and August Zinsser III, *The Trust Business* (Washington, American Bankers Association, 1982), p. 10.

by ongoing existence, capital strength, constant accessibility, and impartiality. The customer of a major bank's trust department gains the benefit of group judgment and a high degree of specialization in such areas as income tax structure, business valuation, and management of real property.[4]

As a group, commercial banks have become the nation's most important fiduciary entities. Table 10.1 shows the 1981 performance of the ten largest banks in the trust field; these banks alone handle trust assets with a market value of over $722 billion, and their trust activities generated income for 1981 of over $874 million.

The banks' preeminent position has been achieved despite numerous and aggressive competition, again coming in many cases from organizations that are not subject to equivalent restrictions. The various trust operations of commercial banks are constrained in many ways. For example, before they can begin offering trust services, they usually must obtain specific state and/or federal approval and meet capital requirements. Federal Reserve Regulation F applies to trust policies and performance at member

[4]Edward W. Reed, Richard V. Cotter, Edward K. Gill, and Richard K. Smith, *Commercial Banking* (Englewood Cliffs, N.J.: Prentice-Hall, 1976), p. 352.

Table 10.1. 1981 Trust Data

Rank in Trust Income	Bank Name	Trust Income[a]	Trust Assets[b]
1	Morgan Guaranty Trust (New York)	$ 164	$ 35.2
2	Citibank, N.A. (New York)	126	33.6
3	Bank of New York	94	101.1
4	Chase Manhattan (New York)	89	181.7
5	Bankers Trust Co. (New York)	75	50.5
6	Manufacturers Hanover Trust (New York)	73	119.2
7	Bankamerica Corp. (San Francisco)	68	36.6
8	Chemical New York	65	109.4
9	United States Trust Company (New York)	61	21.9
10	Northern Trust (Chicago)	58	32.9

Source: American Banker (June 30, 1982):24.

[a]Trust income is in *millions* of dollars.
[b]Trust assets are in *billions* of dollars.

banks. Each bank's trust department is subject to separate federal and/ or state examination, as well as separate internal audits under the supervision of a Directors' Trust Committee. Any bank wishing to engage in trust operations must segregate and pledge specific securities of unquestioned quality, as a means of guaranteeing that the trust assets under its control are protected.[5]

Regulations of the Internal Revenue Service, Securities and Exchange Commission, and Federal Reserve (in the case of all bank holding companies) apply to various aspects of trust services at commercial banks. The insurance companies, law firms, brokerage houses, and investment management and estate planning firms that compete with banks in the trust field do not have to contend with all these restrictions.

Additional competition for commercial banks has resulted from the provision of the Depository Institutions Deregulation and Monetary Control Act of 1980, which conferred trust powers on savings banks and savings and loan associations. The S&Ls, in particular, have been quick to take advantage of this new statute. A Senior Vice President of one prominent S&L sees trust services as the means of enhancing his institution's effort to reshape itself into a general financial-services organization, since they will tie customers to it more closely, and reduce the possibility of their moving to competing entities.[6]

Employee Benefit and Individual Services

Just as governments and corporations have developed strategies to prosper in a period of economic uncertainty, affluent individuals have reviewed their financial goals and tax situations, and have evaluated alternatives to help them achieve their objectives. Professional asset management for these individuals has become a vital service of bank trust departments. It includes a detailed analysis of each person's financial picture, and results in specific recommendations that may include tax-shelter and estate-planning provisions. Two major examples are found in the "sweep" account and the range of individual retirement accounts.

A "sweep" product enables a bank to give its customers an opportunity

[5]American Bankers Association, *The Commercial Banking Industry*, p. 299.
[6]Kenneth A. Southworth, in "What Savings and Loans Are Doing in Trust," *United States Banker* (March 1982):50.

to buy high-yielding money market instruments as an adjunct to their demand deposit relationships. Many bank trust departments now offer this type of vehicle, originally introduced by banks in 1974.[7] Computer technology is used to monitor the daily balance in a customer's NOW or checking account; any excess above a predetermined figure is invested in mutual fund shares. If the account balance falls below the defined figure, shares are redeemed and the proceeds used to replenish it. The "sweep" product may lose some of its attractiveness through the widespread adoption of money market accounts by banks, authorized by the Garn-St. Germain Act of 1982.

A second major area of trust services for individuals came into being through the Keogh Act and subsequent amendments, enabling self-employed persons and workers who were not covered by qualified pension plans to set aside money each year toward retirement. When Congress extended the original legislation so that individuals could establish IRAs (Individual Retirement Accounts) even if they already had pension-plan coverage, the market expanded tremendously. Again, competition for Keogh and IRA relationships is intense among both thrift institutions and nonbanks.

Employee Benefit Accounts

The twentieth century has witnessed many significant developments in the general area of pension and profit-sharing plans, as social pressures have led increasing numbers of employers to establish trusts for the benefit of their workers. Assets underlying private pension plans are now approximately $600 billion, and are increasing at an annual rate of 12 to 15 percent.[8] The Economic Recovery Tax Act of 1981, and amendments to the original ERISA (Employee Retirement Income Security Act) legislation favor increases in employee benefits, and both workers and their unions, driven in many cases by uncertainty regarding Social Security, have sought still greater protection for retirement. Commercial banks are a major force

---

[7]John W. McGonigle, "Banks Have Legal Guidelines for Offering Sweep Accounts," *American Banker* (May 3, 1982):4.
[8]Nancy Buckwalter, "Employee Benefits—Where the Trust Industry Is Growing," *United States Banker* (June 1982):42.

in the accumulating, investing, disbursing, and accounting control of both pension and profit-sharing trusts.

Trust Marketing

It is ironic that the history of banks in the trust field indicates that they have become the largest fiduciary group without having given serious attention to strategic planning, cost accounting, or marketing. A senior officer at one major bank cites this history: "There was always a feeling that it was inappropriate to market trust services. Trust departments were generally set up to handle the affairs of wealthy people, and they did things for free."[9]

Today, the fundamentals of marketing and planning are stressed as banks seek to make their trust units both competitive and profitable. Detailed market research is the first step in the process.[10] It enables a bank to assess its position relative to competitors, and to evaluate them quantitatively and qualitatively. Demographic studies can be performed or obtained to show age groups and personal-income concentrations in a community. Publicly held corporations must announce each pension and profit-sharing plan they implement; this publicity can help shape the bank's marketing effort. The number of estate tax returns filed in a community each year is a matter of public record, and provides an indication of the potential market for such services as investment management, financial counseling, and estate planning.

Trust marketing may be conditioned by pricing factors. State laws establish the maximum fees that banks can charge for certain trust services. The cost of the personnel and other resources needed to perform the services may disclose that the potential income does not justify the effort; trust departments inherently require tax, legal, investment, and analytical specialists, who create higher per capita salary expenses.

In addition, trust operations are both labor- and paper-intensive because of the detailed record-keeping that must be performed, and the volume

[9]William E. Semmes, in "Chemical Applies Marketing Methods to Modernize Its Trust Department," *American Banker* (August 12, 1982):12.
[10]A comprehensive study of suggested procedures may be found in Phillip D. White, "The Role of Marketing Research in the Personal Trust Business," *Trusts & Estates* (November 1982):10–15.

of securities buy-and-sell orders, dividend checks, coupons, and tax returns that must be processed. In some cases, banks have addressed this problem by "farming out" the actual data processing work to outside firms, while preserving their own direct liaison with clients.

Comprehensive management information systems are also critical in fiduciary operations. The market value and composition of each individual portfolio must be known at all times, as well as the amount of each individual security held by the bank. *Pro forma* computer printouts may be used to show the effects of alternate decisions in investment management. A bank's relative performance in managing equities held in pension and profit-sharing plans must be measured against the results achieved by competitors, and against such yardsticks as the Dow-Jones Index.

In addition to the growth of employee benefit trusts and various types of retirement accounts, there are many encouraging factors suggesting that trust services, if properly marketed, monitored, and priced, can make significant profit contributions to a bank. According to the study conducted in 1972 by Louis Harris, 3 percent of the 3,168 respondents were already using one or more trust services at commercial banks. The same survey cited higher levels of income and sophistication among consumers as indicators of further potential growth in the trust field for banks.[11] Because of the burden of federal, state, and local taxation, increasing numbers of individuals have become interested in tax shelters, investment management, and estate planning. A study performed by the United States Trust Company in 1979 disclosed that over 500,000 Americans had a net worth of at least $1 million; such individuals become automatic candidates for personal trust services.[12] As the dividend-disbursing, employee-benefit, and investment activities of corporations grow, they can also use the facilities of bank trust departments.[13]

However, consideration must also be given to some recent negative indicators. A study conducted in 1982 for the Massachusetts Bankers Association found that the same consumer sophistication identified by Louis Harris in 1972 now makes the affluent individual more critical of banks. Among the 1,456 interviewees in this statewide study, an astonishingly high 58 percent said that trust relationships with banks were either "a

[11]*The Second Study: The American Public's and Community Opinion Leaders' Views of Banks and Bankers* (Philadelphia, The Foundation for Full Service Banks, 1972):77.
[12]"The Affluent Society," *Time* (July 9, 1979):54.
[13]Terrence F. Martell and Robert L. Fitts, "Potential Customers of Bank Trust Departments," *The Bankers Magazine* (May–June 1979):74.

poor way'' or ''one of the worst ways'' to make one's money grow, and the consensus among respondents with annual incomes over $50,000 was that banks ''cannot manage money as well as some other institutions.''[14] Clearly, consumers are shopping for increases in the perceived value of their financial relationships, and bank marketing, particularly in the trust area, must focus on an educational effort to offset the strong competition. The capability of commercial banks to provide every type of personal, corporate, and institutional trust services already exists. What is needed is an integrated, well-planned approach to trust marketing that will define products clearly, identify the markets to which they should be sold, and highlight the specific advantages and benefits to the users.

CASH MANAGEMENT SERVICES

As noted earlier in this text, one of the most fundamental changes in American commercial banking can be attributed largely to the new thinking of corporate financial officers and affluent individuals who control demand deposit balances. They no longer leave large excess balances in non-interest-bearing accounts. Checking account balances are used to offset the costs of services provided; to the maximum extent, surplus funds are put to work to generate income. A wide range of investment opportunities exists today, and the holder of $1 million can earn hundreds of dollars by investing that sum for one twenty-four hour period. Therefore, there is an increasing willingness to listen to any suggestions a bank can make for expediting and monitoring the inflow and outflow of funds. The generic term for the services provided in this area is *cash management*. The term may be subdivided under three headings: deposit services, disbursement services, and information services.

One of the basic premises in the total concept of cash management is that an issued check is nothing more than a piece of paper until its payee can convert it into usable funds. Several days may be required for a check to complete its life-cycle; it may be delayed in the postal system, the

---

[14]Peter Merrill, ''Strategic Implications of Consumer Demand,'' *American Banker* (December 29, 1982):5.

payee may be slow in depositing it, and the bank of deposit may not be able to route it promptly to its drawee so that settlement will occur. The American banking system is characterized by huge amounts of *float*, representing deposited checks that are in the process of collection. The recipient of a check is anxious to reduce float, as are the banks of deposit; at the same time, the issuer wants to use float to his or her advantage, so that the reduction of balances is delayed and funds can be invested.

Over 30 years ago, major commercial banks began offering a service known as *lock box* to their large corporate customers in order to reduce the time needed for mail, deposit, and collection processing. Under lock box service, a bank acts as an agent for its customer. It operates a post office box to which the customer's incoming payments are directed, picks up all mail from that box, examines all checks for negotiability, prepares the daily deposit, and forwards the checks to drawees by whatever means will provide quick availability. The customer receives daily input regarding all deposited checks, in whatever form is required for posting to accounts receivable ledgers.

Those customers whose remitters are dispersed throughout the country frequently establish several strategically located lock boxes, so that incoming mail time is kept to a minimum. A typical pattern might include San Francisco, Dallas, Chicago, Atlanta, and New York.

In discussing their techniques for reducing float, lock box banks stress the fact that their messengers can pick up mail at the Post Office around-the-clock; for example, First National Bank of Atlanta states that it makes forty-eight such collections each day.[15] The service also operates on weekends and many holidays.

In its early stages, lock box was felt to apply only to those large corporations that receive relatively few checks each month, but whose incoming payments are for large dollar amounts. The benefits to these firms, through reduced float and increased availability, were the selling points. However, new technology has made it possible to revise the original approach. Lock box service is used today not only by major corporations, but by utilities, insurers, and thrift institutions—all of whom receive large volumes of small-dollar payments. Those payments can now be quickly and efficiently processed in equipment that reads the optically scannable

---

[15]Robert M. Garsson, "Banks Speeding Up Collections of Cash Receipts by Timing Postal Delivery," *American Banker* (December 29, 1982):2.

data on checks and documents, and generates magnetic tape output. That tape can be transmitted directly to the user's computer to update receivables and generate reports of overdue payments. This form of daily reporting is also widely accepted by large corporations, in lieu of the photocopies of deposited checks that were formerly supplied. A study conducted in 1980, by Greenwich Research Associates among 660 decision-makers at "Fortune 1,000" companies, disclosed that almost two-thirds were receiving daily input directly through computers.[16]

In addition to reducing daily float, and thereby increasing the user's availability of funds, lock box service also generates substantial savings for that user by decreasing the clerical work needed to receive, examine, and deposit incoming checks. In the case of those prospects whose receipts are large in volume but small in amount, this can be the selling point to be stressed.

In the area of deposit services, *automated depository transfer checks* exemplify another cash management technique responding to specific customer needs. They are no-signature, preprinted instruments, prepared by institutions called concentration banks. They may be used by customers who receive payments at regional lock box points, or by any other entity whose incoming flow of funds is generated at many locations. The concentration bank receives daily input regarding each deposit made in the user's network of bank accounts, and prepares a check on each bank for the deposited amount. A single deposit is made every day to move the deposited funds from each location into a single account, giving the customer prompt availability at a per-item cost significantly less than a system of wire transfers would create. The bank designated as the concentration bank occupies a preferred position among the user's depositories, since its work is relatively minimal and it receives a major share of each day's deposit activity.[17] Among the many users of this service, the United States Army may serve as a prototype; 260 military installations throughout the country deposit receipts from officer's and NCO clubs, post exchanges, and other sources into some 900 local bank accounts each day. First National Bank of Chicago, as the concentration bank, gathers in the funds from each of these accounts so they can be invested or disbursed.[18]

---

[16]Sandra G. Carcione, "Electronic Cash Management: The Corporate Toy Grows Up," *Bank Marketing* (February 1981):16.

[17]Carcione, "Electronic Cash Management: The Corporate Toy Grows Up," p. 14.

[18]John Morris, "Army, Coast Guard Battle Idle Balances," *American Banker* (June 22, 1982):3.

The burgeoning area of EFTS creates additional opportunities for innovative banks in the cash management field. Individual-to-business preauthorized debits (e.g., payments to insurance companies), individual-to-business GIRO bill payments, and business-to-individual direct deposit of payroll, dividends, and pensions are among the examples.[19]

Under the heading of disbursement services, *account reconciliation* and *microfilm storage of paid checks* are among the most common. The former provides the customer with a computerized list, in check number order, of all paid and/or outstanding items. The latter, as an adjunct to this service, eliminates the burden of receiving, storing, and accessing paid items, since the bank retains a microfilm record of each check and can provide an authenticated copy whenever requested for tax, legal, or auditing purposes. The recent emphasis on truncation is closely allied to the marketing of microfilm storage of canceled checks.

To control disbursements and use float to their own advantage, many corporations today employ a cash management technique designed to lengthen the time required for issued checks to be presented to the drawee bank and actually debited to an account. The common term for this system is *remote disbursements*. By using it, a corporation can offset the use of lock box by the payees of its checks, whose objective is to reduce the same time period. A system of remote disbursements may use accounts with banks at strategically distant points (e.g., Montana and Alaska) so that issued checks will take longer to complete their life-cycle.

Under the traditional system of check collection through the Federal Reserve, sending banks received credit from the Fed in zero, one, or two days, regardless of the time required for actual presentation to drawees and settlement or return by them. The result was a steady buildup in "Fed float;" that is, sending banks were being allowed to use funds the Fed had not yet received. During 1979 and 1980, average daily Fed float was over $6 billion.[20] In order to reduce this exposure, the Fed went on record as being strongly opposed to remote disbursement arrangements, and member banks were directed to discontinue direct marketing of the service.

The Monetary Control Act of 1980 required the twelve Federal Reserve Banks to do everything possible to eliminate Fed float and to begin charging

[19]Joseph J. Bonocore, "Making Cash Management More Marketable," *The Bankers Magazine* (November–December 1980):50.
[20]George C. White, Jr., in "After a Decade, Where Is EFT Headed?," *ABA Banking Journal* (May 1980):88.

a fee to the sending banks in situations where it could not be eliminated.[21] Through operational improvements in its check-collection procedures, including the electronic transmission of check data,[22] average daily Fed float was reduced to $3.4 billion by year-end 1981.[23] The Fed mandate for pricing float offers a major incentive for the increased use of cash management techniques, specifically including applications of EFTS to the inflow and outflow of funds.[24]

Cash Management Consulting

The marketing of a specific cash management service is often preceded by a detailed study of the corporation's or institution's present flow of receipts and disbursements. Many major banks have developed specialized units to perform this consulting function. In a typical situation, an analysis of the prospect's incoming checks is performed for a one-month period, and each date of mailing, receipt, depositing, and assumed availability is recorded. From this raw data, computer-generated reports can be prepared to show the costs and benefits of the various possible configurations of lock boxes. In other instances, studies can be performed to determine the appropriate balance levels for each bank account, and to show the potential income that could be derived from the investment of excess funds.

Cash Management Information

An executive with one of the nation's largest insurance companies has said that the term "cash management" is actually a misnomer in today's corporate environment, since his firm never sees actual cash. Instead, the daily operations of its treasury department are based on the output of computer terminals, and all decisions regarding transfers or investments are made by using printouts of receipts, bank balances, and projected

[21]Federal Reserve Bank of New York, *Annual Report* (1981):26.
[22]Federal Reserve Bank of New York, "Electronic Presentment of Checks," *Circular 8573* (May 17, 1979).
[23]Federal Reserve Bank of New York, *Annual Report* (1981):26.
[24]Carcione, "Electronic Cash Management: The Corporate Toy Grows Up," p. 18.

disbursements.[25] His comment reflects the current state of the art in the broad area of cash management.

Originally, cash management services focused exclusively on deposits and disbursements of funds. More recently, a third field has been added through the offering of services that are designed purely to furnish timely and complete information to customers on the status of their various bank accounts. Through increasingly sophisticated technology, banks are now able to provide the decision-makers in businesses, agencies of government, and correspondent banks with up-to-the-minute data on various types of transactions. Terminals in the user's office or factory provide access to bank computers, under strict security and using local telephone lines. The range of information services available to users is limited only by the innovativeness of the banks with which they deal, and their responsiveness to the users' needs. Those needs may be summarized in three basic questions:[26]

How much "money" do I have?

Where is that "money" located?

What investment or transfer decisions can I make, based on this information?

In the simplest type of service, a single bank provides its customer with early-morning information as to the "book" and "available" balances in an account as a result of all debits and credits for the prior business day. It is also possible for the same user to contact the bank's computer at a later point in time during the same day, to determine what checks have been deposited and paid. In a recent survey, 63% of the corporate respondents were using this system of computerized balance reporting.[27]

In an expanded version of the basic service, a single bank may be designated to consolidate balance information from all the user's accounts and to furnish the information in a single printout through the terminal. Typically, the information from each bank is obtained from one of the many national data-gathering companies in this field. The service can also be enhanced by allowing the user to initiate transfers of funds directly

[25]Robert Field, in "The Frantic New Pace of Cash Management," *Institutional Investor* (June 1981):183.

[26]Carcione, "Electronic Cash Management: The Corporate Toy Grows Up," p. 13.

[27]Suzanne Wittebort, "The Frantic New Pace of Cash Management," *Institutional Investor* (June 1981):183.

through the terminal. Information on current investment opportunities and yields, as well as foreign exchange quotations may be included.

As corporate and institutional cash managers evaluate their banks, they increasingly focus on the ability of those banks to provide a broad spectrum of daily information that is critical to investment and transfer decisions. High interest rates, economic uncertainties (e.g., concern about daily collections of receivables), the need to put float to advantageous use, and the emphasis on reduction of interest-free balances contribute to the demands of those managers for a steady flow of current data. At the largest companies, financial executives have reported using as many as 15 specific cash management services, and computerized reporting systems have become steadily more important as part of the total "package."[28]

Future Potential

Cash management services are among the fastest-growing in modern commercial banking, and appear to have an unlimited future. There can be no doubt that services enabling corporate, institutional, and government customers to expedite the inflow of funds, control disbursements, reduce clerical work, and obtain more timely and complete information will become increasingly popular. A survey conducted in 1973, of 161 corporate financial officers, showed that 80 percent were using lock box, depository transfer checks, wire transfers, account reconciliation, or other specialized services under the generic "cash management" umbrella; while they recognized an obligation to maintain demand-deposit balances with their banks to "pay" for services, they also identified the emphasis placed by their firms on investing any excess funds, over and above those compensating balances.[29]

Because deposits constitute a bank's essential raw material, compensating balances have traditionally been sought as a means of offsetting the expenses incurred in providing cash management services. However, the trend toward direct fees is identified here, just as it is in other aspects of banking. In increasing numbers, prospective users of deposit, disbursement, and information services require banks to respond to detailed proposals that specify the fees involved and that make it clear the balance

[28]"Banks Feeling Rising Pressure to Produce Good Cash Management Services," *American Banker* (January 29, 1981):4.
[29]David I. Fisher, *Cash Management* (New York: The Conference Board, 1973), p. 48.

compensation is not to be considered. A continuation of this trend will increase the pressures on banks to know in advance what fees are necessary to cover all service-related expenses and generate profits. Each shift from balances to fees creates the problem of further erosion of the bank's deposit base, with a resulting shrinkage in its loanable and investable funds.

This point illustrates the basic dilemma in the marketing of cash management services to major corporations, institutions, correspondent banks, and agencies of government. If the marketing effort is successful, the customer has become educated in ways of putting funds to profitable use. It is unrealistic to assume that that customer's increased sophistication will result in balance increases; the likelihood exists that balance attrition will take place. The best that the marketing bank can hope for is that the attrition will affect other depositories; however, this again may not be realistic.

Many corporate financial officers have been frank in publicizing the results of their new focus on cash management techniques. American Can Company reports that it has freed up $20 million in balances and generated $4 million in annual pretax profits by using these techniques. The Equitable Life Assurance Society has reduced its number of bank accounts from 350 to 125, while the Borden Company's banking relationships have decreased from 500 to 200. J. C. Penney uses three banks for payroll purposes, rather than the eleven it formerly designated, and saves $425,000 each year. Occidental Petroleum has generated annual profits of $600,000 by reducing its collection float. General Motors Corporation now uses debits through Automated Clearing Houses to draw funds from dealers' accounts, instead of using checks for that purpose.[30] Each such report prompts other financial officers to seek ways of achieving the same basic objectives, and the erosion of the banks' total deposit base accelerates accordingly.

As part of its overall profit-center planning, a bank must be aware at all times of the income that results from marketing, implementing, and managing its cash management services. Only in this way can the institution know whether the product line is actually having a favorable impact on earnings. It is also extremely helpful to maintain a liaison with existing users of cash management services, and to conduct periodic surveys among them to determine their level of satisfaction with the bank's performance.

[30]Wittebort, "The Frantic New Pace of Cash Management," pp. 180–182.

Quality and timeliness of service are critical, and such surveys disclose problem areas. They may also help the bank identify new areas of customer needs. An institution can substantially enhance its image by providing innovative responses to those needs, thus gaining a competitive advantage.

As mentioned earlier, the entire area of cash management services is no longer confined to corporations, institutions, correspondent banks, and government units; it now extends into the homes of consumers, and a "cash manager" is as likely to be found in a residence as in the headquarters of a corporation. Retail banking and cash management will inevitably be tied together in many new ways. The same technology that enables a corporate treasurer to access a terminal each morning and obtain current and complete information regarding bank balances will apply to home terminals, and the consumer will make financial decisions accordingly.

11 Regulatory Constraints

Because of the four far-reaching and dramatic developments during the 1960s—the introduction of the negotiable C/D, the widespread acceptance of the bank card, the new emphasis on many applications of EFTS, and the advent of the bank holding company—that decade has been characterized as one of the most significant in American banking history. Each of these developments not only had an immediate impact on the industry, but also guaranteed that it would never again be the same.

The introduction of the large-denomination negotiable C/D helped to convert banking from a demand- to a time-deposit orientation, creating a new emphasis on liability management and heightening the importance of interest expense. The bank card opened up a new world of retail services, and provided the key to consumer use of many EFTS innovations. The rise to prominence of the bank holding company (BHC) occurred near the end of the ten-year period but like the other developments, is important for its potential as well as for its historical significance. At a time when competitors are exerting new, more numerous, and more intense pressures on the commercial banking system, the BHC provides the best vehicle for coping with those pressures and meeting the competitive challenge.

HISTORICAL DEVELOPMENT

The restrictive policies of many states on branch banking led many institutions to seek some method of circumventing the regulations in order to serve more customers, in different ways, in their geographic areas. One method of establishing a presence in more than one locality, even when state laws specifically prohibited actual branching, was through a system known as *chain banking*.

The Federal Reserve has defined chain banking as a system in which a network of separately chartered commercial banks is created, with the controlling interest in each bank held by a single group of individuals.[1] Interlocking directorates among the banks in the network are commonplace. Although chain-banking networks were typically established in states where branching was prohibited, their existence went unchallenged by those states in most cases. Many of them exist today as components of other organizations.[2]

In the second half of the nineteenth century, a new organizational pattern appeared in the form of the holding company. The operations of these entities became known as *group banking*.

In any type of business, a holding company may be formed as a corporate entity that exercises control over other companies through stock ownership. Although it was not legally defined as such by Congress until 1933,[3] the *bank* holding company was one in which one or more commercial banks appeared as part of the overall organization. Holding companies that controlled banks in several cities or towns were able to circumvent state restrictions and operate in a manner tantamount to actual branching. By 1920, a large-scale trend in this direction had been identified, and in many cases the holding company with one or more banks in its structure became a multi-million-dollar enterprise, often engaged in such diversified areas as real estate, securities, investments, and restaurant chains.[4] Many of the holding companies that controlled a bank during the years of the Great Depression achieved a higher survival rate than the independent banks.

Until 1933, group banking did not come under federal or state supervision, simply because a holding company was not considered on the same basis as a bank. From today's perspective on bank regulation, it is interesting that the courts that were consulted on group banking generally held

---

[1]"Chain Banking Systems," *Federal Reserve Bulletin* (April 1947):463.

[2]Henry C. Rohlf, "One-Bank Holding Companies," *Thesis* (New Brunswick, N.J.: Stonier Graduate School of Banking, Rutgers University, 1971), p. 3.

[3]Pauline B. Heller, *Handbook of Federal Bank Holding Company Law* (New York: Law Journal Press, 1976), p. xvii.

[4]Michael A. Jessee and Steven A. Seelig, *Bank Holding Companies and the Public Interest* (Lexington, Mass.: D. C. Heath, 1977), p. 7.

that banks should be run by their principals, with minimum interference by government agencies.[5]

In 1927, the Federal Reserve identified the growing trend toward group banking,[6] and, by 1929, holding companies included 8 percent of all commercial banks, controlling 19 percent of total bank loans and investments.[7]

In some cases, a holding company was formed specifically to unify and strengthen a number of banks. Northwest Bancorporation and First Bank System, both headquartered in the Twin Cities, exemplify this type of voluntary association formed during the Depression. The former now controls eighty-five banks in seven states and, as of 1979, reported total assets of $11 billion; First Bank System includes ninety-one banks and trust companies in five states, with 1979 assets of $10.3 billion.[8] Many of the banks in both groups had enjoyed correspondent relationships with one another. By being absorbed into the holding companies, the smaller institutions gained capital, liquidity, and increased customer loyalty resulting from stronger financial backing, and they were able to weather the economic storms of the early 1930s.

The tidal wave of bank failures during the Great Depression prompted Congress to begin a series of investigations, designed to determine whether the speculative nonbank operations of holding companies had contributed to the financial crisis. One result of these hearings was the inclusion in the Banking Act of 1933 (the Glass-Steagall Act) of the first federal attempt to regulate the operations of any holding companies that controlled commercial banks.

BHC LEGISLATION

The Act of 1933 required that bank holding companies divest themselves of any investment business, and that they submit to regular examinations by federal agencies. It is the former provision that remains in force today, and prevents commercial banks from underwriting revenue bonds of municipalities or engaging in the securities business.

[5]George S. Eccles, "Registered Bank Holding Companies," in Herbert V. Prochnow and Herbert V. Prochnow, Jr., Eds., *The Changing World of Banking* (New York: 1974) p. 85.
[6]Board of Governors, *Annual Report* (1927), p. 2.
[7]Jessee and Seelig, *Bank Holding Companies and the Public Interest*, p. 6.
[8]Joseph Asher, "Golden Jubilee for 2 Holding Companies in Twin Cities," *ABA Banking Journal* (June 1979), p. 104.

In actuality, other than imposing these limitations, the 1933 Act did little to restrict the operations of bank holding companies. It did not require BHCs to register with the Federal Reserve if their group banking systems consisted exclusively of state-chartered banks, it permitted further acquisitions of banks by existing BHCs, and it made no mention of the possible competitive effects of further expansion.[9]

In addition, through a "grandfather clause," the Act allowed then-existing multibank BHCs to continue operations across state lines. The present First Interstate (formerly Western) Bancorp exemplifies the results of this clause. It now operates 901 banking offices in 476 communities in 11 western states.[10] Each of its constituent banks is identified with the "First Interstate" name.

Between 1933 and 1956, numerous bills were introduced in Congress to impose additional restrictions on BHCs; however, despite the efforts of the Comptroller of the Currency and the Federal Reserve, none passed. On one occasion, the Fed expressed its concerns in the following message to Congress:[11]

> Bank holding companies are being used to defeat the expressed will of Congress regarding the establishment of branches, and to gather under one management many different and varied enterprises wholly unallied and wholly unrelated to the conduct of a banking business.

Congressional hearings during 1955 and 1956 eventually resulted in new legislation specifically aimed at the group banking movement. The Bank Holding Company Act of 1956 defined a BHC as any entity that directly or indirectly controlled 25 percent or more of the voting stock of *two or more* banks, or in any way controlled the election of a majority of the boards of directors of *two or more* banks.[12] It also required all such BHCs to register with the Federal Reserve, and ordered them to divest themselves of any component engaged in activities that were "not related to banking *per se.*"

From our contemporary perspective, perhaps the most important feature of the 1956 Act was the "blanket" exemption it granted to BHCs if

[9]Rohlf, "One-Bank Holding Companies," pp. 10–11.

[10]"Western Bancorp," *Business Week* (February 23, 1981):134, and First Interstate Bancorp, *Annual Report* (1981):5–6.

[11]Board of Governors of the Federal Reserve System, *Annual Report* (1943), p. 9.

[12]Jessee and Seelig, *Bank Holding Companies and the Public Interest*, p. 10. Emphasis added.

they controlled only one bank. Although all the implications of that exemption were not apparent in 1956, they eventually provided the basis for the formation of a new type of organizational structure, the *one-bank holding company*. John Bunting, former Chairman of the First Pennsylvania Corporation, has referred to this genesis as "one of banking's few authentic revolutions."[13]

During the 1960s, many commercial banks found themselves hampered by legislative constraints in their efforts to diversify and grow, limited in their ability to generate increased profits, and subject to greater competitive pressures than ever before. The introduction of the large-denomination negotiable C/D had made them liability managers, rather than merely asset managers, and created new problems of interest expense. Savings and loan associations were steadily increasing their deposits at the expense of commercial banks. Members of multibank BHCs were restricted in their attempts to enter other lines of business by the 1956 Act; banks that were not members of BHCs became defendants in litigation brought by data processing, travel, and insurance firms and associations anxious to prevent them from diversifying and competing.[14]

In attempting to cope with these pressures, banks resorted to a variety of management techniques. First, in some cases, they chose to make significant increases in their portfolios of municipal bonds, thus gaining tax-exempt income to offset their rising costs. Second, others expanded their traditional loan-to-deposit ratios, with a consequent increase in both interest income and risk. A third alternative required severe programs for cost-cutting, although the inflation rate of the 1960s hampered this effort.[15]

However, the most attractive option remained that of diversifying into various financial activities and services. National banks were given more freedom in this respect through a series of rulings by James Smith, then Comptroller of the Currency. It was his position that they could perform financial services that were "closely related to banking" as long as, in his judgment, their solvency and liquidity would not be impaired. His rulings precipitated a number of requests by state-chartered banks for conversion to national charters, as well as a subsequent relaxation in the

---

[13]"One-Bank Holding Companies: A Banker's View," *Harvard Business Review* (May–June 1969):99.

[14]Paul S. Nadler, "The One-Bank Holding Company," in Prochnow and Prochnow, Jr., *The Changing World of Banking*, p. 144.

[15]Edward W. Reed, Richard V. Cotter, Edward K. Gill, and Richard K. Smith, *Commercial Banking* (Englewood Cliffs, N.J.: Prentice Hall, 1976), p. 48.

policies of regulatory agencies. The Fed responded by amending its Regulation Y, which governs group banking, and thus gave a more liberal interpretation to the concept of nonbank services.[16]

Throughout the 1960s and 1970s, as shown in Table 11.1, multibank BHCs grew steadily, both in numbers and in importance. Despite the restrictions on their activities, they provided a mechanism for expansion, especially in those states where full-scale branching was restricted or prohibited.

Table 11.1.

Year	Multibank BHCS	Bank Affiliates	Banking Offices	Deposits[a]	% of U.S. Bank Deposits
1956	47	428	1,211	14.8	7.5%
1960	42	426	1,463	18.3	8.0
1965	48	468	1,954	27.6	8.3
1968	71	629	2,891	57.6	13.2
1970	111	895	4,155	78.1	16.2
1973	251	1,815	9,328	239.1	35.1
1975	289	2,264	12,160	297.5	37.8
1977	306	2,301	12,863	324.6	34.6

Source: Stephen A. Rhoades, "The Competitive Effects of Interstate Banking," *Federal Reserve Bulletin* (January 1980):2.
[a]Deposits in billions of dollars.

However, it remained obvious that maximum freedom to compete and diversify would require a new type of organization. Analysis of the 1956 Act made it clear that it applied *only* to BHCs that controlled two or more banks. Hence, holding companies in which only one bank was involved could engage in factoring, leasing, mortgage financing, real estate investment, and insurance by availing themselves of the exemption.

The situation was brought to a head in 1965 when the Meadow Brook National Bank, a major institution that subsequently became the National Bank of North America, was acquired by the CIT Financial Corporation.[17] This acquisition was resented by many commercial banks because it was

[16]Jesse and Seelig, *Bank Holding Companies and the Public Interest,* p. 33.
[17]National Bank of North America, as noted earlier, was acquired by National Westminster Bank in 1979.

legal for a nonbank conglomerate or holding company to purchase a bank, whereas the converse was legally restricted or prohibited.

In this context, it may be parenthetically noted that the 1956 Bank Holding Company Act defines a bank as an entity that accepts demand deposits and makes commerical loans. If an institution were to divest itself of either activity, it would lose its legal status as a bank. The fact that several firms had used this loophole to buy banks that had sold off their loan portfolios led Chairman Paul Volcker of the Federal Reserve Board to ask Congress, in December 1982, for a stricter definition of the term "bank," and a tightening of the regulations covering this point.[18] Shortly thereafter, the Dreyfus Company, a major mutual-fund firm, purchased the Lincoln State Bank of East Orange, New Jersey after having arranged for that bank to sell its entire loan portfolio to another institution. Thus, Lincoln State became a nonbank, and its acquisition was not opposed by the FDIC. However, the Federal Reserve expressed its objections to the acquisition, and held out the possibility that it might institute litigation to prevent it from being consummated. Dreyfus thus became the first firm in the securities industry to seek entry into the area of commercial banking.[19]

In 1965, the then First National City Bank of New York was the first major institution to counter the CIT acquisition. It established a new, one-bank holding company, Citicorp, with the bank as the major component. Because only one bank was involved, the 1956 Act did not restrict the operations of the new holding company, and Citicorp began a program of diversification and expansion that by 1980 had enabled it to operate some 400 consumer finance, Edge Act, mortgage banking, and loan production offices in 38 states and the District of Columbia.[20] In steadily increasing numbers, commercial banks throughout the country established similar organizational structures by exchanging all outstanding shares in the bank for shares in a new, one-bank BHC. the latter then formed subsidiaries to perform various services.

As bank after bank hastened to join the movement, fears and reservations about the ultimate effects were expressed in many quarters. William McChesney Martin, then Chairman of the Federal Reserve Board, served

---

[18]Lisa J. McCue, "Volcker Hits Loophole Letting Commercial Firms Own Banks," *American Banker* (December 2, 1982):1.

[19]Robert A. Bennett, "Dreyfus Buys Bank in New Jersey," *The New York Times* (December 28, 1982):D1.

[20]Rhoades, "The Competitive Effects of Interstate Banking," p. 3.

as a spokesman for many concerned parties: "The greatest risk is in concentration of economic power. . . . A bank might deny credit to other borrowers only on condition that they agree to do business with the affiliated firm."[21]

Questions were also raised regarding the posture a one-bank BHC might assume if one of its affiliates were experiencing financial difficulties. Would the bank's resources then be used, perhaps at the expense of depositors' interests, to help that affiliate survive? Another member of the Federal Reserve Board, Andrew Brimmer, stated the case emphatically: "Banks have got a mother-hen complex. Every bank holding company will do whatever it can, at considerable cost, to avoid failure of an affiliate."[22]

In some cases, banks themselves must be held responsible for the concern expressed by Brimmer and frequently restated by others.[23] First Wisconsin Corporation, parent of the First Wisconsin National Bank, bought $14.8 million in loans from its Real Estate Investment Trust (REIT), admitting the possibility of incurring losses as a result but claiming that the action was necessary to protect stockholders in the BHC.[24] United California Bank took similar action when a foreign subsidiary of its BHC failed.[25]

Although the banks, both individually and through policy statements of the American Bankers Association, stated their intention of operating prudently and confining their activities to areas directly related to banking itself, the concerns and fears of their critics continued to be heard. The major banks' trend toward assumption of even greater economic power was a prime topic.[26]

Wright Patman, then Chairman of the House Committee on Banking and Currency, led a movement to revise the Act of 1956, and largely through his efforts a series of amendments to it became the content of Public Law 91-607, signed into law by President Nixon on December 31, 1970 and subsequently incorporated by the Fed into Regulation Y. Two of the amendments served the following basic purposes:

---

[21]In Federal Reserve Bank of Chicago, *Conference on Bank Structure and Competition* (April 1977), p. 117.

[22]In "An Early Warning System to Spot Sick Banks," *Business Week* (October 26, 1974):92.

[23]Jack M. Guttenberg and Bernard Shull, "Bank Holding Companies and Abuse of the Power to Grant Credit," in *Conference on Bank Structure*, p. 129.

[24]*Business Week* (October 26, 1974):92.

[25]Martin Mayer, *The Bankers* (New York: David McKay Co., 1974), pp. 384–385.

[26]"The New Breed in Banking," *Business Week* (September 15, 1973):90.

1. They brought *all* BHCs, specifically those that involved only one bank, under the jurisdiction of the Federal Reserve, and gave the Fed full power to determine which activities of BHCs were permitted.

2. Through a "grandfather clause," they allowed BHCs, with specific Fed approval, to continue to engage in nonbank activities that would otherwise be prohibited, provided that those activities had been engaged in continuously since June 30, 1968.[27]

Section 4(c)(8) of these amendments gave the Fed authority to determine if any nonbank activity proposed by a BHC were "so closely related to banking, or managing or controlling banks, as to be a proper incident thereto."[28] It also established the Fed as the judge of whether performing that activity would produce public benefits outweighing any possible adverse effects.[29]

Within one month after the amendments had been signed into law, the Fed published its first list of approved and prohibited activities for BHCs. Since that time, the Fed has rendered a great many decisions on applications by BHCs to offer new services or make acquisitions. The approved list has been expanded from time to time, and Section 225.4 of Regulation Y now states that a BHC, having filed an application to engage in a permitted activity, may automatically begin doing so unless the Fed renders an adverse ruling within 45 days.[30] The most recent listing of permissible activities is shown in Table 11.2.

Examples of decisions by the Fed on this point include those acquisitions of finance companies that have been approved, and others that have been denied on the grounds that the benefits did not outweigh the possible adverse effects. In one noteworthy case, the application by a major one-bank BHC to acquire a nuclear-fuel leasing operation was denied. It was the feeling of the Fed that the bank in that BHC would have been required to provide substantial financing, and "might have sapped its financial strength in so doing."[31]

"Tie-in" transactions, in which a customer who purchases one service from a bank is required to buy another, are prohibited under the 1970 Act, as are all restrictions by banks on customers' dealings with other

---

[27]Jessee and Seelig, *Bank Holding Companies and the Public Interest*, p. 20.
[28]Reed et al., *Commercial Banking*, p. 50.
[29]Jessee and Seelig, *Bank Holding Companies and the Public Interest*, p. 20.
[30]*Federal Reserve Bulletin* (January 1979):64.
[31]In Jessee and Seelig, *Bank Holding Companies and the Public Interest, op. cit.*, p. 71.

Table 11.2. Permissible Nonbank Activities for Bank Holding Companies Under Section 4(c)8 of Regulation Y, May 1, 1982

Activities permitted by regulation	Activities permitted by order	Activities denied by the Board
1. Extensions of credit[b] Mortgage banking Finance companies: consumer sales, and commercial Credit Cards Factoring	1. Issuance and sale of travelers checks[b,d]	1. Insurance premium funding (combined sales of mutual funds and insurance)
2. Industrial bank, Morris Plan bank, industrial loan company	2. Buying and selling gold and silver bullion and silver coins[b,d]	2. Underwriting life insurance not related to credit extension
3. Servicing loans and other extensions of credit[b]	3. Issuing money orders and general-purpose variable denominated payment instruments[a,b,d]	3. Real estate brokerage[b]
4. Trust company[b]	4. Futures commission merchant to cover gold and silver bullion and coins[a,b]	4. Land development
5. Investment or financial advising[b]		5. Real estate syndication
6. Full-payout leasing of personal or real property[b]	5. Underwriting certain federal, state, and municipal securities[a,b]	6. General management consulting
7. Investments in community welfare projects[b]	6. Check verification[a,b,d]	7. Property management
8. Providing bookkeeping or data processing services[b]	7. Financial advice to consumers[a,b]	8. Computer output microfilm services
9. Acting as insurance agent or broker, primarily in connection with credit extensions[b]	8. Issuance of small denomination debt instruments[a]	9. Underwriting mortgage guaranty insurance[c]
10. Underwriting credit life, accident, and health insurance		10. Operating a savings and loan association[a,e]
		11. Operating a travel agency[a,b]
		12. Underwriting property and casualty insurance[a]
		13. Underwriting home loan life mortgage insurance[a]
		14. Orbanco: Investment note issue with transactional characteristics

Table 11.2 (Continued)

Activities permitted by regulation	Activities permitted by order	Activities denied by the Board
11. Providing courier services[b]		
12. Management consulting for unaffiliated banks[a,b]		
13. Sale at retail of money orders with a face value of not more than $1000, travelers checks and savings bonds[a,b]		
14. Performing appraisals of real estate[a]		
15. Audit services for unaffiliated banks		
16. Issuance and sale of travelers checks		
17. Management consulting to nonbank depository institutions		

Source: David D. Whitehead and Pamela Frisbee, "Positioning for Interstate Banking," Federal Reserve Bank of Atlanta, *Economic Review* (September 1982):17.

[a]Added to list since January 1, 1975.
[b]Activities permissible to national banks.
[c]Board orders found these activities closely related to banking but denied proposed acquisitions as part of its "go slow" policy.
[d]To be decided on a case-by-case basis.
[e]Operating a thrift institution has been permitted by order in Rhode Island and New Hampshire only.
[f]Subsequently permitted by regulation.

banks. The net effect is to preclude any actions that might be construed as creating restraint of trade.[32]

In rendering a negative decision in 1977, on the proposed acquisition of a savings and loan association by a BHC, the Board of Governors stated

[32]Reed et al., *Commercial Banking,* p. 51.

that such acquisitions were not "a proper incident to banking."[33] However, on two occasions in 1982, the Fed relaxed this viewpointand allowed BHCs to take over troubled thrift institutions. It may be noted that Congress has not enacted specific legislation on this issue.

In April 1982, Interstate Financial Corporation, owner of the Third National Bank (Dayton, Ohio) was allowed to acquire the Scioto Savings Association in the same state.[34] In a far more significant case, Citicorp, as was noted earlier in this text, received approval to acquire Fidelity S&L Association (San Francisco). This was the first time an interstate acquisition had been approved by the Fed.[35]

The Douglas Amendment

A third amendment to the Bank Holding Company Act of 1970, named after its sponsor, Senator Paul Douglas, is the amendment most frequently cited as a major obstacle to banks and BHCs in their efforts to expand geographically. The Douglas Amendment prohibits BHCs from acquiring more than 5 percent ownership of a bank in another state, unless the laws of that state specifically permit such acquisitions.[36] At year-end 1982, Alaska, Maine, and New York were the only states that had enacted reciprocity statutes, providing for mutual acceptance of out-of-state banks and BHCs.[37]

Spokespersons for commercial banks have been both numerous and vocal in expressing their opposition to the Douglas Amendment and its restraints at a time when competitors not affected by it are expanding without regard to state boundaries. The former President of Bank of America, A. W. Clausen, has said that "The Douglas Amendment . . . and a host of branching prohibitions and limitations in state laws . . . have become bastions for special interest groups trying to protect their turf

[33]Robert M. Shafton, "Significant New Powers Seen for Thrifts and Banks," *American Banker* (February 23, 1982):1.

[34]Linda W. McCormick, "BHC-Thrift Mergers," *American Banker* (April 6, 1982):1.

[35]"Citicorp Move May Open Door to Interstate Banking," *Gannett Westchester Newspapers* (October 17, 1982), p. BB-10.

[36]Larry A. Frieder, in "An Orderly Transition to Interstate Banking," *The Bankers Magazine* (March–April 1981):51.

[37]"New York Senate Clears Interstate Bill," *American Banker* (June 11, 1982):19.

from outside competition."[38] He has also described the McFadden Act
and Douglas Amendment as "costly legislative antiques,"[39] and his view
is shared by those who note that an American bank can with little difficulty
open a branch in a foreign country thousands of miles away, but cannot
cross a state line one mile away.

Interstate Banking

Discussions of the term "interstate banking" must be conditioned by a
semantic distinction. If the term is construed to mean full-scale banking
across state boundaries, it remains true that the combination of the
McFadden Act and Douglas Amendment precludes this. However, if one
takes a different view of the words, BHCs and individual banks are obviously already involved in various forms of interstate banking, through
acquisitions and *de novo* installations.

   BHCs have concentrated on expansion in many areas of nonbank services that the McFadden Act does not cover. They have established loan
production and Edge Act offices, new EFT networks, and finance company
and mortgage banking subsidiaries; in addition, consumer lending (including bank-card marketing) is being conducted without regard to state
lines. Two court decisions in 1980 helped make this expansion possible.

   First, the United States Court of Appeals for the District of Columbia
supported a 1966 ruling of the Comptroller of the Currency, which allows
national banks to establish loan production offices across state lines, as
long as the facilities were not operated as *de facto* branches. In the second
instance, the Supreme Court ruled in favor of Bankers Trust Company
of New York, which had sought to establish a nonbank subsidiary in Florida that would offer investment advisory services.[40]

   Bankers who have advocated changes in the McFadden Act and Douglas Amendment are not without strong opposition within their own industry. Smaller institutions, both commercial banks and thrifts, have long
opposed the invasion of their communities by the money-center giants.
In discussing the many offices Citicorp now operates throughout the

[38]Address to the Financial Analysts Federation (San Francisco, May 14, 1979), *Bank Stock Quarterly* (October 1979):19.
[39]In Peter J. Brennan, "The McFadden Act," *ABA Banking Journal* (September 1979):49.
[40]Emmett J. Rice, "The Prospects for Interstate Banking," Address to the South Carolina Bankers Association, Myrtle Beach (April 25, 1981).

country, Walter Wriston has said that a change in interstate-banking laws would simply mean that the existing signs on those offices would be replaced by new ones, identifying them as branches.[41] Representatives of smaller banks, hearing his comment, naturally fear that their institutions may be swallowed up or forced out of existence.

Hostility to concentrations of financial power can still be seen in a basically populist attitude that supports the existence of a fractionalized and geographically restricted banking system. For example, the Conference of State Bank Supervisors sees full-scale interstate banking as a serious threat to the supervisory role of the individual states.[42]

Despite such opposition, bankers continue to focus on the holding company as the single best hope for the future if their industry is to compete, grow, and prosper. This hope is not based solely on the fact that the BHC may open the door to eventual interstate banking; rather, it reflects an opinion that the BHC is the only vehicle through which a full range of financial services can be provided.

The point must be stressed that BHCs generally have benefited customers of banks, as well as the banks themselves. The record of the Fed, in considering requests by BHCs for acquisitions of nonbank entities, clearly indicates that approval was granted only after clear advantages for the public sector had been identified. In a study of twenty-four such approvals, benefits such as lower interest rates on loans, lower service charges, choices for sources of a particular service, and continuation of services in a geographic area were cited as justifying factors by the Fed.[43]

Fears that expansion of BHCs would create undue concentrations of economic power do not appear to have been justified. One survey showed that the percentage of statewide deposits held by BHC member banks grew by 10 percent or more in only six states from 1968 to 1973; in twenty-two cases, the percentage actually declined, leading to the conclusion that independent, small banks were perfectly capable of maintaining their market shares.[44] Nonbank service organizations have also demonstrated benefits that outweigh any reduction or elimination of competition.[45]

---

[41]Laura Gross, "Citicorp Interstate Plans Rely on Office Conversions," *American Banker* (January 22, 1981):1.

[42]John D. Hawke, "The Interstate Banking Euphoria," *American Banker* (November 30, 1981):4.

[43]Jessee and Seelig, *Bank Holding Companies and the Public Interest*, p. 64.

[44]Ibid., pp. 142–143.

[45]Ibid.

The shrinkage of demand deposits in the banking system has not been accompanied by a corresponding decline in the demand for financial services; quite the contrary is true. The corporate financial officer who has found it both feasible and profitable to draw down surplus balances and invest them, also seeks the "package" of services that will further improve overall cash management. For major corporations today, as for correspondent banks, units of government, and individuals, balances are placed with those banks proving most responsive to total financial needs. Loans, lines of credit, leasing and factoring, international, trust, and concentration and disbursement services provide the justification for keeping balances with banks. Institutions that cannot or do not provide those services are most likely to suffer competitively. To meet their customers' wants and needs, it is logical for them to establish subsidiaries through the holding company to provide a coordinated group of products. The BHC framework offers the best possibility for meeting both wholesale and retail banking needs, and for serving as wide a clientele as possible, both at home and abroad.

Those bankers who believe that full-scale interstate banking is inexorably on its way can point to developments during 1981 and 1982 to support their opinion. New legislation enacted by some states during those years, along with rising costs of deposits and onerous tax structures, provided the impetus for major commercial banks to take significant actions toward moving across state boundaries and, in so doing, they could enhance their current earnings and establish a base for the future.

In February 1981, the Delaware legislature passed the Financial Center Development Act, eliminating usury ceilings, providing for a favorable tax rate on bank earnings, and abolishing interest-rate ceilings on consumer loans and bank-card fees. As a result, Chase Bank (USA) was established in that state, focusing primarily on consumer lending; J. P. Morgan & Co., Inc. (the BHC for Morgan Guaranty Trust Company) also won approval to establish a subsidiary in Delaware; and the First National Bank (Baltimore) decided to move its card operations to that state. Under the 1981 law, Delaware's tax on bank earnings of $30 million per year is 2.7 percent—approximately one-tenth of the tax rate in New York.[46]

As a major lender to consumers in the New York area, Citibank found itself the victim of that state's usury laws, which in 1981 created a negative

[46]Michael Schroeder, "Delaware Commission Accepts. . . . Interstate Bid," *American Banker* (July 30, 1981):1.

spread between the bank's cost of funds and its interest on installment loans. When the South Dakota legislature enacted a bill abolishing all interest-rate ceilings and allowing out-of-state banks to establish subsidiaries there, Citibank promptly moved its entire consumer credit operations to that state.

In the expectation that prohibitions on interstate banking would eventually be removed, Chase Manhattan Corporation also entered into an arrangement with Equimark Corporation (Pittsburgh) and its chief subsidiary, Equibank, investing a total of $125 million and receiving in return, among other things, an option to acquire all Equibank stock *if* interstate banking becomes legal.[47]

The State of Florida provides two final examples of the actions taken by major commercial banks to position themselves across statelines. Florida laws allow out-of-state institutions that owned banks or trust companies in Florida before 1972 to expand their current market operations. Therefore, NCNB Corporation (North Carolina) and Chemical New York Corporation have entered into agreements, involving very substantial sums of money, with Florida banks in the hope that full scale interstate banking will become a reality in the not-too-distant future.[48]

BANK MERGERS AND BRANCHING

During the 1950s, many of the largest mergers in American banking history took place, particularly in New York City. At year-end 1978, six of the ten largest banks in the country, each of them a component of a BHC, were headquartered in that city; each of them had participated in a merger during the 1950s. The need or desire to expand a specialized service area or to acquire branches, and thus enter the retail field, was usually the rationale for the merger.

From the legislative standpoint, there was little to limit such mergers by way of formal statutes. The one standard that appears to have been

[47]"Chase Builds a Bridge for Going Interstate," *Business Week* (August 3, 1981):20.
[48]"$134 Million Deal NCNB's Third in Florida," *American Banker* (June 2, 1982):1; "Chemical's Coup in Florida Banking," *Business Week* (November 16, 1981):56.

the primary consideration in each case was the degree of capital adequacy in the merging institutions.[49] However, as the trend continued, questions were raised about the competitive effects of mergers and the resulting concentration of power. In 1960, Congress addressed these questions and drew up the Bank Merger Act, the principal provision of which stated that a single authority would, from that time, rule on all mergers and acquisitions involving commercial banks. The decision of that authority would be final in all cases. For all national banks, the Comptroller of the Currency would have jurisdiction; for state member banks, the Fed; for insured nonmembers, the FDIC; and for all others, the individual state banking departments. It was the intention of the Senate Banking and Currency Committee to have this Act eliminate all conflicts and jurisdictional questions among the several regulatory authorities.[50]

The 1960 Act ordered the single designated authority to consider four factors in each application for merger: the financial condition and history of each bank, the competency and character of their management teams, the prospects for profitability and growth of the merged bank, and the interests of the community to be served. Mergers were not to be approved unless the probable benefits to the depositors and community clearly offset any adverse effects that might result from reduced competition.[51]

The United States Supreme Court then brought commercial banking under the provisions of the Clayton and Sherman Antitrust Acts, through its decisions in the Lexington and (more particularly) Philadelphia cases.[52] In the latter, the Court stated that Section 7 of the Clayton Act

does require that the forces of competition be allowed to operate within the broad framework of government regulation of the industry. The fact that banking is a highly regulated industry critical to the nation's welfare makes the play of competition not less important but more so.[53]

[49]Howard D. Crosse and George H. Hempel, *Management Policies for Commercial Banks,* 2nd Ed., (Englewood Cliffs, N.J.: Prentice-Hall, Inc., 1973), p. 27.
[50]Cross and Hempel, *Management Policies for Commercial Banks,* p. 29.
[51]"Federal Laws Regulating Bank Mergers," Federal Reserve Bank of Cleveland, *Economic Review* (January 1971):18.
[52]Details of both decisions may be found in Crosse and Hempel, *Management Policies for Commercial Banks,* p. 30.
[53]*U.S. v. Philadelphia National Bank,* 374 U.S. (1963), p. 372.

For that reason, the Court determined that a merger would be illegal if it produced "a firm controlling an undue percentage share of the relevant market, and resulted in a significant increase in the concentration of firms in that market."[54]

Through these decisions, the Court not only subjected banking to antitrust laws for the first time; it also contravened the will of Congress as expressed in the 1960 Act. The decisions made antitrust considerations the ultimate test for bank acquisitions and mergers, rather than the ruling of a designated authority. This enabled the Office of the Attorney General to intervene in mergers whenever such action seemed appropriate. In effect, the Justice Department was empowered to determine the potential anticompetitive effects of a merger, and to oppose it in a federal court.

In two subsequent decisions, the Supreme Court made it clear that the burden of proof in all merger or acquisition proposals is on the banks themselves, rather than on the Justice Department. They must be prepared to show that the benefits of the proposal outweigh the reduction in competition, and that those benefits cannot reasonably be attained through other means.

As a result, banks have generally avoided any mergers of a horizontal nature—that is, those that would directly change the market structure in a community. Instead, they have sought mergers that involve banks in other geographic markets.

In addition, there has been evidence of a marked reluctance on the part of many banks to enter into negotiations for mergers at all. They are aware that some previous mergers, approved by designated authorities but opposed by the Department of Justice, were in litigation for years.[55]

On June 14, 1982, the Department of Justice publicized its new guidelines for mergers. These included the theory of probable future competition, and indicated that the Department would most likely challenge any merger proposal in which the acquired bank's or firm's market share was 20 percent or more.[56]

[54]Ibid., p. 363.

[55]Stephen A. Rhoades, "The Competitive Effects of Interstate Banking," *Federal Reserve Bulletin* (January 1980):1–3.

[56]Anthony S. Winer, "Applying the Theory of Probable Future Competition," *Federal Reserve Bulletin* (September 1982):531–532.

BRANCH BANKING

The controversial topic of full-scale branching has been mentioned frequently in this text. It is one of the most visible components of a system whose hallmark is a diversity unmatched elsewhere in the world. That diversity exists not only among types of banks (money-center and small community, wholesale or retail orientation or a combination of the two, unit and branch, member and nonmember), but also among the authorities who regulate and examine them. It results from the often-reinforced, longstanding view that American banking should be as decentralized as possible, and that each state should have sovereign authority over branching within its borders.

Federal statutes and Supreme Court decisions have repeatedly upheld that authority. Thus, although a trend toward more extensive branching has been noted in recent years (as mentioned earlier, several states have liberalized their laws on this subject[57]), the most recent statistics indicate that fifteen states allow branch banking only on a limited scale, and eleven states continue to prohibit it. In addition, in four of the unit banking states (i.e., those that do not allow branching), Kansas, Nebraska, Oklahoma, and West Virginia, there is no significant group banking activity.

It is reasonable to assume that without such statutes and decisions, American banking might have developed along the same lines as the systems found in other countries, with a strong central bank (usually a direct agency or instrument of the government) and a relative handful of nationwide institutions.

Fears of undue concentration of financial power in the hands of a few banks characterized much of the history of the industry in the United States. For example, Massachusetts, New York, and Rhode Island all had laws on their books at one time stating that no individuals could operate a banking business except at their own legal place of residence.[58] The abuses of the "wildcat banking" era, when banks opened remote, nearly inaccessible facilities for the presentation and redemption of their notes, were cited as evidence that branch banking was inherently wrong.

---

[57]Donald T. Savage, "Developments in Banking Structure, 1970–81," *Federal Reserve Bulletin* (February 1982):79.
[58]Crosse and Hempel, *Management Policies for Commercial Banks,* p. 17.

As recently as 1925, only 3.1 percent of state banks and 1.3 percent of national banks operated any branches.[59] By contrast, 6,859 commercial banks (46.2 percent of the total) operated 38,353 branches at year-end 1980.[60]

It is interesting to note that consumers do not always concur with many banks' desire for more freedom to branch. Over one million voters in Colorado took part in a 1980 referendum, and by a three-to-one margin, rejected a proposal for statewide branching.[61] Similarly, in those states that persist as "unit banking" jurisdictions (i.e., where no branching is permitted), various associations of small, independent banks still hold that extensive branch banking inevitably leads to excessive concentrations of power in the hands of a few institutions. They believe that the one-office community bank, operated by local management, serves customers at least as well as any larger entity could.

The McFadden Act, which extends branching options to national banks in their individual states *only* to the extent that state-chartered banks have the same privileges (and thus makes national banks subject to state laws, rather than to the rulings of the Comptroller of the Currency), is the legislation most frequently cited in contemporary discussions of branching. Its timeliness, validity, and rationale are particularly questioned at a time when American commercial banks cannot buy institutions in other states but foreign banks can; when EFT services and twenty-four-hour foreign exchange markets make such laws anachronisms; and when nonbank competitors can offer, in every state, money market funds with check-writing privileges and unregulated interest rates.[62]

John Heimann, former Comptroller of the Currency, held that statutory restrictions on branching imposed a burden on both citizens and their communities,[63] and two Presidential Commissions and the Comptroller of the Currency's Advisory Committee have stated that less-restricted branching might well be in the public interest.[64] Nevertheless, the matter continues to rest with the banking departments and legislatures of the fifty states.

---

[59]Peter J. Brennan, "The McFadden Act," *ABA Banking Journal* (September 1979):49.
[60]Savage, "Developments in Banking Structure," p. 82.
[61]"Voters Reject Statewide Branching," *American Banker* (November 6, 1980):1.
[62]Willard C. Butcher, "Unshackle the Banks," *Chief Executive* (Spring 1982):3.
[63]In "Banking in Transition," *The Bankers Magazine* (September–October 1978):22.
[64]Reed et al., *Commercial Banking*, pp. 33–34.

FEDERAL REGULATION OF BANKING

Without exception, every commercial bank in the United States is subject to one or more regulatory units of government. Through the chartering process, a set of government controls is imposed before a bank can open its doors and accept its first deposits. Throughout a bank's entire life-cycle, representatives of governments examine it, scrutinize its financial reports, and make decisions about its ability to expand and offer services.

The early colonists believed that a minimum of government banking regulation was desirable. Their basic premise was that banks should be given the same freedom to operate as other merchants. That notion vanished in the nineteenth century, by which time it had become apparent that banking is, *per se*, different from all other industries. Bankers must accept the notion that what they do, and the manner in which they do it, are legitimate areas for concern and supervision by governments. An industry that handles a trillion dollars of deposited funds, and whose daily operations so vitally affect the entire economy, cannot expect to go unregulated.

The difficulty lies not in the fact that such regulation exists, but rather in its extent and in its overlapping nature in so many cases. For example, national banks are under the jurisdiction of the Comptroller of the Currency, yet by law, must be members of both the Federal Reserve and the FDIC. The Comptroller is responsible for the annual audit of all such banks, but the other two agencies may conduct their own examinations whenever they feel it is necessary or appropriate. All state-chartered member banks are regularly examined by the Federal Reserve, but are also subject to regulation and examination by the FDIC, to which they must belong. State banking authorities also examine and regulate this category of banks. A state-chartered, insured nonmember is similarly subject to both the FDIC and the regulations of its own state. Only two percent of all commercial banks fall into the final category: they are uninsured nonmembers, subject only to state laws and examinations.

In addition to regulating state-chartered members, the Fed is also responsible for all BHCs, the foreign branches of all member banks, and all Edge Act subsidiaries. Mergers are subject to the approval of the Department of Justice. As publicly held corporations, BHCs fall under the jurisdiction of the Securities and Exchange Commission. The restrictive provisions of the Glass-Steagall Act have already been mentioned in this text.

The National Banking and Currency Acts of 1863 and 1864 created a dual banking system, under which a commercial bank may have either a national or a state charter. Today, it is interesting that two prominent figures on the banking scene have used identical words to describe the effects of that system. During his term as Chairman of the Federal Reserve Board of Governors, Dr. Arthur Burns stated that it "fosters competition in laxity . . . (and) should be substantially reorganized."[65] Four years later, William Proxmire, then Chairman of the Senate Committee on Banking, Housing, and Urban Affairs, made this comment: "Banks are free to pick and choose which of the three federal agencies shall regulate them. This system leads to competition in laxity, with regulation at the lowest common denominator level."[66]

Their choice of words reflects their view that federal agencies might lower their standards to attract new members or retain existing ones. Indeed, banks *can* select their regulators by converting from one type of charter to another, as several hundred banks, with assets of over $11 billion, did during the 1970s.[67]

Senator Proxmire also went on record in favor of consolidating the Office of the Comptroller of the Currency, the Fed, and the FDIC into a single unit, as a means of eliminating what he referred to as "burdensome and overlapping duplication."[68] His view has been shared by contemporary advocates. For example in December 1982, Vice President George Bush announced the formation of a study group to consider consolidation of the federal regulatory agencies,[69] and Dr. Carol S. Greenwald, former President of the National Consumer Cooperative Bank, has said that "Consolidation is needed for equity. . . . [It] would achieve gains in efficiency and reduce or eliminate weaknesses in the present system."[70]

However, consolidation has also had its vocal and numerous opponents.

[65]In "An Early Warning System to Spot Sick Banks," *Business Week* (October 26, 1974):88.
[66]In "Banking in Transition," p. 29.
[67]Carol S. Greenwald, "Who's Regulating the Regulators?" *The Bankers Magazine* (March–April 1981):41.
[68]In "Banking in Transition," p. 22.
[69]Kennneth B. Noble, "Study of Financial Regulators," *The New York Times* (December 11, 1982):D3.
[70]In "Who's Regulating the Regulators?":41–42.

State bank associations and supervisors have opposed it, since they consider it inimical to the continued existence of the dual banking system.[71] John Heimann, former Comptroller of the Currency, criticized it because it gave too much power to one organization and put an end to state regulation.[72]

Critics of the existing regulatory structure claim that it does not treat state and national banks on the same basis, generates pressures to lower standards for the involved agencies, causes duplication of effort with accompanying inefficiency and expense, and causes delays in actions to curb unsound practices. They have also pointed to situations that reflect inconsistent regulatory policies, as in the proposed acquisition by the Dreyfus Fund of a bank in New Jersey.[73] Those who favor continuation of the present system claim that it works well, prevents undue concentration of power in a single authority, and provides for flexibility in regulation.[74]

It has also been pointed out that under the present system, the Federal Reserve, by virtue of its role as the supervisor of all BHCs, has assumed a position significantly superior to the other federal agencies, and may be able to circumvent their rights and powers. The same critics feel that the rapid expansion of the holding company movement has occupied so much of the Federal Reserve's time and effort that attention to monetary policy may have been neglected. Because the 1970 Act places the Fed in a position of authority over nonmember banks in BHCs as well as members, some observers believe this degree of control may not be entirely appropriate.[75]

Attrition from the Federal Reserve System in recent years has been a major source of concern to its Board of Governors. Although the Monetary Control Act addressed this by making *all* banks subject to reserve requirements, and thus eliminating a primary reason for that attrition, it did not mandate membership in the system.

Frank Wille, former Chairman of the FDIC, has suggested a regulatory approach that would entail the formation of two new agencies, each headed by a federal official. One of these, overseeing all state banks, would assume the regulatory powers the Fed now holds over state-chartered members.

---

[71]Lucille S. Mayne, "Restructuring the Federal Bank Regulatory System," *The Bankers Magazine* (September–October 1978):72.
[72]Walter E. Headley, "Severn Crucial Decisions," *American Banker* (February 2, 1977):7.
[73]Noble, "Study of Financial Regulators,":D3.
[74]Jessee and Seelig, *Bank Holding Companies and the Public Interest*, p. 157.
[75]Ibid.

The other would become responsible for all national banks. Holding companies, depending on the type of charter held by their largest bank, would be supervised and examined by either. The Wille proposal also calls for a five-member Federal Banking Board, consisting of the heads of the two agencies, one member of the Federal Reserve Board of Governors, and two individuals named by the President. This new agency would establish uniform policy for all commercial banks.[76]

In the Philadelphia case, the Supreme Court created a host of new problems by determining that, as a result of the "cluster" of services and products offered by commercial banks, their industry constitutes a unique line of commerce and that these institutions therefore compete *only* with one another:

> Commercial banks are the only financial institutions in which a wide variety of financial products and services . . . are [sic] gathered together in one place. The clustering of financial products and services in banks . . . makes possible access to certain products or services that would otherwise be unavailable.[77]

Therefore, the Court held that any merger might, *per se,* constitute restraint of competition, since the number of banks in a local geographic market would be automatically reduced.[78] The Court reaffirmed this position in two subsequent merger decisions.[79]

The logic behind these decisions was difficult for many bankers to understand or accept at the time; it is even more unfathomable today.[80] Henry C. Wallich, Member of the Fed's Board of Governors, has said that the decisions do not reflect the realities of today's marketplace,[81] and recent regulatory and technological changes make it more important than ever before that the Court's basic premise be reassessed, whether through legislative or judicial processes.[82] The fact is that commercial banks *do not* compete exclusively with one another today, if indeed they did in 1963,

[76]Jessee and Seelig, *Bank Holding Companies and the Public Interest,* p. 157.
[77]*United States* v. *Philadelphia National Bank,* 374 U.S. 321 (1963).
[78]Mayne, "Restructuring the Federal Bank Regulatory System," p. 74.
[79]*United States* v. *Phillipsburg National Bank,* 399 U.S. 350 (1970) and *United States* v. *Connecticut National Bank,* 418 U.S. 656 (1974).
[80]Selected criticisms are cited in F. Jay Cummings, "Commercial Banking as a Line of Commerce," Federal Reserve Bank of Dallas, *Economic Review* (September 1982):12.
[81]With Walter A. Varvel, "Evolution in Banking Competition," Federal Reserve Bank of Richmond, *Economic Review* (March–April 1981):3.
[82]Cummings, "Commercial Banking as a Line of Commerce."

nor do they have the exclusivity in offering a "cluster" of products and services that the Court imputed to them. Rather, they

> face intensive competition across a rapidly broadening scope of product and geographic markets from . . . thrifts and nonfinancial firms. . . . They are experiencing an all-out invasion from both traditional and new competitors.[83]

Thrift institutions not only offer time and savings accounts, and checking accounts with overdraft privileges and debit/credit cards; their ability to provide various types of loans was substantially broadened through the Monetary Control Act of 1980 and the Garn-St. Germain bill of 1982. They also compete aggressively for IRA and Keogh accounts. Commercial credit, factoring, insurance, and captive finance companies extend huge amounts of credit to various categories of borrowers. Credit unions have become a significant force in the deposit, payment, and credit areas that were traditionally the province of banks. Money market funds, at their peak in 1982, held over $230 billion, much of which was assumed to have come from disintermediation of bank and thrift deposits. Major corporations, themselves the banks' largest customers, lend to one another through the commercial paper market, bypassing the banking system.[84] As a result of all these developments, today's bankers hear a question that was never posed to their predecessors: "Why do we need a bank at all?"[85]

The federal banking legislation that was passed many years ago, and is still largely intact, had an essentially negative tenor; it reflected the view that bankers had been guilty of excessive efforts to compete with one another, and had neglected the proper business of commercial banking. Therefore the areas of activity open to banks became limited. This may have curbed previous excesses, but it inhibited flexibility and innovation.

The holding company has been an effective countering device; indeed, with both the Department of Justice and the Supreme Court in virtually automatic opposition to merger and acquisition proposals by American banks,[86] it is perceived as the only vehicle through which banks can broaden their range of services and effectively compete for funds. The

---

[83]Varvel and Wallich, "Evolution in Banking Competition" p. 8.

[84]Paul S. Nadler, *Commercial Banking in the Economy*, 2nd Ed. (New York: Random House, 1973), p. 176.

[85]Jane B. Quinn, "Savings Without Banks," *Newsweek* (July 16, 1979):82.

[86]Nadler, *Commercial Banking in the Economy*, pp. 177–178.

BHCs that control two of the three largest commercial banks may be cited as examples. In 1976, Bankamerica Corporation listed a total of twenty-three domestic banking subsidiaries (including Edge Act offices in four states), five foreign banking subsidiaries, and thirteen nonbank subsidiaries as evidence of its ability to serve customers through data processing, insurance, real estate, and other financially related functions throughout the world.[87] More recently, the Chase Manhattan Corporation listed twenty-eight foreign subsidiary and associated banks, twenty foreign subsidiary and associated companies, and twenty-two domestic subsidiaries.[88] Yet holding companies still raise regulatory problems when their components include national banks; the holding company automatically falls under the jurisdiction of the Federal Reserve, but the national bank, which is usually its major element, remains under the Comptroller of the Currency. Various state laws may also affect those operations of the BHC that fall within state jurisdictions. If the Fed, as the agency responsible for the BHC, is to conduct an examination of its total financial position, it must rely on the Comptroller's audit of the bank, and conduct its own inquiry into the operations of all the nonbank subsidiaries and affiliates.

During the 1970s, in their efforts to compete effectively within the framework of so much federal and state regulation and supervision, several commercial banks began to take advantage of the Federal Reserve's list of permitted BHC activities, and acquired special types of financial institutions known as industrial banks. Technically, these are not banks or savings and loan associations; they are state-chartered entities, legally authorized in eleven states to offer a limited range of financial services. They can accept consumer deposits and extend various forms of commercial and personal credit. Major bank holding companies, including Citicorp, Bankamerica Corporation, Manufacturers Hanover Corporation, Chemical New York Corporation, and First Pennsylvania Corporation were among those obtaining Federal Reserve approval to acquire existing industrial banks or to establish *de novo* institutions of this type. Because industrial banks are exempt from Regulation Q, there is no ceiling on their interest rates, and they can effectively compete with thrift institutions.[89]

[87]Bankamerica Corporation, *Annual Report* (1976).
[88]Chase Manhattan Corporation, *Annual Report* (1981).
[89]Karen W. Arenson, "A Bank Bridge over State Lines," *The New York Times* (April 20, 1979):D1.

The State of the Art

As today's commercial banker surveys the financial marketplace, he or she recognizes that the thrifts and nonbanks have attracted an increased share of the nation's total activity. The banker cannot complain about the competition as such; rather, the complaint reflects the fact that competitors do not fall under the same regulatory and statutory restraints as the banks. A "financial services" organization that can cross state lines with impunity, is not required to set aside reserves with the Fed, and is not subject to all the regulations that federal and state authorities impose on banks, obviously enjoys a very significant competitive advantage.

If banks are to be allowed to compete more effectively, either their competitors must be subjected to the same regulations so that the "playing field" becomes more level, or the banks themselves must be given more freedom. Walter Wriston, among others, has said that the former is not the viable alternative:

> The solution is *not* to take away the freedoms that make our nonbanking competition more vigorous. It is to let us compete under regulations framed . . . on the real world . . . [and] to give us the flexibility to provide that competition which always improves services to the public.[90]

A final summation of the same viewpoint has been provided by Kenneth A. Randall, former Chairman of the FDIC:

> In our imperfect world, there is the branch that we may want to start but that branching laws will not permit, the banking market that we can't reach because it's just into the next state or county, . . . and the financial service that has not been approved by the Federal Reserve.[91]

Accepting deposits, processing payments, and granting loans have been considered parts of the unique franchise of commercial banking; therefore, all types of federal and state restrictions were felt to be justified for the commercial banking system. The justification has long since disappeared, but the restrictions remain—and the banks see themselves at a severe competitive disadvantage as a result.

[90]In "Banking in Transition," p. 35.
[91]In Prochnow and Prochnow, Jr., *The Changing World of Banking*, p. 324.

12 The New World of Banking

The commercial banker was primarily an asset manager, who loaned and invested, on a selective basis, the demand deposits that provided him with a steady flow of raw material and formed the basis for his bank's deposit structure. Acronyms such as MICR, ACH, NOW and EFTS had not yet been coined. Networks of foreign branches did not exist to any real extent; international transactions for customers were handled through overseas correspondent banks. Checking account statements, with all paid checks, were sent out to every customer on the last business day of every month. Only one major bank in New York City actively sought installment loan applications from individual wage-earners; its competitors expressed little or no interest in that type of credit, and focused their attention on commercial lending. Individuals who requested savings accounts or home mortgage loans were politely referred to correspondent savings banks or S&Ls, except when so-called "compound interest" or "thrift" accounts were opened as a special accommodation to existing checking-account customers. All checks that would create account overdrafts were individually referred to officers for approval before being posted. Automated teller facilities and demand deposit accounting systems did not exist. Direct lending to foreign governments was done on a limited basis, if at all. The banker's vocabulary did not include such terms as Eurodollars, sweep accounts, credit cards, share drafts, or CDs. Any thought that consumers might be able to obtain balance data through a home terminal, pay bills by telephone, or conduct a significant part of their banking business through off-site automated units was a sheer flight of fancy.

Does the foregoing paragraph describe the state of the art in some ancient, long-forgotten period in American banking history? Not at all. Every condition, management philosophy, and service (or lack of service) mentioned in it existed in 1950, when the author of this text began his career with one of the country's largest commercial banks. In every instance, the obvious changes that have occurred provide an inkling of the revolution that has taken place in commercial banking in the intervening years.

The word *revolution* is not an overstatement in this context. Indeed, it is the only term that can be accurately used in referring to all that has happened to banking in little more than three decades. Internal changes have introduced new services and technology, and have revised the method of supplying old ones. External changes have stripped banking of its traditional exclusivity in many service areas. This revolution is far from over; it is producing additional changes in the financial marketplace even as this text is being written. Note Martin Mayer's comment in 1974: "Like all revolutions, the one in banking can be admired or loathed, depending on one's other attitudes. What it should not be is ignored—yet not one American in a thousand has any idea about what has happened."[1]

All available evidence contradicts Mayer's generalization in every respect. The average American *is* fully aware that a revolution has occurred. The banking industry, whose leaders have sometimes been described as unable to adjust to changing times and lacking in vision,[2] has been completely transformed in a multitude of ways, and the consumer—like the corporate treasurer or the financial officer of a government agency or correspondent bank—has been quick to take advantage of this fact.

Every holder of a bank card or certificate of deposit, every customer with a traditional or new type of NOW account, every user of the 26,000 ATMs that are now seen at financial institutions throughout the country, every consumer who follows industry's lead by reducing demand deposit balances to a minimum, and every person who is exposed to radio, newspaper, television, magazine, and billboard advertising of banks cannot help but be aware of the new world of banking.

The dynamics of change have been repeatedly stressed throughout this

---

[1] In *The Bankers,* (New York: David McKay Co., 1974), p. 5. Reprinted by permission.
[2] Kenneth A. Randall, in Herbert V. Prochnow and Herbert V. Prochnow, Jr., Eds., *The Changing World of Banking* (New York: Harper & Row, 1974), p. 322.

text. The shift from basic asset allocation to complex liability management, the advent of diversified operations and services provided through entities under the holding-company umbrella, the dawning of a "less-check" society, and the expansion of global activities by both American and foreign banks have been mentioned. They offer further evidence that the revolution not only has taken place, but *is* noticed. Similarly, any member of the 2,000 households that will take part in a pilot project for home banking, scheduled for August 1983, *must* be cognizant of the dramatic potential in the new world of banking. Those individuals will test a home-terminal service combining account data, funds transfers, bill payments, sports and weather news, shopping opportunities, video games, and financial and business features.[3]

The new world of banking is one in which the profession, once characterized by Paul Nadler as having the motto "never do something for the first time,"[4] is coming to recognize that traditional attitudes, stereotyped approaches, and hidebound thinking are no longer viable. The "old breed" of bankers saw their industry as one in which banks competed only with one another and not with a Sears, an American Express, a Merrill Lynch, or a National Steel. Because the bank and its officers were known in the community, advertising was viewed as both unnecessary and undesirable. The entire commercial banking industry spent less than $50 million on all forms of advertising in 1950, the year referred to at the beginning of this chapter.[5] If, as Mayer has stated, most Americans are unaware of the changes that have taken place in banking, the huge increases in advertising expenses since 1950 have been wasted.

The New World of Bank Marketing

That relatively new emphasis on bank advertising is in itself evidence of a new attitude. Traditionally, the banking industry paid little attention to the theories and strategies of marketing, and the very word *salesman* was considered to have strongly pejorative connotations. The banker was a prestigious, trustworthy figure in the community; the salesman was viewed by bankers as a huckster, a peddler, or a used-car dealer.

---

[3]John Morris, "BancOhio in Home Banking Test," *American Banker* (January 20, 1983):2.
[4]In Prochnow and Prochnow, Jr., Eds. *The Changing World of Banking*, p. 381.
[5]Howard D. Crosse and George H. Hempel, *Management Policies for Commercial Banks*, 2nd Ed. (Englewood Cliffs, N.J.: Prentice-Hall, 1973), p. 281.

To the contemporary and progressive banker, the word *salesperson* is no longer derogatory; marketing is the key to success. The effective banker is a salesperson who can motivate use of the institution's products and services by customers and prospects. Today's bank Marketing Department is often an integrated unit that not only supplies data on the profit potential of a new product or branch site, but also directs the total program of advertising and promotions, serves as a source of competitive intelligence, and conducts sales training. It translates Maslow's theory of human needs into sales messages aimed at the appropriate segments of the bank's market. It puts into action management's recognition of and commitment to the principle that business decisions can be made *only* after consideration has been given to user wants and needs, as well as to profit factors.

Thus, in the new world of banking, an integrated marketing effort includes the following:

Clear identification of the product or service itself

Determination of the customer segments and geographic areas to which it will be targeted

Statement of the customer benefits to be stressed

Identification of the promotional methods to be used in soliciting customers

Pro forma profit statements, showing the net effect after all budget requirements and projected expenses have been met.[6]

In money-market cities, where many competing banks and other financial institutions coexist, there may be few or no real differences among the services offered. If all competitors are delivering those services in a timely, thorough, and accurate manner, the bank that achieves a dominant position in any one area can usually point to the effectiveness of its marketing program as the reason.

Organizing or restructuring the marketing unit and effort in order to meet changing conditions begins logically with an identification of existing problems. One major bank in New York City identified three of these: "Calling officers didn't have time to make the calls they should; they weren't motivated to sell, and many who were didn't really know how to sell; and current customers didn't use many of the bank's services."[7]

[6]N. W. Pope, "Drawing Up a Plan and Seeing to It That It Works," *American Banker* (February 2, 1983):4.
[7]J. Wilmer Mirandon, "Mobilizing for Personal Selling," *Burroughs Clearing House* (June 1973):20.

These problems were solved first by organizational restructuring so that business development officers could concentrate on selling and could be freed from administrative duties and details, and second by instituting programs designed to train the staff in selling skills, self-motivation, cross-selling, and interpersonal communications. The new world of banking requires the services of individuals who understand and apply the principles of human relations in their cultivation of customers. By empathizing with the latter group, they focus the services of the bank on customer needs and simultaneously convey impressions that it is both "progressive" and "caring."[8]

The quasi-educational aspect of marketing is of particular importance in the EFTS field. Many consumer reservations, uncertainties, and fears have already been identified. New programs that seem highly desirable from the bank's viewpoint cannot be successfully "sold" unless the consumer is convinced that they will benefit him or her, rather than just the institution itself. The new world of banking must mirror that of America's new society, in which there are so many individuals who are more sophisticated, affluent, receptive to change, and aware of yield opportunities.

Banks must prove to these individuals that the new systems are secure, cost-effective, and accurate, and are not intended to remove personal control over one's financial transactions. The danger to the banks lies in the posssibility of "concentrating on the technology and forgetting about the user, upon whom the real success of EFTS will depend."[9] When a senior officer of the National Bank of Detroit, demonstrating the effectiveness of a new network, obtains cash and balance information through an ATM in Chula Vista, California,[10] the result is impressive. However, the average consumer may have little or no interest in this system, simply because it does not reflect his or her particular need.

The deposit structure of the commercial banking system today clearly shows the new sophistication of customers. Demand deposits continually shrink as a proportion of the total, and while Table 12.1 shows the changes that took place in 1982, it does *not* include the new types of money market and Super-NOW accounts that were introduced at the end of that year and in early 1983. A bank marketing effort today that aims at attracting interest-free demand deposits is doomed to failure. Rather, the effort must

[8]Ray C. Brewster, "More Psychology in Selling," *Harvard Business Review* (July–August 1953):91.
[9]George C. White, Jr., "EFTS Update," Speech delivered to New York City Chapter, Bank Administration Institute Conference (March 16, 1978).
[10]Laura Gross, "Cirrus Network Used Interstate," *American Banker* (January 18, 1983):1.

**Table 12.1.   Changes in Deposit Structure
All U.S. Commercial Banks, 1982**

	November 1982	December 1981	Increase
Total Deposits[a]	1,316	1,206	110
Demand	338 (25.7%)	322 (26.7%)	16
Savings	245	223	
Time	733	661	
Savings and Time	978 (74.3%)	884 (73.3%)	94

Source: Federal Reserve Bulletin, December 1982, p. A18.
[a]In billions of dollars.

focus on services and relationships that will offer customers an attractive interest rate while giving the bank an adequate profit margin. Alternatively, the marketing program can focus on generating sufficient fees, in keeping with the new trend in the financial marketplace.

As mentioned earlier, corporate financial officers are no longer willing to maintain interest-free balances, either as compensation for credit facilities or as a form of payment to the bank for services rendered. Rather, they want to free-up balances and gain tax deductions by paying direct fees. In many cases, major commercial banks have not only accepted the pressures created by customers; they have initiated a move toward fees themselves. Fee income is not as sensitive to the cost of money, and is not subject to the forces that keep rates of return down. The 1981 Annual Reports of five leading banks specifically identified management moves toward fees, and actual dollars of noninterest income at all insured commercial banks have more than doubled since 1977.[11]

In banking's new world, the three traditional and basic functions—accepting deposits, processing payments, and extending credit—remain essentially unchanged. It is the scope, type, substructure, and method of delivery of those functions that have been modified and expanded.

First, the era of the large, relatively inactive, interest-free checking account is gone. The deposit function in the future must concentrate on various forms of savings and time deposits, all of them with interest expense an integral part of their operations. One of the major paradoxes in

[11]Carol T. Karkut, "The Growing Importance of Fee Income in Strategic Planning," *The Magazine of BANK ADMINISTRATION* (January 1983):20.

banking in recent years can be found in the marketing of cash management services, which allowed financial officers—and, more recently, consumers—to monitor balances more closely than ever before, and to draw down and invest excess funds.

Disintermediation, in the past, described the outflow of funds from banks to thrift institutions, and from the latter group to money market funds or to other investment media. More recently, the word has assumed a new meaning, as internal disintermediation has taken place. The banks' experiences in December 1982 and January 1983 provide a case in point.

With the passage of the Garn-St. Germain Act in 1982, the Depository Institutions Deregulation Committee was able to direct commercial banks and thrifts to offer new types of accounts with unlimited interest rates as a form of direct competition with the funds. Within two weeks following the introduction of the first of these new accounts (December 1982), the Fed reported that $52 billion had been deposited in them. However, only one-sixth of that amount came from outside sources (including money market funds); the remainder came from lower-yielding passbook accounts or from interest-free demand deposits. Thus, the banks were generally doing nothing more than paying additional interest for funds that were already part of their deposit base.[12] The ratio of demand to time and savings deposits, cited earlier, can be expected to decrease still further as more funds move into the new accounts.

Second, the payments function in commercial banking has also changed tremendously in recent years. Payment mechanisms used by the banks in moving funds among themselves (e.g., CHIPS and SWIFT), and by their customers in disbursing, have been radically altered, and although the total "checkless" society, as first envisioned, may never arrive, EFT services still hold the potential to become the most important development in terms of total impact on the banking system.

That impact can only be increased through the effects of the Monetary Control Act of 1980, which directed the Federal Reserve to implement a system of explicit pricing for its services to banks—specifically including the collection of checks. The Fed's per-item charges must be passed along to customers, and that may accelerate the move toward EFTS.

Finally, in the third traditional area of banking, that is, the credit function, the type and scope of loans made to accommodate the total customer market have undergone significant changes. The new emphasis on personal

[12]Charles P. Alexander, "A Big Brawl in Banking," *Time* (January 17, 1983):34.

overdraft privileges, the use of bank cards to incur debt, the expansion of global leasing and factoring operations, the formation of syndicates with foreign banks to provide large loans in many parts of the world, and the acquisitions of small loan companies by many BHCs exemplify the trend toward new types of lending.

THE IMPACT OF EFTS

Two of the Hunt Commission's co-directors have stressed the point that EFTS will not only affect the deposit, payment, and credit functions, but will have an impact on the geographical and numerical composition of the banking industry:

> Businesses will be able to utilize the services of banks at considerable distances, . . . thus permitting even small businesses to utilize banks which are not in the same community. This will intensify competition in bank markets . . . [and] raises the question of the continued viability of the thousands of small banks that are now geographically protected.[13]

It is the last point that is likely to create extended controversy in the new world of banking. If full-scale operations across state lines become feasible for commercial banks—as they now are for many thrift institutions—through the use of automated facilities, the customer in a given community will have access to institutions in major moneymarket centers, and will no longer have to depend on the limited resources of the local banks. The advantages of a unique location may then disappear, and Paul Nadler,[14] among others, has predicted a significant reduction in the future number of banking organizations as a direct result of this innovation.

The question of actual survival, posed under this scenario, receives additional impetus from the new money market and "Super-NOW" accounts. Large banks obtain much of their deposits from businesses, which are not eligible for the latter type of account; however, the smaller regional banks rely more heavily on consumer deposits and are therefore more

---

[13]Donald P. Jacobs and Almarin Phillips, "Hunt Proposals," *American Banker* (February 5, 1975):4.
[14]In Prochnow and Prochnow, Jr., Eds., *The Changing World of Banking*, p. 388.

vulnerable. If they cannot, for competitive reasons, maintain loan rates high enough to cover the costs of the new accounts and show a profit, they may have no alternative but to merge with stronger institutions or go out of business.[15]

If existing regulatory constraints are relaxed so that banks enjoy the same freedom from which S&Ls and nonbank competitors (e.g., American Express, Sears, and Merrill Lynch) now benefit, physical visits to the banks by customers will diminish in importance. Many transactions will be initiated through terminals in airports, supermarkets, and other convenient locations. Further refinement of EFTS capabilities, coupled with effective marketing, will lead to far wider acceptance of systems that make the consumers' homes their financial-services centers as at-home banking spreads.

For corporations, the banks may assume a larger role in processing receivables and payables, including direct deposit activity if businesses can be motivated to use electronic funds transfers in lieu of checks.[16]

In the new world of banking, the institutions themselves may bear little or no physical resemblance to today's structures. High-rent locations, vaulted ceilings, Gothic architecture, and large expanses of open space will be replaced in many cases by far more functional, efficient, and inexpensive minibranches, storefront facilities, and automated installations. Those networks of branches that are now permitted by state laws will undoubtedly be reduced in size.

MARKETING EFTS

Two of the foregoing sections of this chapter are directly connected in the discussion of this "new world." Modern marketing and EFTS are tied to each other, and the future of banking's profitability and growth depends largely on that linkage.

The network of automated clearing houses (ACHs) has been established and its components interconnected. The in-bank hardware and software are, for the most part, now in place at banks throughout the country. All

[15]Alexander, "A Big Brawl in Banking," p. 35.
[16]George C. White, Jr., "Innovations in Cash Management," *Bank Administration* (March 1975):58.

that is needed is a customer base large enough to drive transaction costs down and make EFT programs and systems flourish. Yet the potential marketplace, with but a few significant exceptions, has remained openly opposed or, at best, apathetic.

Those significant exceptions include the federal government's programs for direct deposit of Social Security payments and Armed Forces payrolls, the Hinky Dinky project, and the increasing volume of transactions now being handled through some 26,000 ATMs. These successes have been widely publicized. Unfortunately for the prophets of a totally checkless society, so have the failures. A California S&L abandoned its commitment to ATMs and closed down its 130-terminal system.[17] Bill payment by telephone through the EFT facilities of over 400 banks replaced 80 million checks in 1982, yet it has never achieved the popular acceptance that was predicted for it in the 1970s.[18]

If electronic funds transfers are to play as important a role in the new world of banking as was originally anticipated and hoped for, a far more effective marketing campaign is essential. The banks must devise ways to overcome consumers' fears of loss of privacy, use of their accounts by unauthorized parties, and loss of personal control over finances. The campaign must be a positive one, placing its stress on the direct benefits to the users. It is self-defeating to try to force-feed a system to a public that has strong reservations about it, or to market that system solely on its advantages for the selling banks. Today's sophisticated consumer immediately asks, "What's in it for me?" As the competitors' ranks grow and their own marketing becomes ever more aggressive, consumers are given a new and wider freedom of choice. If commercial banks wish to attract and retain retail business, the motivating factors can come only from a strongly educational marketing program.

To counter the competition and sell their own systems and services, banks must create an image of themselves as innovative: a quality they have so long and so often been said to lack. Thrift institutions, credit unions, money market funds, and retailers have achieved their gains at the banks' expense, by learning consumer needs and wants and becoming innovators in responding. Their example must be followed in filling voids in the financial marketplace by introducing new service products and marketing integrated "packages."

[17]Robert A. Eisenbeis, "A Framework for Evaluating the Debate Over EFTS," in *Conference on Bank Structure and Competition,* Federal Reserve Bank of Chicago (April 1977):303.
[18]Robert M. Garsson, "Telephone Bill Paying," *American Banker* (January 5, 1983):8.

The individual worker, who believes that direct deposit of payroll automatically creates a loss of privacy in his or her household, *can* be convinced that this is not necessarily true. The corporate financial officer *can* be "sold" on the concept that electronic payments generate benefits that more than offset the loss of float. The prospective user of an ATM *can* be reassured that proper security measures have been implemented, and that transaction costs will be lower than those for checks—particularly since explicit pricing for check collection is now mandated.

The financial community, in marketing various applications of EFTS, must also be aware of the many potential liabilities it faces. A host of federal laws and legal concerns must be addressed, if the banks are to protect themselves and avoid systems-related litigation, regulatory enforcement actions, or both.[19]

Funds do not now and will never steadily flow into the banking system on an automatic basis. In the new world of banking, marketing demands the creativity and flexibility that will attract those funds. There will always be observers—some of whom may occupy positions of authority in regulatory agencies— who will look at the manner in which banks are preparing corporate payrolls, handling rent and tax collections, leasing all types of equipment, and performing a host of ancillary and peripheral services, and who will say, "But that isn't banking!" Yet, in every case, there *is* some form of relevance to traditional banking functions.[20]

These observers would undoubtedly look askance at a home-banking system known as *Prestel*, which combines a television set with a special receiver to give the user access, in his or her office or home, to a huge data bank. In Great Britain, Barclays Bank has adapted this system to allow customers to enter personal information, through the terminal, to apply for loans. Further adaptations resemble many of the home-terminal systems mentioned earlier. They include a printout on the TV screen, allowing users to scan a store's catalogue list and initiate purchases. Immediate account debiting can result.[21]

Certainly systems of this type represent a major departure from traditional banking functions, but that fact cannot be the basis for underestimating, attacking, or ignoring them. If commercial banks do not seize

[19]August Bequai, "Legal Liabilities of EFT Systems," *The Magazine of BANK ADMINISTRATION* (January 1983):25–27.
[20]Paul Nadler, *Commercial Banking in the Economy, 2nd Ed.* (New York: Random House, 1973), p. 202.
[21]" 'Prestel': A Glimpse at the Future," *American Banker* (May 22, 1979):7, and "TV Turns to Print," *Newsweek* (July 30, 1979):74.

the opportunity to develop and market services of this type wherever feasible and legal, there is no doubt that a competitor of some type will.

MANAGEMENT FOR THE FUTURE

The past is known and has been recorded. The present has been analyzed. Can the future be foreseen with any degree of certainty? If commercial banks are to achieve their objectives of generating profits while rendering services, what are the most significant challenges they seem likely to face? How may their objectives be attained? What actions and reactions can one logically expect?

A synthesis of all that has been said and written on these topics indicates an interplay of several critical abilities that will be required for the growth and profitability of individual banks, as well as the industry as a whole.

Ability to Meet the Challenge of Nonbanks

Savings and loan associations, regulated by a separate federal agency, and frequently unhampered by the state laws that restrict commercial banks, have long displayed an ability to attract business away from the latter. Although the number of S&Ls shrank from 4,240 in 1980 to 3,620 in 1982, acquisitions by such conglomerates as National Steel, infusions of federal aid, and mergers have made the surviving associations stronger and better able to compete.[22] The additional powers granted to S&Ls under the Monetary Control Act of 1980, will also prove helpful. Finally, in recent years, several S&Ls have "gone public" to gain the capital that will enable them to compete more effectively.[23]

The Chairman of Sears has publicly stated his plans to make the firm a leader in the entire area of consumer financial services.[24] Since 1979, it

[22]Alexander, "A Big Brawl in Banking."

[23]"The S&Ls: The Conversion Era," *Financial World* (July 1, 1979):38.

[24]Harry Taylor, "Deregulation . . . Vital for Industry Survival," *American Banker* (April 20, 1982):24.

has been possible for a client to telephone Fidelity Management and Research Company in Boston on a toll-free number, buy shares in a daily-
income fund, and have the privilege of withdrawal through a free checking
account.[25] The holder of a Merrill Lynch Cash Management Account may
likewise obtain many of the services and benefits that were once part of
banking's exclusive fiefdom.[26] The inroads made on banking by the credit
unions, whose assets exceed $62 billion, were noted by a former Comp-
troller of the Currency.[27] Retailers, unregulated by the Fed, the FDIC, or
the state banking departments, offer many financial services through their
outlets.[28]

General Motors Acceptance Corporation, operating across state lines
and not subject to reserve requirements or regulation by the Federal Reserve, reported net earnings of $348 million in 1981, and over $600 million
for 1982.[29] Citicorp was the *only* bank holding company to report 1982
earnings in excess of $500 million, and only three BHCs in the United
States had 1982 net incomes larger than GMAC's 1981 figure.[30]

The only logical action banks can take in the face of this intense competition from many sources calls for a concerted, ongoing effort to seek
legislative relief. This should not take the form of a vendetta, in which
reprisals are sought against competitors. Rather, it should clearly and
forcefully make the point that current regulatory and antitrust constraints
are, in many cases, anachronisms that cannot be justified.

For many years, commercial banks exerted this type of effort toward
deregulation, and both the Monetary Control Act of 1980 and the Garn-
St. Germain Act of 1982 included that word in their complete official titles.
However, the two statutes have *not* brought to banking the deregulation
for which its spokespersons had hoped. Rather, both Acts have given
more freedom to, and conferred additional powers on, the savings banks
and S&Ls, and the direct benefits to commercial banks have been relatively minimal. The banker who analyzes the text of the 1980 Act, and

[25]"Everyone is Stepping into Everyone Else's Turf," *Forbes* (April 16, 1979):134.

[26]Robert A. Bennett, "Merrill Vies for Bank Customers," *The New York Times* (July 9,
1979):D1.

[27]John G. Heimann, "A Conversation with the Comptroller," *The Bankers Magazine* (January–February 1979):30.

[28]Stuart Greenbaum, "The Future of Commercial Banking," *American Banker* (June 12,
1979):4.

[29]John Holusha, "GM Profit Up 49.5% in 4th Quarter," *The New York Times* (February 8,
1983):D1.

[30]"Top 10 Earning Banks," *American Banker* (January 24, 1983):3.

notes the expanded authorities it gives to credit unions and thrifts, can hardly be blamed for skepticism as to what "deregulation" means.

The Depository Institutions Deregulation Committee, in implementing the provisions of the Garn-St. Germain Act, allowed commercial banks and thrifts to offer "Super-NOW" accounts, without interest-rate ceilings, but with unlimited withdrawal privileges. These accounts are available to individuals, government agencies, and certain nonprofit organizations.[31] Yet required reserves against them were set at only 4% for thrifts versus 12% for commercial banks, thus enhancing the competitive advantage of the former group.[32] Clearly, *deregulation* has different connotations for different groups.

It is not unreasonable to propose that the banks invite America's major corporations, which have always relied on them to meet their credit needs, to join with them in the effort to obtain legislative relief and greater freedom to operate. Further disintermediation from the commercial banking system can create a situation in which the banks find themselves unable to meet the loan requests of all these corporate clients. The result would inevitably be a system of credit allocation, with an increase in interest rates and a detrimental effect on the nation's economy.

In terms of the number of banks that went out of existence (42), in 1982, the industry experienced its worst year since 1940.[33] Corporate treasurers should ask themselves whether nonbank competitors could ever replace the existing industry and fill the potential credit vacuum.

The ability of commercial banks to diversify into new, financially oriented areas is the key to continued maintenance of their role as the pillars of the economy. If they wish to become, and are able to become, the type of "financial supermarket" once predicted as their future format, they may draw some degree of encouragement from the fact that an institution offering a complete range of congeneric services appealed to 45 percent of the respondents in a nationwide study conducted in 1972.[34] Unfortunately, many existing competitors are now in a better position than commercial banks to respond to that public appeal.

[31]Federal Reserve Bank of New York, "Depository Institutions Deregulation Committee," *Circular 9429* (December 29, 1982).
[32]Laura L. Mulcahy, "Reserve Rules Give Thrifts Edge," *American Banker* (January 6, 1983):1.
[33]Arthur J. L. Lucey, "Deregulation: Learn from It," *American Banker* (January 19, 1983):4.
[34]Louis Harris, *The Second Study: The American Public's and Community Opinion Leaders' Views of Banks and Bankers in 1972* (Philadelphia: The Foundation for Full Service Banks, 1972), p. 118.

At the same time, the bankers must recognize the opposition they can expect to encounter in their quest for greater freedom and flexibility. Fears of undue concentration of power in the hands of a relatively small number of banking giants will be voiced; public awareness of bank failures and problems in recent years will be expressed; and potential litigation must be considered.

Ability to Manage Global Lending

Many of America's major commercial banks have significantly increased their credit exposure in some of the world's problem areas in recent years, and as a result, face a dilemma that gained a great deal of public attention in 1982 and 1983. A study conducted among 130 banks disclosed that their loan charge-offs in 1982 increased 72 percent, from $226 million to $389 million; their loss expenses rose from 2.5 percent of gross income to 3.6 percent.[35] The dilemma lies in the fact that write-offs by the banks of a large part of the total debt of less-developed countries (LDCs), estimated at $600 billion at year-end 1982,[36] would further damage their earnings and impair their further lending ability. Conversely, a rigorous effort to compel repayment might lead the borrowers to simply repudiate their obligations.

The concerns felt by the banks on this subject have been shared by the Securities and Exchange Commission, which has imposed new guidelines requiring BHCs to divulge detailed information on their loans to and investments in "problem nations."[37]

There is a sober new awareness of the effects that nonperforming LDC loans are having on the banks' bottom lines, . . . on their own credit ratings and funding costs as well as on the viability of the international credit system.[38]

[35]Sanford Rose, "Massive Rise in Defaults Crimps Bank Earnings," *American Banker* (February 1, 1983):1.
[36]Robert Samuelson, "U.S. Is Linked to Debt Patterns of Developing World," *American Banker* (February 1, 1983):5.
[37]Andrew Albert, "Banks Reminded to Disclose Their Loans to Poor Nations," *American Banker* (January 18, 1983):3.
[38]Linda Sandler, "Can Crisis Cofinancing Save the World?" *Institutional Investor* (February 1983):55.

In February 1983, several senior bankers appealed to Congress for federal assistance in the event that some of their "Third-World" borrowers were to become bankrupt. At the same, members of the International Monetary Fund, to which the United States is a major contributor, were meeting to decide how much money the Fund needed to help the heavily indebted nations, and prevent them from defaulting on their loans.[39] The bankers' request for federal aid met with this comment from Chairman St. Germain, of the House Banking Committee: "U.S. banks have ignored prudent practices and domestic needs in search of the quick buck and the sky-high interest rates offered by desperate borrowers caught in an international financial squeeze."[40]

The suggestion has been advanced that only a joint effort by the lending banks—notwithstanding any antitrust statutes—with the International Monetary Fund can avert a major global crisis. In the new world of banking, this is a problem that cannot be ignored.

Ability to Meet the Challenge of Foreign Banks

The President of Manufacturers Hanover Trust Company has cited the presence of over 300 foreign banks in the United States, their ability (under "grandfather" clauses in the International Banking Act of 1978) to operate across state lines, and the acquisitions of such major institutions as Marine Midland, Crocker Bank, and the National Bank of North America by foreign interests as serious competitive problems in the new world of banking.[41] As of September 1982, branches and agencies of foreign banks in the United States reported outstanding loans of $126 billion, or 12.8 percent of the national total.[42] In California and New York, where their presence is most strongly felt, foreign banks are the lenders on some 30 percent of all commercial loans. Concern is also caused by the fact that the true financial condition of foreign banks is not always easy to determine, since accounting standards vary from one country to another.

The question has been raised about possible reciprocal action by foreign

[39]Andrew Albert, "Lawmakers, Bankers Clash on IMF Aid," *American Banker* (February 10, 1983):1.
[40]Clyde H. Farnsworth, "Banks' Bid for Aid Stirs Old, Deep Resentments," *The New York Times* (February 10, 1983):D1.
[41]Taylor, "Deregulation . . . Vital for Industry Survival."
[42]*Federal Reserve Bulletin* (January 1983):A76.

governments if American laws were enacted to curtail the above-mentioned trend. Given the contributions of American banks to the global economy and the financial structure of so many foreign countries, the threat of such action today has diminished. More important is the threat of a real concentration of domestic banking in the hands of foreign interests that may be in conflict with our own. In the new world of banking, the development method that can meet the challenges of foreign banks and offset the advantages they enjoy will be vital to the growth and profitability of many institutions.

Ability to Adjust to Asset/Liability Management

As the dynamics of change in the deposit base of American commercial banks intensify, the emphasis on effective management of assets and liabilities becomes ever more critical. The new world of banking is one in which all the activities involved in attracting funds from depositors and investors, determining the proper deposit "mix," and maintaining an appropriate profit margin affect current profits, as well as the banks' possible eventual survival.

Commercial banks are traditionally highly leveraged financial intermediaries, with borrowed funds supplying over 90 percent of their assets.[43] As increasing numbers of depositors in every category reduce their interest-free balances and move funds into various forms of time, savings, and NOW relationships, and as the phase-out of interest-rate ceilings required by the Monetary Control Act progresses, the problems of liability management become even more severe. Use of the Federal Reserve's discount window, purchases of Fed funds for liquidity purposes, borrowings in the Eurodollar market, use of repurchase agreements, and issues of capital notes and/or debentures are among the most common techniques used by banks to fund their operations. However, in addition to employing any or all of these methods, each bank must directly relate its marketing effort to its program of funds management.

Escalating interest expense cannot be avoided in today's financial marketplace, but no bank needs "loss leader" relationships. The costs of acquiring and retaining funds must always be matched against the rate of return generated by the use of those funds.

[43]Edward W. Reed, Richard V. Cotter, Edward K. Gill, and Richard K. Smith, *Commercial Banking*, 2nd Ed. (Englewood Cliffs, N.J.: Prentice-Hall, 1980), p. 125.

A classic case of "rate wars" among banks, and the problems they create, occurred when the new money market accounts were introduced in December 1982. In their anxiety to attract new deposits, some banks—particularly those in the southeastern United States—offered rates of 20 percent or more, at a time when Treasury-bill rates were declining. One institution stopped offering the new account after its rate of 25 percent brought in four times the deposits it had sought.[44]

One observer has estimated that money-market and "Super-NOW" accounts may reduce community banks' earnings by as much as 30 percent, and those of regional banks by 9 to 13 percent, unless effective programs of asset and liability management recover the costs of those relationships.[45] Modern technology can play an important role in this effort. Full-scale computer models can be designed to suggest portfolio changes, and show the effect of various decisions on bottom-line earnings.[46]

The continuing and essential *caveat* in this effort involves a basic management decision. Does the bank truly want to be "all things to all people?" Many institutions in the new world of banking have no such lofty ambition. Rather, they are implementing a policy of market segmentation, using all the data available through demographic research to identify their optimum targets. George Vojta, formerly Executive Vice President of Citibank, and more recently Chief Financial Officer of Phibro-Salomon, has stated flatly that "The day of the general approach to the market is over. Successful . . . [banks] will organize and manage accordingly."[47]

The notion of "Full Service" banking does not necessarily mean that every type of institution must provide every type of service to every category of customer. Rather, in the new world of banking, it can be construed to mean that a particular institution will concentrate on the services it is best equipped to offer to those customers who appear to provide it with the maximum earnings potential. A Senior Vice President of Bankers Trust Company confirms this view:

> Will bank-customer relationships get stronger or weaker? . . . If they get stronger, this will partly be a function of how well and carefully a bank has

[44]Jerry Adams, "Rate War Abates in Southeast," *American Banker* (January 4, 1983):1.
[45]Lucey, "Deregulation: Learn from It," p. 4.
[46]Roger L. Hayes and Robert A. Meyer, "Financial Modeling Support for Asset-Liability Management," *The Magazine of BANK ADMINISTRATION* (January 1983):28–32.
[47]In *Institutional Investor* (January 1983):12.

chosen its niches and customized its services to suit those niches. Service focus and anticipation of customer needs will determine who survives.[48]

Ability to Organize and Staff to Meet Future Needs

In the new world of banking, there must be a basic recognition of the fact that the systems of internal organization and personnel administration that got the job done in the past are no longer necessarily valid. The market-place, the work force, and the technology that makes new services possible have all experienced tremendous change; banks must keep pace with them and adapt to them.

There must be a willingness to restructure internally, and to revise traditional philosophies in order to address specific market segments. An equivalent willingness will break down the banks' former strong parochial attitudes, so that the expertise of individuals from specialized nonbanking areas can be introduced and utilized. This applies especially in such areas as cost accounting, marketing, corporate planning, data processing, and industrial engineering and psychology—fields in which commercial banks traditionally have lacked the ability to perform well.

If their market-research data indicates that such a decision is appropriate, banks must be ready to move into areas that open up new horizons of customer service. The acquisitions of Charles Schwab & Co. by Bank of America; Kahn & Co. (Memphis) by Security Pacific National Bank; and Rose & Co. by Chase Manhattan provide a case in point. Regulators have held that because discount brokers do not underwrite securities or solicit trades in particular stocks, banks can enter their business without violating the Glass-Steagall Act of 1933.[49] Discount-brokerage houses provide the acquiring banks with an entirely new area of service opportunities,[50] but the breakdown of the barriers between the banking and brokerage businesses may have a serious impact on some firms in the

---

[48]G. Lynn Shostack, "Where Will the Trends of 1982 Lead Us?" *American Banker* (December 29, 1982):4.
[49]"Chase Is Proceeding with Plan to Acquire Rose & Co. Brokerage," *The Wall Street Journal* (February 17, 1983):5.
[50]Lisa J. McCue, "Acquisition of Brokerage Approved," *American Banker* (January 6, 1983):1.

latter field.[51] Every customer of a brokerage firm is automatically a candidate for bank services, and Security Pacific, through its acquisition of the Kahn firm, immediately added 30,000 new accounts to its data base for future marketing.

Banks must also be ready to implement expanded systems of management information, so that decision-making is expedited and simplified. Given the ever-expanding abilities of modern computers, there is no reason for a bank to operate without knowing fully the profitability of each department, service, or branch, or the extent of its credit exposure in each country and industry.

Finally, new procedures in human resource management are needed if banks are to attract, develop, motivate, and retain those individuals who will best be able to respond to the challenges facing them.

THE DYNAMICS OF CHANGE

Resistance to change is a common trait among humans. There is an innate tendency not to disturb the *status quo,* and to ask why any new technique or approach is necessary. In actuality, however, change is only the real enemy of those who cannot accept and adjust to it. History is replete with evidence of this in organizations and organisms alike. The dinosaur was unable to cope with change and went out of existence. Individuals who remain hopelessly tied to the past, and cannot relate to the present, fail— inside and outside the work environment. American railroads could neither see the implications of change nor respond to it, and lost their status as a result. The lessons are there, plainly written, for commercial bankers to see and understand.

Every contemporary topic, issue, and problem in commercial banking relates to this same principle. If banks are to avoid going the way of the dinosaurs and railroads, they must anticipate change and be in a position to capitalize on it. Their role must be active, rather than merely reactive. This is a formidable challenge, but one that carries with it an opportunity and a potential reward that may well be greater than any provided in the past.

[51]Shostack, "Where Will the Trends of 1982 Lead Us?"

Bibliography

Anderson, Stanley W., *The Banker and EFT*. Washington: American Bankers Association, 1982.

Austin, Douglas V., and Booker, Gene S., *Modern Techniques in Bank Management*. Boston: Warren, Gorham & Lamont, 1969.

Baker, James C., and Bradford, M. Gerald. *American Banks Abroad*. New York: Praeger, 1974.

Berliner, William M. *Managerial and Supervisory Practice: Cases and Principles,* 7th Ed. Homewood, Ill.: Richard D. Irwin, 1979.

Blevins, Ronald L., Clarke, John M., Mitchell, III, James J., Zalaha, Jack W., and Zinsser, August. *The Trust Business*. Washington: American Bankers Association, 1982.

Bowden, Elbert V. *Revolution in Banking*. Richmond, Va.: Robert F. Dame, 1980.

Candilis, Wray O. *The Future of Commercial Banking*. New York: Praeger, 1975.

Compton, Eric N. *Savings and Time Deposit Banking*. Washington, D.C.: American Bankers Association, 1982.

Conboy, Jr., James C. *Law and Banking*. Washington, D.C.: American Bankers Association, 1982.

Coombs, Charles A. *The Arena of International Finance*. New York: Wiley, 1976.

Corson, John J., and Steiner, George A. *Measuring Business's Social Performance: The Corporate Social Audit*. New York: Committee for Economic Development, 1974.

Crosse, Howard D., and Hempel, George H. *Management Policies for Commercial Banks,* 2nd Ed. Englewood Cliffs, N.J.: Prentice-Hall, 1973.

Davis, Robert W. (Ed.) *Comparative Digest of Credit Union Acts*. Washington, D.C.: Credit Union National Association, 1981.

Drucker, Peter F. *Management: Tasks, Responsibilities, Processes*. New York: Harper & Row, 1974.

———. *The Practice of Management*. New York: Harper & Row, 1954.

————. *Preparing Tomorrow's Business Leaders Today.* Englewood Cliffs, N.J.: Prentice-Hall, 1969.

Fisher, David I. *Cash Management.* New York: The Conference Board, 1973.

Flannery, Mark J. *An Economic Evaluation of Credit Unions in the United States.* Boston: Federal Reserve Bank of Boston, 1974.

Franks, J. R., and Broyles, J. E. *Modern Managerial* Finance. Chichester, England: Wiley, 1979.

Friedman, David H. *Deposit Operations.* Washington, D.C.: American Bankers Association, 1982.

Fulmer, Robert M. *The New Management,* 2nd Ed. New York: Macmillan, 1978.

————. *Practical Human Relations.* Homewood, Ill.: Richard D. Irwin, 1977.

Glueck, William F. *Personnel: A Diagnostic Approach,* Rev. Ed. Dallas: Business Publications, 1978.

Hammond, Bray. *Banks and Politics in America.* Princeton: Princeton University Press, 1957.

Harris, Louis. *The Second Study: The American Public's and Community Opinion Leaders' Views of Banks and Bankers in 1972.* Philadelphia: The Foundation for Full Service Banks, 1972.

Hawke, Jr., John D., and Petersen, Neal L. *The New Community Reinvestment Act and Consumer Credit Rules: Regulatory Compliance and Bank Marketing.* New York: Harcourt, Brace, Jovanovich, 1979.

Heller, Pauline B. *Handbook of Federal Bank Holding Company Law.* New York: Law Journal Press, 1976.

Hendrickson, Robert A. *The Cashless Society.* New York: Dodd, Mead, 1972.

Herrick, Tracy G. *Bank Analyst's Handbook.* New York: Wiley, 1978.

Herzberg, Frederick, Mausner, Bernard, and Snyderman, Barbara B. *The Motivation to Work.* New York: Wiley, 1959.

Humble, John W. *How to Manage by Objectives.* New York: AMACOM (A Division of American Management Associations), 1972.

Hunt, Alfred L. *Corporate Cash Management and Electronic Funds Transfers.* New York: AMACOM (A Division of American Management Associations), 1978.

Hutchinson, Harry D. *Money, Banking, and the United States Economy,* 4th Ed. Englewood Cliffs, N.J.: Prentice-Hall, 1980.

Jacoby, Neil H. *Corporate Power and Social Responsibility.* New York: Macmillan, 1973.

Jessee, Michael A., and Seelig, Steven A. *Bank Holding Companies and the Public Interest.* Lexington, Mass.: Lexington Books (D. C. Heath), 1977.

Kepner, Charles H., and Tregoe, Benjamin B. *The Rational Manager.* New York: McGraw-Hill, 1965.

Lamb, W. Ralph. *Group Banking: A Form of Banking Concentration and Control in the United States.* New Brunswick, N.J.: Rutgers University Press, 1961.

Lesikar, Raymond V. *Business Communications: Theory and Application.* Homewood, Ill.: Richard D. Irwin, 1972.

Lundborg, Louis B. *Future Without Shock.* New York: Norton, 1974.

Maslow, Abraham. *Motivation and Personality.* New York: Harper & Row, 1954.

Mason, John M. *Financial Management of Commercial Banks.* Boston: Warren, Gorham & Lamont, 1979.

Mayer, Martin. *The Bankers.* New York: David McKay Co., 1974.

McDonald, Jay M., and McKinley, John F. *Corporate Banking.* Washington, D.C.: American Bankers Association, 1981.

McKie, James W. (Ed.). *Social Responsibility and the Business Predicament.* Washington, D.C.: Brookings Institution, 1974.

McKinney, George W., Brown, William J., and Horvitz, Paul M. *Management of Commercial Bank Funds,* 2nd Ed. Washington, D.C.: American Bankers Association, 1980.

Myers, Margaret G. *A Financial History of the United States.* New York: Columbia University Press, 1970.

Nadler, Paul S. *Commercial Banking in the Economy,* 2nd Ed. New York: Random House, 1973.

Oppenheim, Peter K. *International Banking,* 3rd Ed. Washington, D.C.: American Bankers Association, 1979.

Pezzullo, Mary Ann. *Marketing for Bankers.* Washington, D.C.: American Bankers Association, 1982.

Prochnow, Herbert V. (Ed.). *The One-Bank Holding Company.* Chicago: Rand McNally, 1969.

————, and Prochnow, Jr., Herbert V. (Eds.). *The Changing World of Banking.* New York: Harper & Row, 1974.

Reed, Edward W., Cotter, Richard V., Gill, Edward K., and Smith, Richard K. *Commercial Banking.* Englewood Cliffs, N.J.: Prentice-Hall, 1976.

Robichek, Alexander A., Coleman, Alan B., and Hempel, George H. *Management of Financial Institutions: Notes and Cases.* Hinsdale, Ill.: Dryden, 1976.

Rockefeller, David. *Creative Management in Banking.* New York: McGraw-Hill, 1964.

Roeber, Richard J. C. *The Organization in a Changing Environment.* Reading, Mass.: Addison-Wesley, 1973.

Russell, Thomas. *The Economics of Bank Credit Cards.* New York: Praeger, 1975.

Schellie, Peter D. *Manager's Guide to the 1980 Monetary Control Act.* Washington, D.C.: American Bankers Association, 1980.

Staats, William, F. *Money and Banking.* Washington, D.C.: American Bankers Association, 1982.

Summers, Donald B. *Personnel Management in Banking.* New York: McGraw-Hill, 1981.

Teplitz, Paul V. *Trends Affecting the U.S. Banking System*. Cambridge, Mass.: Cambridge Research Institute, 1976.

Thompson, Thomas W., Berry, Leonard L., and Davidson, Phillip H. *Banking Tomorrow; Managing Markets Through Planning*. New York: Van Nostrand Reinhold, 1978.

Welfling, Weldon. *Mutual Savings Banks*. Cleveland: The Press of Case Western Reserve University, 1968.

Wood, Jr., Oliver G. *Commercial Banking: Practice and Policy*. New York: D. Van Nostrand, 1978.

Index